THE LAW OF ATTACHMENT
AND GARNISHMENT

2nd Edition

by
Margaret C. Jasper

For Reference
Not to be taken from this room

Oceana's Legal Almanac Series
Law for the Layperson

2000
Oceana Publications, Inc.
Dobbs Ferry, New York

Library of Congress Control Number: 00-134131

ISBN 0-379-11346-5

Oceana's Legal Almanac Series: Law for the Layperson
ISSN 1075-7376

©2000 by Oceana Publications, Inc.

To My Husband Chris

Your love and support
are my motivation and inspiration

-and-

In memory of my son, Jimmy

Table of Contents

ABOUT THE AUTHOR..vii

INTRODUCTION ix

CHAPTER 1:
OVERVIEW OF DEBT COLLECTION LAW

TYPES OF DEBT.. 1
Secured Debts... 1
Unsecured Debts... 2

DEBT COLLECTION... 2

METHODS OF DEBT RECOVERY.................................. 3
In General 3
Attachment and Garnishment................................ 3
Attachment and Garnishment Distinguished.................. 4
Restraining Notice.. 4
Property Execution 5
Wage Execution 5
Bank Execution 6
Real Property Execution 6
Construction Lien.. 7

SATISFACTION OF JUDGMENT AND RELEASE OF LIEN.......... 7

BANKRUPTCY 7

WRONGFUL ATTACHMENT OR GARNISHMENT 8
Malicious Prosecution Action 8
Liability on the Attachment or Garnishment Bond 9
Abuse of Process Actions 9
Damages 9
Compensatory Damages..................................... 9
Punitive Damages 9

SECURED TRANSACTIONS UNDER ARTICLE 9 OF THE
UNIFORM COMMERCIAL CODE (U.C.C.) 10

CHAPTER 2:
ATTACHMENT

IN GENERAL 15

GROUNDS FOR ATTACHMENT 15

PREJUDGMENT REMEDY. 15

THE ORDER OF ATTACHMENT 16

LIMITATIONS ON PREJUDGMENT REMEDIES 17
Bond Requirement 17

LEVIES 17
Levy By Service 18
Levy By Seizure 19
Duties Following Levy 19
    Vacating the Attachment Order *19*
    Inventory *19*
    Statement of Garnishee *19*
Motion to Modify or Discharge Attachment 20
Priority of Orders of Attachment 20

CHAPTER 3:
GARNISHMENT

IN GENERAL 21

PROCEDURE 21
Order of Garnishment. 22
Levies. 24
    Intangibles *24*
    Tangibles *24*

DUTIES AND LIABILITIES OF GARNISHEE 25

DEBTS AND PROPERTY SUBJECT TO GARNISHMENT 26
Personal Property 26
Real Property. 26
Beneficiary Distribution under an Estate 27
Trust Funds or Property and Income from Trusts 27
Bank Accounts. 27
Life Insurance 27
Debts 28

WAGE GARNISHMENT. 28
Consumer Credit Protection Act. 29
    Protection Afforded Under Title III *29*
    Employer Violations *30*
    Subsequent Wage Garnishments *30*
    Child Support and Alimony Orders *30*

CHAPTER 4:
EXEMPTIONS

IN GENERAL 31

PURPOSE OF EXEMPTIONS 31

TYPES OF EXEMPT PROPERTY 32
Homestead 32
Wages and Income 32
Tools and Implements Used in Debtor's Trade or Business 33
Motor Vehicles. 33
Animals 33
Household Goods and Furniture 34
Insurance and Annuities. 34
Pension and Retirement Benefits 34
Miscellaneous Items 35

ASSERTION OF THE EXEMPTION 35

USE OF FORCE TO RETURN EXEMPT PROPERTY
AND REMEDIES 36

CHAPTER 5:
THE UNIFORM FRAUDULENT TRANSFER ACT

FRAUDULENT TRANSFERS 37

THE UNIFORM FRAUDULENT CONVEYANCE ACT 37

THE UNIFORM FRAUDULENT TRANSFER ACT 38
Fraudulent Transfers and Obligations 39
Insolvency. 40
Preferential Transfers to Insiders 40
Available Remedies 40
Liability and Defenses. 41
Timing 41
Statute of Limitations 41

CHAPTER 6:
FEDERAL TAX COLLECTION

THE COLLECTION PROCESS. 43

ENFORCEMENT ACTIONS 43
IRS Tax Liens. 44
Lien Payoff Amount 44

COLLECTION APPEAL RIGHTS 44
Lien and Levy Notices 45
Lien Notice 45

Levy Notice 45

THE DUE PROCESS HEARING. 45

CERTIFICATE OF RELEASE OF FEDERAL TAX LIEN 47

APPENDICES

Appendix 1: Table of State Statutes Governing Debt Collection 49

Appendix 2: Application for Property Execution 53

Appendix 3: Property Execution Exemption Claim Form 55

Appendix 4: Table of Property Exemptions by State 57

Appendix 5: Application for Wage Execution 97

Appendix 6: Income Execution for Support Enforcement 99

Appendix 7: Wage Execution Exemption Claim Form 103

Appendix 8: Table of Wage Exemptions by State 105

Appendix 9: Application for Bank Execution 109

Appendix 10: Bank Execution Exemption Claim Form 111

Appendix 11: Sample Construction Lien Claim Form 113

Appendix 12: Sample Satisfaction of Judgment and Release of Lien. 117

Appendix 13: Applicable Sections—UCC Article 9—
Secured Transactions 119

Appendix 14: Notice of Application for Prejudgment Remedy/Claim for
Hearing to Contest Application or Claim for Exemption 129

Appendix 15: Selected Provisions of the Consumer Credit Protection Act
(15 U.S.C. 1671-1677) 131

Appendix 16: Post-Judgment Interrogatories 135

Appendix 17: Petition for Examination of Judgment Debtor and
Notice of Hearing. 137

Appendix 18: Uniform Fraudulent Transfer Act 139

Appendix 19: IRS Collection Appeal Request 169

Appendix 20: IRS Request for a Collection Due Process Hearing 171

Appendix 21: Federal Tax Lien Act (26 U.S.C. §6321, et seq.)...........173

Glossary...197

Bibliography and Suggested Reading.............................211

ABOUT THE AUTHOR

MARGARET C. JASPER is an attorney engaged in the general practice of law in South Salem, New York, concentrating in the areas of personal injury and entertainment law. Ms. Jasper holds a Juris Doctor degree from Pace University School of Law, White Plains, New York, is a member of the New York and Connecticut bars, and is certified to practice before the United States District Courts for the Southern and Eastern Districts of New York, and the United States Supreme Court. Ms. Jasper has been appointed to the panel of arbitrators of the American Arbitration Association and the law guardian panel for the Family Court of the State of New York, is a member of the Association of Trial Lawyers of America, and is a New York State licensed real estate broker and member of the Westchester County Board of Realtors, operating as Jasper Real Estate, in South Salem, New York.

Ms. Jasper is the author and general editor of the following legal almanacs: Juvenile Justice and Children's Law; Marriage and Divorce; Estate Planning; The Law of Contracts; The Law of Dispute Resolution; Law for the Small Business Owner; The Law of Personal Injury; Real Estate Law for the Homeowner and Broker; Everyday Legal Forms; Dictionary of Selected Legal Terms; The Law of Medical Malpractice; The Law of Product Liability; The Law of No-Fault Insurance; The Law of Immigration; The Law of Libel and Slander; The Law of Buying and Selling; Elder Law; The Right to Die; AIDS Law; The Law of Obscenity and Pornography; The Law of Child Custody; The Law of Debt Collection; Consumer Rights Law; Bankruptcy Law for the Individual Debtor; Victim's Rights Law; Animal Rights Law; Workers' Compensation Law; Employee Rights in the Workplace; Probate Law; Environmental Law; Labor Law; The Americans with Disabilities Act; The Law of Capital Punishment; Education Law; The Law of Violence Against Women; Landlord-Tenant Law; Insurance Law; Religion and the Law; Commercial Law; Motor Vehicle Law; Social Security Law; The Law of Drunk Driving; The Law of Speech and the First Amendment; Employment Discrimination Under Title VII; Hospital Liability Law; Home Mortgage Law Primer; Copyright Law; Patent Law; Trademark Law; and Special Education Law.

INTRODUCTION

Attachment and garnishment are two powerful tools available to a creditor to be used against a debtor. These debt collection methods effectively give the creditor protection and a means of virtually guaranteeing payment of the debt owed to him. Yet there are also safeguards and exemptions available to a debtor so that the debtor is not totally without protection and at the mercy of a creditor.

This almanac presents an overview of debt collection law, and describes and defines the basic characteristics of both attachment and garnishment, and the procedures by which these debt collection methods are implemented. Debtor safeguards, such as statutory exemptions and bankruptcy protection, are also explored. This almanac also provides the reader with a discussion of the federal tax collection process.

The Appendix provides sample documents, applicable statutes, and other pertinent information and data. The Glossary contains definitions of many of the terms used throughout the almanac.

CHAPTER 1:
OVERVIEW OF DEBT COLLECTION LAW

TYPES OF DEBT

A debt is generally defined as an obligation or liability to pay. However, debts may be classified further according to certain factors, such as the type of lender and the rights the lender retained according to agreement, as set forth below.

Secured Debts

A debt is "secured" if the lender, by agreement, has retained some kind of interest in the borrower's property in return for making the loan. Secured debts usually involve large purchases, such as homes, automobiles, appliances and furniture. This security gives the lender some assurance that the debt will be repaid, or that the lender will not suffer a total loss if the borrower defaults. The secured item can be repossessed.

For example, when a home is purchased, the bank or mortgage company which finances the purchase retains the right to foreclose and sell the house if the payments are not made as agreed. The house is the security for the loan.

In addition, if an individual borrows money from a lending institution, such as a bank or finance company, the lender may require the borrower to pledge some item of value as collateral for the loan, such as a car. The loan is secured by the collateral, even though the collateral has nothing to do with the reason for borrowing the money.

A security interest also provides the secured party with the assurance that if the debtor files bankruptcy, the lender may be able to recover the value of the loan by taking possession of the collateral, instead of receiving only a fraction of the borrower's property after it is divided among all creditors, or nothing at all.

As further set forth below, secured debts are governed by Article 9 of the Uniform Commercial Code.

Unsecured Debts

Unsecured debts are those for which the lender has retained no interest in any of the items purchased. Thus, if the debtor defaults on the payments, the lender has no legal right to repossess any of the goods.

Unsecured debts are the most common, and may include: (i) credit card debt; (ii) medical expenses; and (iii) uncollateralized loans.

DEBT COLLECTION

In general, a debtor is one who owes a monetary debt to another, who is known as a creditor. If the creditor prevails in a legal action against the debtor for the amount owed, the court awards the creditor a "judgment" for money damages. The creditor is thereafter known as a judgment creditor and the defendant as the judgment debtor. If the judgment debtor does not voluntarily pay on the judgment amount, the plaintiff may attempt to "execute" on the judgment—i.e., recover the amount owed.

Once a creditor obtains a judgment, collecting a debt from an individual or business that is solvent is not as difficult because the judgment debtor purportedly has some interests to protect, e.g., a good credit rating. However, when the debtor is insolvent, or appears to be "judgment-proof"—i.e., has no discernable assets from which to collect the debt—or is simply reluctant to pay the debt, further debt collection techniques must be employed to recover the money owed the creditor.

"Judgment proof" refers to the status of a debtor who has no assets or wages that can be attached or garnished. For example, an elderly individual, who rents their living space, and survives on social security, without any assets except for those which would be deemed exempt, would be considered "judgment proof." An unemployed college student would also appear to be "judgment proof."

However, if it appears that the debtor's financial situation will change in the future—e.g., the college student will embark on a promising new career after graduation—depending on the jurisdiction, judgment creditors generally have a long time to enforce a judgment and collect the debt, e.g. ten or more years. Once that statutorily-prescribed time period ends, the debt is presumed satisfied unless the judgment debtor has acknowledged the debt or made a payment during that period. Either of these actions would renew and/or extend the time period for collection.

The reader is advised to check the law of his or her own jurisdiction concerning the time within which a debt must be recovered, and whether there are any rights to renew a judgment.

METHODS OF DEBT RECOVERY

In General

There are a number of methods by which a creditor may enforce a judgment and recover a debt from a debtor. For example, the creditor may seize money from a debtor's bank account, attach the debtor's business income or garnish a portion of a debtor's wages. The creditor may also be able to seize personal or real property owned by the debtor, or money owed to the debtor by third parties.

If a creditor creates a lien on the real property of the debtor, the creditor will generally get paid when the property is sold or refinanced. The lien may arise by agreement, statute, or through litigation between the parties. The proceeds from the sale of the debtor's property are used to satisfy the debt to the creditor.

In some states, a lien is automatically created when the court enters its judgment. In others, you must file a document to create a lien. Although recovering a debt by creating a lien may take a long time, it requires little effort on the part of the creditor, who merely waits for the sale or refinance to occur. In addition, every state authorizes a creditor to collect interest on a debt—e.g. 9 percent—while waiting to get paid.

A table of state statutes governing debt collection is set forth at Appendix 1.

Under the law, certain creditors—such as the Internal Revenue Service—are entitled to a priority lien on the debtor's property, in which case the priority creditor's debt—e.g. taxes—must be paid if the debtor becomes insolvent before any other debts are paid.

Federal tax liens are discussed more fully in Chapter 6 of this almanac.

Attachment and Garnishment

As further discussed in this almanac, attachment and garnishment are the two most common remedies available to a creditor to recover money owed by the debtor.

Attachment is a limited statutory remedy whereby a creditor has the property of a debtor seized to satisfy the debt. The process of "attachment and execution" permits a creditor, with the assistance of the sheriff or marshall, to take or "seize" the debtor's personal property—such as a car—and then sell it. Thus, attachment refers to taking legal possession of the debtor's property and execution refers to the sale of the attached property to satisfy the debt.

Attachment is discussed more fully in Chapter 2 of this almanac.

Garnishment refers to the process of taking something belonging to the debtor which is being held by a third party, known as the "garnishee." For example, if a creditor "garnishes" a debtor's bank account, the bank is the "garnishee" because the bank is holding the funds in the debtor's account. A creditor may also "garnish" a debtor's wages to satisfy the debt.

Garnishment is discussed more fully in Chapter 3 of this almanac.

Thus, through attachment and garnishment, a creditor collects, applies or subjects personal property, real property, wages or funds owned by or due to a debtor, to the debt owed to the creditor. Any claim, which is due from one person to another whether arising from a personal loan, installment purchase, tort action, contract action or any other action can be satisfied in whole or part by the use of attachment or garnishment proceedings.

Attachment and Garnishment Distinguished

These two remedies are similar in many respects. Both are statutory remedies, and Federal courts follow state rules as to the availability of one or both remedies. In many states, the terms attachment and garnishment are used interchangeably and, in fact, garnishment is often referred to as a form of attachment. In some states, garnishment is not a separate remedy but rather a proceeding ancillary to attachment, while in other states, garnishment is an independent remedy.

The primary difference between attachment and garnishment is that attachment is directed to property in the possession of the debtor, whereas garnishment is directed to the property of the debtor that is being held by the garnishee. Attached property is seized pending execution whereas garnished property is generally left in the care and custody of the garnishee until surrendered to the creditor.

Restraining Notice

A restraining notice instructs the judgment debtor, or a third party, that he or she cannot transfer or dispose of any assets of the judgment debtor. The restraining notice is not a levy or a lien on the assets. It merely prevents their transfer. Once a creditor acquires a levy or lien on the assets, the sheriff, or other designated enforcement officer, can "execute" and take the property. For the purposes of this almanac, the term sheriff will be used to identify any designated enforcement officer.

Nevertheless, if the property which is the subject of the execution is "exempt," the debtor can make a claim for exemption and the sheriff would be prevented from seizing the exempt property.

Exemptions are discussed more fully in Chapter 4 of this almanac.

Property Execution

The judgment creditor generally makes an application to the court for a property execution. The property execution in effect gives the judgment creditor permission to allow the sheriff to seize the property of the judgment debtor.

A sample property execution application is set forth at Appendix 2.

Upon issuance, the property execution is generally delivered to the sheriff so that he or she can enforce it. The sheriff will then demand payment and place a levy on the judgment debtor's assets. The type, amount and whereabouts of the debtor's assets are specified and included with a copy of the execution sent to the sheriff.

The sheriff is obligated to levy any property specifically identified by the creditor so as to avoid dissipation of the assets. The manner in which a levy takes place generally involves delivery of the execution to the custodian of the property, inspection and inventory of the property, and may also involve the physical relocation of the property. Property subject to execution may be sold at a public auction.

The judgment debtor has the right to petition the court if he or she believes that the property specified in the property execution is exempt.

A property execution exemption claim form is set forth at Appendix 3 and a table of property exemptions by state is set forth at Appendix 4.

Wage Execution

The judgment creditor generally makes an application to the court for a wage execution. The wage execution in effect gives the judgment creditor permission to attach the debtor's salary, commonly known as a wage garnishment. Depending on the jurisdiction, the judgment creditor is entitled to a statutorily prescribed percentage of the debtor's net pay, e.g. 10 to 25 percent.

A sample wage execution application is set forth at Appendix 5.

Following issuance of the wage execution, the sheriff will generally serve the judgment debtor's employer with a wage garnishment. The employer must then deduct the statutory amount from the debtor's paycheck and forward it to the sheriff. The sheriff deducts their fees, and sends the balance to the judgment creditor.

A sample income execution for child support enforcement is set forth at Appendix 6.

The federal government has limited wage garnishment so that no amount may be withheld for any week unless the debtor's disposable earnings exceed thirty times the federal minimum hourly wage as prescribed in the Fair Labor Standard Act in effect at the time the earnings are payable.

The judgment debtor has the right to petition the court if he or she believes that income subject to the wage execution is exempt.

A wage execution exemption claim form is set forth at Appendix 7 and a table of wage exemptions by state is set forth at Appendix 8.

Bank Execution

The judgment creditor may also make an application to the court for an execution on the bank account of the judgment debtor. The bank execution gives the judgment creditor permission to allow the sheriff to seize the proceeds of the account of the judgment debtor.

A sample bank execution application is set forth at Appendix 9.

Following issuance of the bank execution, the sheriff will generally serve the execution on the judgment debtor's bank. The bank generally must notify the judgment debtor of the execution. After a prescribed period of time,—e.g., 15 days—if the judgment debtor does not claim an exemption, the bank must turn the funds over to the sheriff, who deducts their fees, and sends the balance to the judgment creditor.

The judgment debtor has the right to petition the court if he or she believes that the money in the bank account is exempt. For example, the funds may be social security or unemployment compensation income, which is exempt.

A bank execution exemption claim form is set forth at Appendix 10.

Real Property Execution

A judgment creditor may also file a lien against the debtor's home. A lien is a legal assertion that the creditor has a claim for a specific amount against certain property. Once the lien has been created, state statutory law governs how the lien is executed against the debtor's property.

However, unless the debt is significant, it is not usual for the creditor to proceed with a foreclosure and sale of the home, as this is a costly undertaking. Nevertheless, the mere filing of a lien against one's home is often enough to get a debtor to negotiate a settlement. In any event, the debtor is prevented from refinancing or selling the home until the lien is satisfied.

Some states provide the debtor with a certain level of protection under a law generally known as a "homestead exemption." Depending on the jurisdiction, this may completely protect the debtor's home from a foreclosure sale, or at the very least, may provide the debtor with the exemption amount if the home is sold.

Again, however, if the collector is a taxing authority, a homestead exemption may not be applicable. Further, if the debtor defaults on his or her mortgage, the lender can foreclose on the property and force a sale.

Depending on the jurisdiction, the law may provide a redemption period following a forced sale of the debtor's home. During this period of time, the debtor may be able to regain ownership to the property by paying off the debt, as well as court costs and other expenses. The reader is advised to check the applicable redemption laws of his or her jurisdiction.

Construction Lien

A construction lien—also referred to as a mechanic's lien—is a claim created by law which allows for a lien to be placed against the real property of the debtor for the purpose of securing a priority of payment of the price of work performed and materials furnished.

A sample construction lien claim form is set forth at Appendix 11.

SATISFACTION OF JUDGMENT AND RELEASE OF LIEN

When a judgment is paid, a satisfaction of judgment and release of lien, if applicable, must be filed with the proper authorities within a certain time period after the payment is made. A copy of the satisfaction of judgment is usually required to be sent to the judgment debtor. If the judgment is paid, in part, a partial satisfaction of judgment may be filed.

A sample satisfaction of judgment and release of lien is set forth at Appendix 12.

BANKRUPTCY

If the debtor does not have the funds to satisfy the judgment, a debtor who faces execution on his or her property can file bankruptcy to provide the debtor with some breathing space to reorganize and/or rid the debtor of some or all of his or her debts. When faced with an imminent foreclosure sale, or wage garnishment, the filing of a bankruptcy action stays—i.e. temporarily suspends—any further legal action being taken against the debtor and the debtor's property.

Bankruptcy was provided by the federal government as a means for a debtor to get rid of a large number of his or her debts, so that they can begin a fresh start. These are known as "dischargeable" debts. However, once a debtor files bankruptcy, and the debts are discharged, he or she is precluded from doing so again for a period of approximately six years.

The bankruptcy court will generally review a statement of the debtor's financial condition and list of assets and liabilities. If it is determined that there are assets of value which are not statutorily exempt, the court may order those assets to be sold and the proceeds to be paid out to the creditors.

The debtor may be entitled to select exemptions available under the bankruptcy law or their own state's law, whichever provides the debtor with the maximum protection. Therefore, the reader is advised to check the law of his or her jurisdiction in this regard.

There are, however, certain debts which are not dischargeable. These may include federal and state taxes, child support, student loans, and debts which were omitted in the bankruptcy filing papers, unless it is demonstrated that the creditor knew of the filing and failed to make a claim. Further, the bankrupt debtor is still required to make payments on debts which are secured—e.g., an automobile loan—or the debtor must return the secured property.

For a more detailed discussion of individual bankruptcy law, the reader is advised to consult this author's legal almanac entitled Bankruptcy Law for the Individual Debtor, also published by Oceana Publishing Company.

WRONGFUL ATTACHMENT OR GARNISHMENT

Although many precautions are taken by the courts in issuing attachment or garnishment orders, there are times when the order is improperly or fraudulently obtained. In these cases, the debtor has some options to pursue to obtain compensation for his or her damages, as set forth below.

Malicious Prosecution Action

A malicious prosecution action requires the debtor to show that he or she was the successful party in an action which determined the validity of the attachment. Further, the debtor must usually show that the attachment was brought by the creditor maliciously, without probable cause. The debtor must further show that he or she was damaged in some respect. Most states require a wrongful sequestration of property or the arrest of the person before the court will entertain a malicious prosecution suit. Even if the creditor eventually wins in the primary suit against the debtor, the attachment may still be wrongful if adequate grounds did not exist. Each state has its own requirements for malicious prosecution suits. Some states require a showing of malice on the part of the creditor while other states require a showing of a lack of probable cause.

Liability on the Attachment or Garnishment Bond

Another remedy for wrongful attachment is for the debtor to sue on the attachment or garnishment bond, if one was required. Most states generally require that before an attachment or garnishment shall issue, the plaintiff creditor must post a bond conditioned to pay the costs and damages which the defendant debtor may sustain if the order was wrongfully issued. The right to bring an action on such a bond depends upon the obligations specifically set forth in the bond.

Abuse of Process Actions

The abuse of process action is generally brought where there has been an excessive garnishment or attachment—i.e., where the creditor has attached more of the debtor's property or obtained a greater garnishment against him than was necessary to secure the debt owed.

Damages

The statutes of each state determine the type and extent of damages recoverable in an action for wrongful attachment or garnishment. Normally, the defendant can recover all the actual damages which he sustained as a natural result of the wrongful attachment or garnishment. Unusual, remote or speculative damages are not recoverable.

Compensatory Damages

Compensatory damages are those damages which attempt to place the debtor back in the position he was in prior to the wrongful act. If property has been lost or destroyed, the debtor may recover the value of the property at the time it was seized. If the goods were damaged, the debtor may recover the value prior to the damage. Damages caused by a detention of the property may be recoverable as well as the loss of profits or injury to his business, the loss due to depreciation in value of the property, loss of use of the property, and the loss of interest. Damages for mental suffering may also be recoverable if caused by the wrongful garnishment or attachment. Many states permit the debtor to recover the cost of attorney's fees and court costs.

Punitive Damages

The debtor may also be entitled to punitive damages. Punitive damages are those damages awarded as a punishment against the wrongdoer, and are supposed to act as a deterrent against further wrongdoing. Punitive damages are usually awarded in actions where the attachment or garnishment, in addition to being wrongful, was also done maliciously, willfully and without probable cause. In other words, the attachment was issued for the purpose of harassing or oppressing the debtor, rather than to preserve legal rights. For example, punitive damages have been awarded in suits where there was an attachment of exempt property with knowledge of the exemption or where false grounds were alleged.

SECURED TRANSACTIONS UNDER ARTICLE 9 OF THE UNIFORM COMMERCIAL CODE (U.C.C.)

UCC Article 9 governs *secured* transactions. Because a security agreement is also a contract, it must comply with any other state laws governing contracts. Thus, the reader is advised to further check the law of his or her own jurisdiction when researching a specific issue.

Article 9 applies to any transaction which is intended to create a security interest in personal property or fixtures, including goods, documents, instruments, general intangibles, chattel paper or accounts; and to sales of chattel paper or accounts. Article 9 also applies to security interests created by contract, as set forth in the statute. The purpose of Article 9 is to include all *consensual* security interests in personal property and fixtures under one Article.

Exclusions from Article 9 include but are not limited to landlord's liens, transfers of employee wage claims; governmental transfers; transfers of insurance claims; transfers of real estate liens or leases; and transfers of tort claims. In addition, statutory liens are not governed by Article 9, but by the individual statute that creates them. Statutory liens may take priority over a perfected security interest unless the statute provides otherwise.

Unless the secured party is in possession of the collateral pursuant to agreement—i.e., the collateral is "pledged"—a security interest is not enforceable against the debtor or third parties, and cannot attach until the debtor has signed a security agreement. The agreement to provide for a security interest must be in writing, signed by the debtor, and must describe the collateral.

The requirement of a writing is for evidentiary purposes in case a future conflict arises over the terms of the agreement and the identity of the collateral. Therefore, if the collateral is pledged, the need for a writing is of less importance and thus not required by the statute. Additional terms in a security agreement may include the amount of the debt and terms of repayment; and risk of loss and insurance provisions.

Value must be given in return for the security interest in order for it to attach. Value refers to any consideration sufficient to support a simple contract. For example: Buyer purchases a washing machine from Seller on an installment basis. Buyer and Seller agree that Seller will retain a security interest in the washing machine in case Buyer reneges on the payments.

The sale of the washing machine to Buyer is the consideration which supports the contract.

A security interest cannot attach until the debtor has rights in the collateral. A pledged security agreement exists when the debtor transfers the collateral to the secured party in exchange for a loan. An example of a pledged security agreement would be where an individual leaves an item with a pawnbroker in return for a cash payment and the right to redeem the item.

The "perfection" of a security agreement allows a secured party to gain priority to the collateral over any third party. In general, the secured party is protected against any subsequent creditors and transferees of the debtor. In addition, the secured party's interest is superior to those of unsecured creditors in bankruptcy proceedings instituted by or against the debtor.

To perfect a security agreement, the filing of a financing statement is generally required unless an exception exists, as set forth in the statute. The purpose of the filing is to give public notice of the security interest. In general, most financing statements, other than those regarding land-related collateral, must be filed with the register of deeds in the county of the debtor's residence.

The financing statement generally must contain:

1. The names and addresses of the debtor and the secured party;

2. A description of the collateral; and

3. The signature of the debtor.

However, if the security agreement itself contains the above information, its filing may be sufficient to comply with this section.

Again, an exception to the filing requirement exists if the secured party takes possession of the security interest. If filing or possession takes place prior to attachment, the security interest is perfected at the time the requirements of attachment are met as set forth above.

If the secured party assigns a perfected security interest to another, the perfected status of the security interest against creditors of the original debtor remains intact, and no further filing is required.

Article 9 defines *collateral* as property subject to a security interest, including accounts and chattel paper. Chattel paper refers to a writing which evidences both a monetary obligation and a security interest in goods. The collateral may remain in the possession of the debtor, or may be placed in the possession of the secured party, while the debt remains unpaid.

If the secured party is in possession of the collateral, he is required to use reasonable care in preserving the collateral. However, the obligation to pay reasonable expenses are chargeable to the debtor, and also secured by the collateral. A type of such expense is insurance coverage. Thus, the risk of accidental loss or damage to the collateral is borne by the debtor if there is insufficient insurance coverage.

The secured party is entitled to hold any increase or profits received from the collateral as additional security, other than money. If the collateral generates any money, the secured party must turn it over to the debtor, or apply it to reduce the secured obligation. Collateral may be repledged by the secured party provided it does not impair the debtor's right to redeem the collateral.

If the secured party fails to meet the obligations imposed under the statute, he is liable for any resulting loss. However, the secured party does not thereby lose his security interest.

If the secured party is aware that collateral is owned by a non-debtor, the owner is not liable for the debt. In addition, the owner has the same right as the debtor to: (i) receive a statement of account; (ii) receive notice of and make objections to a secured party's proposal to retain the collateral to satisfy the debt; (iii) redeem the collateral; (iv) obtain injunctive relief; and (v) recover losses caused by the secured party's actions or inactions.

A secured party may release all or a part of any collateral described in a filed financing statement by signing a statement of release. The statement of release must contain: (i) a description of the collateral being released; (ii) the names and addresses of the debtor and secured party; and (iii) the financing statement file number.

Whether a debtor is in default depends on the terms of the security agreement. For example, an agreement will invariably provide that failure to make payments required under the agreement constitutes default.

In addition to any rights and remedies provided in the security agreement in case of default, Article 9 affords the secured party further relief. For example, the secured party may execute against—i.e., reduce the claim to judgment and request the sheriff to levy—the debtor's property, which is then sold and the proceeds applied to the debt. If the agreement covers both real and personal property, he may foreclose on the real property.

In addition, the secured party may take possession of the collateral, if it is not already in his possession, or may sell the collateral and apply the proceeds of the sale to satisfy the claim. Of course, if there is any deficiency after sale—an amount still owing after the sale proceeds have been applied to the debt—the debtor is still liable for the deficiency, unless the underlying transaction is a sale of accounts or chattel paper and the security agreement provides for a deficiency judgment.

At any time before the secured party has disposed of the collateral, the debtor—or another secured party—may redeem the collateral by fulfilling the obligations secured by the collateral, as well as reimbursing the secured party for any expenses reasonably incurred in connection with the debtor's default. This may include legal fees and costs.

If a secured party proposes to retain the collateral in full satisfaction of the obligation, written notice of the proposal must be sent to the debtor absent the debtor's prior renunciation of the collateral. If the debtor fails to object, the secured party may retain the collateral.

Unless the collateral is perishable or subject to a rapid decline in value, the debtor is entitled to reasonable notice of the time and place of any public sale, or of the time after which any private sale is to be made.

If the security agreement secures an indebtedness, the secured party must account to the debtor for any surplus proceeds resulting from a sale of the collateral. However, if the underlying transaction is a sale of accounts or chattel paper, the debtor is only entitled to an accounting and surplus if the agreement provides for it.

The text of Article 9 of the U.C.C. is set forth at Appendix 13.

CHAPTER 2:
ATTACHMENT

IN GENERAL

Attachment is a remedy generally used for the collection of an ordinary debt. It is the process by which a debtor's property—real or personal—is placed in the custody of the law and held as security pending the outcome of a creditor's suit.

This remedy has a two-pronged purpose:

1. It seizes upon property of an alleged debtor in advance of final judgment and holds it to provide the plaintiff with security for satisfaction of any judgment obtained; and

2. It attaches property so that the court has jurisdiction over the defendant where personal jurisdiction cannot be had. It also compels the debtor to appear in court.

Until the case is decided, the debtor cannot dispose of the property or place it beyond the reach of the creditor.

GROUNDS FOR ATTACHMENT

The usual grounds for attachment are:

1. The debtor is a non-resident or foreign corporation;

2. The debtor has left the state or is in hiding;

3. The debtor is about to remove, conceal or dispose of his property with the intent to defraud creditors or frustrate the enforcement of a judgment.

Fraudulent transfers are discussed more fully in Chapter 5 of this almanac.

PREJUDGMENT REMEDY

Unlike the remedy of garnishment, attachment occurs prior to the taking of a judgment against an alleged debtor and pertains to property in the possession of the debtor which is within the territorial jurisdiction of the court in which the creditor seeks to enforce his rights against the debtor. Thus, the main purpose of attachment is to reach the property of the defendant in order to secure a fund for the satisfaction of the creditor's judgment.

Attachment is a provisional remedy—that is, a form of execution against defendant's property in advance of judgment. It is an extraordinary remedy in that the rights of a party may be determined without service of process and sometimes without even his or her knowledge. Since the remedy of attachment is purely statutory, and because it is a harsh remedy, the statutes have been construed strictly and interpreted liberally.

Attachment can be sought in any type of action, except a matrimonial action where the plaintiff seeks a money judgment. In some states, such as New York, attachment is also available in equity actions, such as an action for specific performance, or an action for a permanent injunction.

For the purposes of this almanac, the discussion on attachment will focus on prejudgment proceedings.

THE ORDER OF ATTACHMENT

An order of attachment is a means of providing a plaintiff with security for a money judgment prior to the termination of his or her lawsuit. It is used when a plaintiff is concerned that, once a money judgment is awarded, he or she will not be able to enforce it against a judgment debtor.

Generally, an order of attachment is granted either upon notice to the defendant or ex parte—which means without notice. If the application is made on notice, then the plaintiff is generally granted a temporary restraining order (TRO) preventing the transfer of assets. If a TRO was not granted, the notice method would offer no protection to the creditor because the debtor would be able to dispose of the property before the order of attachment is granted. Thus, the purpose of granting this prejudgment relief is to maintain the status quo—to insure a plaintiff that the defendant will not either make himself judgment-proof, or insolvent in some way.

Nevertheless, most states require an opportunity for a hearing and allow the defendant debtor to contest the application and claim any exemptions to which the debtor is entitled under law. There is a balancing test that courts typically employ in determining whether to issue prejudgment relief. The defendant's due process rights are weighed against the possibility of the defendant becoming judgment-proof.

A Notice of Application for Prejudgment Remedy/Claim for Hearing to Contest Application or Claim Exemption is set forth at Appendix 14.

LIMITATIONS ON PREJUDGMENT REMEDIES

Precisely because prejudgment remedies are very powerful, their use has come under attack in the past. A significant decision addressing this issue was rendered in 1969. In *Sniadach v. Family Finance Corp.*, the Supreme Court held that a Wisconsin statute providing for prejudgment garnishment of wages was unconstitutional. The majority opinion emphasized the hardship that results from wage garnishment and suggested that there be a requirement of notice and a hearing before an order of wage attachment is issued, except in "extraordinary situations."

Unfortunately, an "extraordinary situation" is difficult to define and is rarely invoked. In 1972, in *Fuentes v. Shevin*, the Supreme Court expanded the notice and hearing requirements to include property other than wages. In 1975, in *North Georgia Finishing, Inc. v. Di-Chem, Inc.*, the following basic concepts seem to summarize the current status of prejudgment remedies:

1. Prejudgment remedies are not necessarily unconstitutional;

2. The use of prejudgment remedies is subject to due process limitations;

3. Due process requires notice and an opportunity for an adversary proceeding; and

4. In some situations, a pre-seizure ex parte hearing together with an opportunity for an immediate post-seizure hearing will satisfy the "fairness" concerns.

Bond Requirement

In order to protect the defendant against wrongful attachment, the general practice in most states is to require a plaintiff creditor to post a bond before any injunctive relief can be ordered. The bond guarantees payment of the defendant debtor's costs and damages if it turns out that the attachment was wrongfully issued.

LEVIES

Once issued, the order of attachment empowers a sheriff to seize and possess property belonging to the judgment debtor until the conclusion of the litigation. The order of attachment must specifically state the amount the plaintiff is demanding, which then dictates the amount of property that may be attached. The order gives the sheriff the authority to levy upon any personal property in which the defendant has an interest, or any debts owed to the defendant within the jurisdiction of the court.

A sheriff may levy upon as much property as he or she feels will reasonably satisfy the plaintiff's demand, together with interest, costs, and sheriff's fees and expenses. It is not necessary to levy upon property which will meet the exact dollar amount in the attachment order, but a sheriff should be cautious and exercise discretion.

Generally, attachment creates a lien on the property attached, which is as binding and enduring as a mortgage, and which gives the creditor security and a priority or right greater than persons who subsequently acquire liens on the property.

The act of taking over custody of the property is referred to as a "levy" on the property. What a levy entails depends on the nature of the property. A levy on real property generally entails giving notice to the defendant and the public notice of the lien. The levy of attachment upon personal property requires a seizure or taking possession or control. Although the manner in which seizure of the property may vary among the jurisdictions, the general methods are as follows:

Levy By Service

A sheriff may levy upon any interest of the judgment debtor in personal property or upon any debt owed to him by a third party, by serving a copy of the order of attachment, in the same manner as a summons, upon the third party—known as a "garnishee"—or upon the defendant himself, if he is in possession of the property to be levied upon.

In general, the attachment is effective only if, at the time of service, the garnishee owes a debt to the defendant or is in possession of property in which the defendant has an interest. The levy is then effective for a statutorily prescribed period of time—e.g., 90 days—as to any of the defendant's personal property that comes into the garnishee's possession or any debt that becomes due to the defendant within the effective period of the levy. After expiration of the applicable time period, or such further time as provided by order of the court served on the garnishee, the levy is ineffective except as to that property already within a sheriff's control.

As in a property execution, unless the court orders otherwise, a garnishee served with an attachment is required to transfer all personal property of the judgment debtor to the sheriff forthwith, to pay to the sheriff all debts owed to the defendant as they become due, and to execute any documents necessary to effect transfer of payment. Where the garnishee fails or refuses to make delivery of the defendant's property, remedies are available, but only by a special proceeding in court, which is brought by the judgment creditor or his or her attorney. The sheriff generally does not institute this proceeding.

Levy By Seizure

As an alternative to levying by service of the attachment order, if the property is "capable of delivery," a sheriff may effect a valid levy by serving a copy of the order, in the same manner as a summons, upon the person from whose possession or custody the property is to be taken, and seizing the defendant's property. However, this may be done only at the direction of the plaintiff, and he must provide the sheriff with indemnity against wrongful levy to the satisfaction of the sheriff or the court. As with a property execution, a sheriff need not actually take the property into his possession, but must at least exercise control over the property.

Duties Following Levy

Once a sheriff has attached the defendant's property, it is his responsibility to keep safe all property attached, or debts paid him, in order to satisfy any judgment that may be obtained against the defendant. If the situation requires it, the court may direct the sale or other disposition of the property levied upon.

Vacating the Attachment Order

Within a certain time period following the levy, the plaintiff must make a motion, with notice to the sheriff, the defendant and to any garnishee, for leave to prove the ground upon which the order of attachment was issued. If no such motion is made, the order of attachment shall be deemed vacated. No disposition of the levied property shall be made until final determination of the motion.

Inventory

Within a certain time period after service of an order of attachment, the sheriff must file an inventory of the property seized, the names and addresses of all persons served with the order of attachment, and an estimate of the value of all property levied upon. Money shall be kept in an interest bearing account. If the attachment order has been vacated, the inventory is generally made as soon as possible.

Statement of Garnishee

Within a certain time period following service of an order of attachment upon a garnishee, the garnishee must serve upon the sheriff a statement specifying all debts of the garnishee owed to the defendant, when the debts are due, all personal property of the defendant which is in the possession of the garnishee and the amounts and value of the debts and property specified.

Motion to Modify or Discharge Attachment

A defendant whose property or debt has been levied upon may make a motion, upon notice to the sheriff and to the plaintiff, for an order discharging the attachment, as to all or part of the property or debt, provided he pays sheriff fees and expenses, and gives an undertaking in an amount equal to the value of the property levied upon. In addition, any person with an interest in the property levied upon may make a motion for a vacatur or modification of the order of attachment.

An order of attachment is annulled when: (i) judgment is entered in favor of the defendant; (ii) the plaintiff's judgment is satisfied; or (iii) the underlying action is discontinued. An attachment is not annulled, however, when the plaintiff simply wins a judgment.

Nevertheless, the court may direct the clerk of any county to cancel a notice of attachment and may direct the sheriff to return or release the attached property, subject to the payment of sheriff's fees and expenses.

Priority of Orders of Attachment

Where two or more attachments are delivered to the same sheriff, they are generally satisfied out of the proceeds of personal property in the order in which they were delivered to the sheriff. Where the attachment orders are delivered to different sheriffs, priority is given to the plaintiff whose attachment is served first. Thus, a sheriff must note the date and time of delivery of the order to him and should act upon it as quickly as possible.

CHAPTER 3:
GARNISHMENT

IN GENERAL

Garnishment is generally defined as the action of a judgment creditor to compel a third party owing money to, or holding money for, a judgment debtor to pay the money to the creditor instead of the debtor.

Garnishment is a collection remedy directed not at the defendant, but rather at a third person—known as the garnishee—who owes a debt to the principal debtor, has property of the principal debtor, or has property in which the principal debtor has an interest. Most commonly, garnishees are the debtor's employer and the bank where the debtor maintains his or her bank accounts.

The garnishee in effect becomes a trustee of the debtor's funds for the benefit of the creditor. If a garnishee fails to comply with the garnishment order, the garnishee could be held liable to the creditor.

Although there are limited circumstances under which prejudgment garnishment may be available, garnishment—as opposed to attachment — is generally only available after a valid judgment is obtained against the debtor. For the purposes of this almanac, the discussion on garnishment will generally apply to the post-judgment garnishment of property.

Since garnishment is a powerful tool, there are rigid statutory guidelines and exemptions which are regulated by federal legislation in the Consumer Credit Protection Act.

Selected provisions of the Consumer Credit Protect Act are set forth at Appendix 15.

PROCEDURE

The garnishment procedure is generally started with a notice sent to the judgment debtor advising him or her of the garnishment action, and affording the debtor the opportunity to satisfy the judgment—e.g., by making installment payments. If the judgment debtor does not make arrangements to satisfy the judgment, then the judgment creditor commences a formal garnishment proceeding by filing a petition together with an affidavit stating that there is a sum certain due to the creditor by virtue of a judgment that is due and owing. The name and address of the garnishee and the type of property the garnishee is holding on behalf of the debtor must be included in the affidavit.

Order of Garnishment

Upon proper proof, the court will issue an order of garnishment, also known as a property execution. This order must be served upon the garnishee, in order to afford notice of his responsibilities and to provide time for an answer. The order is also served on the judgment debtor to put him on notice that the procedure has been started. The garnishee is required to respond to the order within a stated time period.

Accompanying the order may be a set of interrogatories—i.e., questions—to assist the judgment creditor in determining the identity and extent of assets being held by the garnishee which belong to the debtor. The garnishee must answer and return the interrogatories to the judgment creditor within a certain period of time from the date of service—e.g. 30 days.

A Notice of Post-Judgment Interrogatories is set forth at Appendix 16.

If the garnishee fails to respond to the interrogatories, the judgment creditor may petition the Court for a hearing at which time the judgment debtor or any other person, including the garnishee, may be examined. At the hearing, the court may issue an order for compliance with the interrogatories, or an order authorizing additional interrogatories. Any person who fails to comply with the discovery orders issued by the court may be held in contempt and liable for attorney's fees necessitated by a contempt hearing for failure to respond to the interrogatories.

A Petition for Examination of Judgment Debtor and Notice of Hearing is set forth at Appendix 17.

In the garnishee's answer, the garnishee may set up any defenses to the garnishment action it may have against the principal debtor, and must assert all defenses of which the garnishee has knowledge. For example, the garnishee may plead as a defense the fact that: (i) he is not indebted to the defendant; (ii) the debt has already been paid (iii) there are adverse claims to the property; or (iv) there are other garnishment proceedings pending.

Some other defenses are that the debtor is no longer employed by the garnishee or that the garnishee had already paid over the funds to the principal debtor before he was served with the notice of garnishment. The garnishee may also assert as a defense the exemptions allowable to the debtor especially if wages or earnings are the subject of the garnishment.

The garnishee may also set off any of its claims against the principal debtor, but only claims that arose before the garnishment proceedings. For example, a bank may set off against the amount of a deposit that has been garnished, the amount of any matured indebtedness due it by its depositors.

If the garnishee's answer is objected to by the plaintiff, the issues are tried as in other civil cases. The answer is admissible in evidence and the admissions are binding against the garnishee. If the answer is not objected to, then it is accepted as true. If the answer admits the indebtedness to the principal debtor, the court will render judgment against the garnishee for the admitted amount, and any property held by the garnishee will be ordered turned over to the court to satisfy the creditor's judgment.

Once the order of garnishment is issued, the sheriff will "execute" on the garnished property—i.e., collect the money from the garnishee. A valid property execution must generally specify the date on which the judgment or order was entered, the court in which it was entered, the amount of the judgment or order and the amount due thereon, and shall also identify the parties in whose favor and against whom the judgment or order was entered.

When an execution is issued to a sheriff, the date, hour, and minute of delivery are generally recorded on the execution to protect the judgment creditor's rights against other executions. When two or more executions issued against the same judgment debtor are delivered to the same sheriff, the executions must be satisfied out of the judgment debtor's property in the order in which the executions were delivered to the sheriff. Where two or more executions issued against the same judgment debtor are delivered to different enforcement officers, and personal property levied upon is within the jurisdiction of all the officers, the enforcement officer who is first to levy will secure the priority.

Once a valid execution has been issued to a sheriff, a notice, commonly referred to as a "notice of execution," may be mailed to the judgment debtor. This type of notice merely informs a judgment debtor of the issuance of an execution against his property and warns him that, if he does not remit the monies due, certain of his assets are subject to levy and sale. This notice sometimes prevents the need for service of an execution and subsequent sale because the judgment debtor may be persuaded by the notice to remit the amount demanded.

Levies

A levy—i.e., the seizure of the property subject to the execution—may be initiated by the sheriff by serving a copy of the execution together with an inventory of the property levied upon. The levy occurs when the sheriff takes the debtor's property into his custody, physically or constructively, to satisfy a money judgment. There are two different types of personal property which may be levied upon: (i) intangible and (ii) tangible.

Intangibles

If the debtor's property is "not capable of delivery," for example, a debt owed to the judgment debtor or money in a bank account, a levy is made by serving a copy of the execution on the garnishee. This type of execution is usually entitled "execution with notice to garnishee." An inventory is not taken when levying upon intangibles.

With respect to property "not capable of delivery," a levy will be effective only if the person served owes a debt to the judgment debtor at the time of service, or is in possession or custody of property "not capable of delivery" in which the judgment debtor has an interest at the time of service. Otherwise, the levy is ineffective, even though the person served thereafter acquires such property.

Tangibles

If the debtor's property is "capable of delivery," a levy is made by physically or constructively seizing the property and immediately serving a copy of the execution, together with an inventory, upon the person from whose possession or custody the property was taken. The inventory must list in detail all property subject to the levy.

With respect to this type of property, a sheriff may take physical possession removing and storing it, or he may retain a custodian at the premises where the property is located to ensure that the property is not removed. Where a physical seizure is made, the property must be properly identified, tagged, and stored in the sheriff's office or in a warehouse under the sheriff's control.

To effect a valid levy on property "capable of delivery," a sheriff may also merely assert "dominion and control" over the specific property levied upon. If this manner of levy is relied upon, as it commonly is, a sheriff must be capable of physically removing the property in order to assert "dominion and control." A valid levy may be made in this manner by:

1. Going to where the judgment debtor's assets are and specifically declaring which items are subject to levy;

2. Serving a copy of the execution;

3. Making an inventory of the property subject to the levy, on the notice of levy form; and

4. Leaving a copy of the paperwork with the person in whose possession or custody the property was found.

A person served with an execution is required to immediately transfer to the sheriff all property of the judgment debtor in his possession or custody, pay the sheriff all debts owed to the judgment debtor as they become due, and execute any documents necessary to effect transfer of payment to the sheriff.

In addition, except at the direction of the sheriff or pursuant to a Court order, the debtor or garnishee is forbidden by law to sell, transfer, assign, or interfere with any property or to pay or dispose of any debt subject to the levy. This restraint is effective until the debtor or garnishee satisfies the judgment or transfers the property to the sheriff or until the levy expires.

Once the garnishee transfers or pays to the sheriff all of the property or all of the debts subject to the levy, the levy generally terminates and is not effective as to property thereafter coming into the garnishee's possession or custody in which the judgment debtor has an interest or any debts thereafter coming due to the judgment debtor.

DUTIES AND LIABILITIES OF GARNISHEE

A garnishee is treated as an innocent person owing money to, or having in his possession property of another, without fault or blame, and indifferent as to who shall have the money. He is in effect a trustee since he must protect the rights of all parties to the property he holds.

A garnishee's obligation and responsibility only extends to funds or property he holds on behalf of the debtor. Normally, the garnishee is not responsible for court costs. Some courts provide a small stipend to the garnishee to cover his administrative costs in processing the garnishment. If, however, the garnishee denies that there are any funds or property in his possession belonging to the debtor, he may be responsible for costs if in fact he did have property of the debtor in his possession.

The garnishee is protected from double liability. Payment by the garnishee to the judgment creditor of the amount owed by the garnishee to the principal debtor protects the garnishee against the debtor. The garnishment procedure may be cut short or terminated by the debtor's payment to the creditor. In that event, the creditor will issue a release to the debtor which will stop the garnishment proceeding.

Generally, a garnishee cannot be placed in any worse condition than he would be if the defendant's claim against him were enforced by the defendant himself, except in cases of fraud or collusion between the defendant and the garnishee.

Some statutes state that the garnishee's liability is determined only as of the date of service of the garnishment and that the liability is limited to the property of the defendant in his possession or under his control and owing by him to the defendant at that time. However, some states require that the garnishment binds property of any debts owed to the defendant coming into the hands of the garnishee after service of the garnishment.

DEBTS AND PROPERTY SUBJECT TO GARNISHMENT

Although wages or earnings are commonly the subject of garnishment, there are many other types of property which may be taken by garnishment proceedings. The property to be garnished is in the possession of a third party such as banks, trustees, firm partnership or corporations. The property sought to be garnished must be owned by the debtor or the debtor must at least have some legal or equitable interest in it at the time the notice of garnishment is served upon the garnishee. The debts or property subject to garnishment are the same as those against which a money judgment may be enforced.

Personal Property

Except for property exempted by statute, as further discussed in Chapter 4 herein, most personal property owned by the debtor is subject to garnishment.

Real Property

Unlike personal property, which may be subject to garnishment, judgments are typically enforced against real property by alternative remedies, such as foreclosure or attachment. Because a debtor's interest in real property is his legal title, this title in the hands of third parties is not subject to garnishment. However, where another person holds legal title and the debtor has some equitable interest, garnishment proceedings may be available.

Nevertheless, the proceeds of sale of real property owned by the debtor and in the hands of a third person, are subject to garnishment. In addition, rents which have accrued but have not yet been paid are regarded as a fund belonging to a landlord while yet in the hands of the debtor, and are subject to garnishment in an action against the landlord garnishee. Future rents are not garnishable because they are considered contingent and speculative.

Beneficiary Distribution under an Estate

Most states do not allow the garnishment of a beneficiary's interest in an estate prior to distribution or settlement of the estate. After final determination of the amount due, but prior to actual distribution of the funds, the fiduciary, as representative of the estate is subject to garnishment since he is holding the funds as a personal debtor of the beneficiary.

Trust Funds or Property and Income from Trusts

Since the beneficiary of a trust has an equitable interest in the trust fund, his interest is subject to garnishment so long as there is express statutory authorization. Of course, the beneficiary's interest must be absolute and definable as opposed to being uncertain or subject to some contingency. The trustee is the proper garnishee in this instance. If the trustee has discretion as to how much income and how frequently the beneficiary is to be paid, then the interest is not definable and is not subject to garnishment. Further, property held by a debtor as a trustee is not subject to garnishment since this property is being held in trust for another.

Bank Accounts

Bank accounts are especially amenable to garnishment. The title to the funds is in the debtor/depositor while the actual possession is in the bank. Thus, the bank is the garnishee. By garnishing the debtor's bank account, the creditor steps into the shoes of the debtor, and acquires only the rights the debtor had in the account. In other words, if the debtor is a trustee on the account and he only holds the funds in a fiduciary capacity, the garnishee need not turn over the funds.

Problems arise when the debtor has a joint account with someone else who is not a debtor. In most instances, if it can be proven that the non-debtor is the true owner of the funds, then garnishment may not be available. Commercial or business accounts are particularly susceptible to garnishment since the exemptions do not apply. Since most debtors maintain bank accounts, creditors usually always search for bank accounts to garnish.

Life Insurance

Generally, the proceeds of life insurance policies are not subject to garnishment because they are contingent upon the death of the insured. In some instances, life insurance policies can be garnished to the extent of accumulated cash surrender value, loan value or dividends earned, subject to exemptions where the beneficiaries are the surviving spouse and/or the children. Annuities can be garnished so long as the payments are due and owing the debtor.

Debts

Any debt which is past due or is to become due, incurred either in or out of the state, and to or from a resident or non-resident, is subject to garnishment or attachment.

WAGE GARNISHMENT

A creditor, who obtains a valid judgment against a debtor, has the right to collect on his judgment through the process of wage garnishment, also known as an income execution. Wage garnishment is a legal procedure by which the earnings of an individual are required by court order to be withheld by an employer for the payment of a debt. Each state has its own statutory scheme setting forth the procedure for garnishment and also establishing the maximum monetary limits of how much of a debtor's salary can be used to satisfy a judgment.

A wage garnishment is often a strong motivation for a debtor to their debt because it is embarrassing to have one's employer made aware of the debtor's financial situation, and to cause the employer extra work in complying with the garnishment.

Unless a judgment is for child or spousal support, a creditor cannot garnish unemployment insurance, workers' compensation awards, relocation benefits or disability or health insurance benefits. Garnishing payments made from a retirement plan is also very difficult because most retirement plans contain "anti-alienation" provisions barring the plan administrator from paying anyone except the plan holder or beneficiary, such as a spouse. Social Security benefits can never be garnished.

As set forth below, federal law affords some protection to wage earners who are the subject of a wage garnishment. In 1971, Congress enacted the Consumer Credit Protection Act which placed federal restrictions on the garnishment of an individual's earnings, including a prohibition against the discharge of an employee due to a wage garnishment, and a limit on the amount of wages that are subject to the garnishment.

This legislation resulted from growing congressional concern over the effects of increasing use of credit in the nation, and the ever-increasing number of personal bankruptcy filings. These filings were prompted by individuals unable to cope with harsh garnishment laws.

The Act does not preempt the field of garnishment entirely but does provide that in those instances where state and federal laws are inconsistent, then the courts are to apply the law which garnishes the lesser amount, or which provides for the greater restriction on an employer's right to discharge an employee whose wages have been garnished.

Consumer Credit Protection Act

Title III of the Consumer Credit Protection Act (CCPA) protects employees from being discharged by their employers due to a wage garnishment. Title III is administered and enforced by the Employment Standards Administration's Wage and Hour Division, and applies to all individuals who receive personal earnings and to their employers. Personal earnings include wages, salaries, commissions, bonuses and income from a pension or retirement program, but does not ordinarily include tips.

Protection Afforded Under Title III

Under Title III, an employee cannot be discharged because their wages have been garnished for any one debt, regardless of the number of levies made or proceedings brought to collect it. It does not, however, protect an employee from discharge if the employee's earnings have been subject to garnishment for a second or subsequent debts.

Title III also limits the amount of an employee's earnings which may be garnished in any one work week or pay period to the lesser of 25 percent of disposable earnings—the amount of employee earnings left after legally required deductions have been made for federal, state and local taxes, Social Security, unemployment insurance and state employee retirement systems—or the amount by which disposable earnings are greater than 30 times the federal minimum hourly wage prescribed by section 6(a)(1) of the Fair Labor Standards Act of 1938.

Other deductions which are not required by law, e.g., union dues, health and life insurance, and charitable contributions, are not subtracted from gross earnings when calculating the amount of disposable earnings for garnishment purposes.

Title III specifies that garnishment restrictions do not apply to bankruptcy court orders and debts due for federal and state taxes. Nor does the Act affect voluntary wage assignments—i.e. situations in which workers voluntarily agree that their employers may turn over some specified amount of their earnings to a creditor.

The Law of Attachment and Garnishment   **29**

Employer Violations

If an employer violates Title III, he may be subject to certain penalties, such as reinstatement of a discharged employee with back pay, and the restoration of improperly garnished amounts. Where violations cannot be resolved through informal means, court action may be initiated to restrain and remedy violations. Employers who willfully violate the law may be prosecuted criminally and fined up to $1,000, or imprisoned for not more than one year, or both.

Subsequent Wage Garnishments

The federally-mandated 25% limitation on a wage garnishment applies to the maximum amount that can be garnished by all of the debtor's ordinary creditors, not just one. Thus, if a debtor is already subject to another garnishment, their wages cannot be garnished further by a subsequent garnishment unless:

1. The first garnishment takes less than 25% of the debtor's disposable income, or

2. The garnishment is for alimony or child support.

Child Support and Alimony Orders

There are special restrictions which apply to court orders for child support and alimony and which allow for greater amounts to be garnished. If a debtor is supporting either or both a spouse and a dependent child and the garnishment for support is for someone else—i.e. a former spouse or another dependent child—then only 50% of the disposable earnings is subject to garnishment. If the debtor is not supporting a spouse or child, then 60% of his disposable earnings is subject to garnishment.

CHAPTER 4:
EXEMPTIONS

IN GENERAL

Federal and state statutes limit the type of property that can be used to satisfy a debt. Property that is not subject to collection is known as "exempt" property. For example, a creditor cannot take certain property related to basic needs, such as food, clothing, and necessities.

Under state "homestead" laws, all or a portion of a debtor's primary residence is exempt. In addition, under federal law, creditors cannot garnish more than 25% of a debtor's wages. Further, income from public assistance, social security, unemployment, pensions, veterans benefits, insurance proceeds, worker's compensation benefits or other disability payments generally cannot be garnished.

PURPOSE OF EXEMPTIONS

An exemption is a privilege or right granted by law, on grounds of public policy, to enable a debtor to retain a portion of his property free from judicial seizure and sale by his creditors. This right of a debtor, to hold his property or a part of it, free from the claims of creditors is statutorily granted. The purpose of the exemption statutes is three-pronged:

1. Protection of the debtor;

2. Protection of the family of the debtor; and

3. Protection of society.

By allowing the debtor to retain certain property free from appropriation by creditors, exemption statutes extend to a debtor an opportunity of self-support so that he will not become a burden on the public. The central and common characteristic of exemption statutes is the shelter they afford to debtors from claims of otherwise unsecured judgment creditors acting under a collection process.

Although exemption is considered to be a shield, it should not be used as a sword by the debtor. The exemption laws are designed to secure to the debtor the necessary means of getting a livelihood while doing as little injury as possible to his creditors.

There are two notable characteristics of state exemption statutes: (i) obsolescence and (ii) extreme variety. All states have some exemption statutes but all states are different. The burden for asserting the right to an exemption is on the debtor.

The protection afforded by the exemption statutes is not absolute. The federal tax lien reaches exempt property and, in most states, state taxes, alimony and child support also reach beyond the exemptions.

TYPES OF EXEMPT PROPERTY

Homestead

Almost all states have homestead exemption laws designed to protect the family home from creditors. The exemption is given not for the benefit of the debtor, but rather for the protection of the debtor's family and in part for the protection of the public which might otherwise be burdened with the support of the debtor.

Homestead laws only protect real property interests of the debtor. However, not all real property interests are subject to the exemption. Most statutes require that the debtor have a family, that the property be occupied and used as a residence, that the debtor be a resident of the state, and that the owner have a specified interest in the property.

Real property which is owned and occupied as the debtor's principal residence, the value of which does not exceed $10,000 above liens and encumbrances, is exempt from satisfaction of a money judgment. Similarly, a lot of land with a dwelling, shares of stock in a cooperative apartment, a condominium apartment and a mobile home are also subject to exemptions. Lands set apart as a family or private burying ground are also usually exempt from creditor's claims.

Wages and Income

Like all exemptions, wage exemptions are intended to protect the family as much as the debtor and so should be very liberally construed, especially if the garnishment is sought against the family's sole income.

To protect the debtor, all states have specific wage exemption statutes, as well as the garnishment restrictions in the Federal Consumer Credit Protection Act, which is more fully discussed in Chapter 3 of this almanac. These statutes afford specific protections as to the maximum amounts of wages that can be garnished.

Where a person is engaged in a business of his own, his profits are not wages within the meaning of the statutes. Thus, wage exemptions are not available for, among others, self-employed CPA's, attorneys, and surveyors. Some statutes also limit exemptions on bonuses, commissions and business expense reimbursements. In addition, tax refunds and worker's compensation payments are not characterized as wages for purposes of wage exemption provisions.

Tools and Implements Used in Debtor's Trade or Business

The majority of state exemption statutes provide that a debtor may keep a specified portion of his tools and implements that are necessary for use in his profession, trade or business. The types of items exempted have also been described as instruments, apparatus, books, materials, stock in trade, equipment, machines etc. The purpose of this particular exemption is to allow the debtor to continue in business in order to generate enough income to support himself and his family.

Issues as to whether a particular article is exempt as a tool or implement and whether these items are necessary or proper in the debtor's trade or business are determined through judicial interpretation of the individual state statute. For example, a seat on a stock exchange was not an exempt working tool of a stockbroker, but an automobile owned by a real estate agent has been held to be exempt.

The interpretations are endless—the exempt or non-exempt status of each individual profession and tool is generally considered on a case by case basis with results that can vary radically from state to state.

Motor Vehicles

Many states provide specific exemptions for motor vehicles which may exist in place of or in addition to a tools of the trade exemption. The term "motor vehicle" has also been held to include trucks, trailers, vans and buses. These exemption provisions generally establish a value ceiling. The value of the vehicle that may be exempted is the debtor's equity since the debtor has no value in collateral to the extent that it is security for a loan.

Animals

Statutes exempting animals range from exempting only animals used in a trade or business, such as farm animals, domestic animals, such as dogs and cats, etc., or specially enumerated animals, such as "five cows and a bull". Some states also allow an exemption to cover food for the animals.

Household Goods and Furniture

Household goods and furniture are protected from creditors under many state exemption statutes. Such statutes may exempt these articles generally or exempt specific household items and then by a general clause exempt all other household goods. What type of property is exempt varies with the individual state and can depend on whether the items are necessary to the debtor, whether the items are normally found in the debtor's residence or whether the items are primarily for personal, family or household use.

Many statutes limit the amount of exemption to a specific value, while others categorize the specific property and may also set value caps. Some examples of items held to be exempt are: antiques, dinnerware, some electronic equipment such as a television, stereo, VCR, appliances, musical instruments, kitchen utensils and sewing machine.

Insurance and Annuities

Most states have enacted exemption statutes which protect insurance proceeds from seizure by creditors. These provisions apply to various types of insurance. Life insurance proceeds are generally exempt form the claims of creditors. Some states allow exemptions for the proceeds of health and accident insurance and disability benefits while others do not provide any statutory exemptions.

Similarly, there are no general rules with regard to annuities. While some states do not provide an exemption, other states, depending on the purpose of the annuity, have provided exemptions. For instance, where the annuity was based on a structured settlement for the wrongful death of a debtor's minor son, or where the proceeds of a life policy were converted into an annuity by the widow beneficiary, the statutes specifically exempted these annuities.

Most states exempt the proceeds of insurance on exempt property where that property is destroyed on the theory that the insurance money represents or stands in the place of the property itself. Thus it allows the debtor to replace the destroyed property, enabling him to continue the purpose of the exemption laws, which is the protection of the family.

Pension and Retirement Benefits

Generally, benefit payments made under the Employee Retirement Income Security Act (ERISA) are exempt. These include railroad pensions, civil service pensions, federal, state and local government pensions, social security, old age and survivor's benefits and veteran's benefits.

Miscellaneous Items

Some states exempt food, provisions and fuel in quantities sufficient to protect the debtor and his family. Wearing apparel which is necessary or primarily for personal, household or family use up to a certain dollar value may also be exempt from creditors. Worker's compensation benefits, books, burial plot, certain amounts of cash, family pictures and heirlooms and jewelry are other types of property which may be exempt.

Since each state's exemptions are varied, the reader is advised to check the law of his or her own jurisdiction when faced with an attachment or garnishment situation.

ASSERTION OF THE EXEMPTION

The duty of making a claim of exemption generally rests primarily on the debtor since it is purely personal to the one in whose favor it exists. Some states require that a debtor affirmatively claim an exemption in order to exercise it, while other states do not have a notice provision.

In order to claim an exemption right, the debtor should place the judgment creditor on notice of the exempt property. For example, if the debtor's bank account only contains proceeds from social security benefits, the judgment creditor, as well as the bank, should be made aware of this fact. A number of statutes require that exemptions be claimed within a specified time period or within a reasonable time prior to the levy or sale.

In general, the debtor must make an application to the court. The affidavit should be filed with the judgment creditor, the sheriff's office, and the debtor's bank. Exempt property which has been seized is generally returned shortly after the sheriff is made aware of the exemption.

If the judgment creditor disputes the debtor's claim of exemption—e.g., if there is a dispute over the value of a car thus raising questions about whether it is exempt—the creditor may request a court hearing. The debtor must be prepared to demonstrate to the court that the property is subject to an exemption—e.g., bring receipts or other evidence of the value of the car. If the debtor prevails, their money or property will generally be released. If the debtor is unable to support their claim for exemption, the debtor should investigate his or her right to appeal the decision.

The reader is advised to check the law of his or her own jurisdiction concerning specific time limitations and procedural steps to claim an exemption.

USE OF FORCE TO RETURN EXEMPT PROPERTY AND REMEDIES

Where an officer attempts to levy on exempt property after being informed of the fact that it is exempt, he is a trespasser and the owner may use as much force as is necessary to prevent the levy. However, the owner is liable if he uses more force than is necessary.

In addition, a debtor is entitled to damages resulting from the wrongful seizure of exempt property. Liability for the wrongful seizure of exempt property or for other injury to exemption rights attaches to those who participate in, or are responsible for, the illegal act. The creditor is liable if he ordered or acquiesced in the abuse of process.

The damages that may be allowed when exempt property is wrongfully seized generally depends on an estimate of the value of loss to the debtor. For example, a debtor who claimed that his truck and tools were wrongfully seized and that he had no way to make the long round trip to available work during the period of seizure, and would have been forced to purchase new tools in order to accept some employment, was entitled to recover the wages he would have received during that time period.

Depending on the state where the debtor resides, he may or may not be able to recover for mental suffering or distress in an action for unlawful seizure of exempt property. Similarly, attorneys fees may sometimes be recovered and in situations where, in defiance and disregard of the law, a party levies on and sells property known to be exempt, the debtor may be awarded punitive or exemplary damages.

CHAPTER 5:
THE UNIFORM FRAUDULENT TRANSFER ACT

FRAUDULENT TRANSFERS

In order to avoid having a piece of property seized, a debtor may attempt to fraudulently transfer the property to another. There are state laws which make this type of property transfer illegal. In doing so, the majority of states have adopted the language of the revised Uniform Fraudulent Transfer Act.

THE UNIFORM FRAUDULENT CONVEYANCE ACT

The Uniform Fraudulent Conveyance Act (UFCA) was the forerunner to the renamed and revised Uniform Fraudulent Transfer Act (UFTA). The UFCA was promulgated by the Conference of Commissioners on Uniform State Laws in 1918. The UFCA was adopted in 25 jurisdictions, including the Virgin Islands. It was also adopted in the sections of the Bankruptcy Act of 1938 and the Bankruptcy Reform Act of 1978 that deal with fraudulent transfers and obligations.

The UFCA was a codification of the "better" decisions applying the English Statute of Elizabeth. The English statute was enacted in some form in many states, but, whether or not so enacted, the voidability of fraudulent transfer was part of the law of every American jurisdiction.

Since the intent to hinder, delay, or defraud creditors is seldom susceptible of direct proof, courts have relied on so-called "badges" of fraud. The weight given these badges varied greatly from jurisdiction. The Conference sought to minimize or eliminate the diversity among jurisdictions by providing that proof of certain fact combinations would conclusively establish fraud. In the absence of evidence of the existence of such facts, proof of a fraudulent transfer was to depend on evidence of actual intent.

An important reform effected by the UFCA was the elimination of any requirement that a creditor have obtained a judgment or execution returned unsatisfied before bringing an action to avoid a transfer as fraudulent.

THE UNIFORM FRAUDULENT TRANSFER ACT

The Conference was persuaded in 1979 to appoint a committee to undertake a study of the UFCA with a view to preparing the draft of a revision. The Conference was influenced by the following considerations:

1. The Bankruptcy Reform Act of 1978 had made numerous changes in the section of that Act dealing with fraudulent transfers and obligations, thereby substantially reducing the correspondence of the provisions of the federal bankruptcy law on fraudulent transfers with the Uniform Act.

2. The Committee on Corporate Laws of the Section of Corporations, Banking & Business Law of the American Bar Association, engaged in revising the Model Corporation Act, suggested that the Conference review provisions of the Uniform Act with a view to determining whether the Acts are consistent in respect to the treatment of dividend distributions.

3. The Uniform Commercial Code, enacted at least in part by all 50 states, had substantially modified related rules of law regulating transfers of personal property, notably by facilitating the making and perfection of security transfers against attack by unsecured creditors.

4. Debtors and trustees in a number of cases have avoided foreclosure of security interests by invoking the fraudulent transfer section of the Bankruptcy Reform Act.

5. The Model Rules of Professional Conduct adopted by the House of Delegates of the American Bar Association on August 2, 1983, forbid a lawyer to counsel or to assist a client in conduct that the lawyer knows is fraudulent.

The Drafting Committee appointed by the Conference held its first meeting in January of 1983. A first reading of a draft of the revision of the Uniform Fraudulent Conveyance Act was conducted at the Conference's meeting in Boca Raton, Florida, on July 27, 1983. The Committee held four meetings in addition to a meeting held in connection with the Conference meeting in Boca Raton.

The Committee determined to rename the Act as The Uniform Fraudulent Transfer Act in recognition of its applicability to transfers of personal property as well as real property. The term "conveyance" appeared to restrict application of the Act to a transfer of personal property. However, the revised Act, like the original Uniform Act, does not purport to cover the whole law of voidable transfers and obligations.

Fraudulent Transfers and Obligations

The basic structure and approach of the Uniform Fraudulent Conveyance Act are preserved in the Uniform Fraudulent Transfer Act. There are two sections in the new Act delineating what transfers and obligations are fraudulent:

1. Both Acts declare a transfer made or an obligation incurred with actual intent to hinder, delay, or defraud creditors to be fraudulent.

2. Both Acts render a transfer made or obligation incurred without adequate consideration to be constructively fraudulent—i.e., without regard to the actual intent of the parties—under one of the following conditions:

(a) The debtor was left by the transfer or obligation with unreasonably small assets for a transaction or the business in which he was engaged;

(b) The debtor intended to incur, or believed that he would incur, more debts than he would be able to pay; or

(c) The debtor was insolvent at the time or as a result of the transfer or obligation.

As under the original Uniform Fraudulent Conveyance Act, a transfer or obligation that is constructively fraudulent because insolvency concurs with, or follows failure to receive adequate consideration, is voidable only by a creditor in existence at the time the transfer occurs or the obligation is incurred. Either an existing or subsequent creditor may avoid a transfer or obligation for inadequate consideration when accompanied by the requisite financial condition or mental state specified in the Act.

Reasonably equivalent value is required in order to constitute adequate consideration under the revised Act. The revision follows the Bankruptcy Code in eliminating good faith on the part of the transferee or obligee as an issue in the determination of whether adequate consideration is given by a transferee or obligee.

The new Act, like the Bankruptcy Act, allows the transferee or obligee to show good faith in defense after a creditor establishes that a fraudulent transfer has been made or a fraudulent obligation has been incurred. Thus a showing by a defendant that a reasonable equivalent has been given in good faith for a transfer or obligation is a complete defense although the debtor is shown to have intended to hinder, delay, or defraud creditors.

A good faith transferee or obligee who has given less than a reasonable equivalent is nevertheless allowed a reduction in liability to the extent of the value given. The new Act, like the Bankruptcy Code, eliminates the provision of the Uniform Fraudulent Conveyance Act that enables a creditor to attack a security transfer on the ground that the value of the property transferred is disproportionate to the debt secured. The premise of the new Act is that the value of the interest transferred for security is measured by and thus corresponds exactly to the debt secured.

Foreclosure of a debtor's interest by a regularly conducted, noncollusive sale on default under a mortgage or other security agreement may not be avoided under the Act as a transfer for less than a reasonably equivalent value.

Insolvency

The definition of insolvency under the Act is adapted from the definition of the term in the Bankruptcy Code. Insolvency is presumed from proof of a failure generally to pay debts as they become due.

Preferential Transfers to Insiders

The new Act adds a new category of fraudulent transfer, namely, a preferential transfer by an insolvent insider to a creditor who had reasonable cause to believe the debtor to be insolvent. An insider is defined in much the same way as in the Bankruptcy Code and includes a relative, also defined as in the Bankruptcy Code, a director or officer of a corporate debtor, a partner, or a person in control of a debtor. This provision is available only to an existing creditor. Its premise is that an insolvent debtor is obliged to pay debts to creditors not related to him before paying those who are insiders.

The new Act omits any provision directed particularly at transfers or obligations of insolvent partnership debtors. Under Section 8 of the Uniform Fraudulent Conveyance Act, any transfer made or obligation incurred by an insolvent partnership to a partner is fraudulent without regard to intent or adequacy of consideration.

The new Act also omits as redundant a provision in the original Act that makes fraudulent a transfer made or obligation incurred by an insolvent partnership for less than a fair consideration to the partnership.

Available Remedies

Section 7 of the Act lists the remedies available to creditors. It eliminates as unnecessary and confusing a differentiation made in the original Act between the remedies available to holders of matured claims and those holding unmatured claims.

Since promulgation of the Uniform Fraudulent Conveyance Act, the Supreme Court has imposed restrictions on the availability and use of prejudgment remedies. As a result, many states have amended their statutes and rules applicable to such remedies. Thus, it is frequently unclear whether a state's procedures include a prejudgment remedy against a fraudulent transfer or obligation.

Liability and Defenses

Section 8 of the Act prescribes the measure of liability of a transferee or obligee and enumerates defenses. Defenses against avoidance of a preferential transfer to an insider under Section 5(b) include an adaptation of defenses available under Section 547(c)(2) and (4) of the Bankruptcy Code when such a transfer is sought to be avoided as a preference by the trustee in bankruptcy.

In addition a preferential transfer may be justified when shown to be made pursuant to a good faith effort to stave off forced liquidation and rehabilitate the debtor. Section 8 also precludes avoidance, as a constructively fraudulent transfer, of the termination of a lease on default or the enforcement of a security interest in compliance with Article 9 of the Uniform Commercial Code.

Timing

The new Act includes a new section specifying when a transfer is made or an obligation is incurred. The section specifying the time when a transfer occurs is adapted from Section 548(d) of the Bankruptcy Code. Its premise is that if the law prescribes a mode for making the transfer a matter of public record or notice, it is not deemed to be made for any purpose under the Act until it has become such a matter of record or notice.

Statute of Limitations

The new Act also includes a statute of limitations that bars the right rather than the remedy on expiration of the statutory periods prescribed. The law governing limitations on actions to avoid fraudulent transfers among the states is unclear and full of diversity. The Act recognizes that laches and estoppel may operate to preclude a particular creditor from pursuing a remedy against a fraudulent transfer or obligation even though the statutory period of limitations has not run.

The text of the Uniform Fraudulent Transfer Act is set forth at Appendix 18.

CHAPTER 6:
FEDERAL TAX COLLECTION

THE COLLECTION PROCESS

Most taxpayers file their tax returns and pay what they owe on time. If they don't, the Internal Revenue Service sends the taxpayer a bill. This begins the collection process. However, the IRS recognizes that sometimes taxpayers are unable to pay what they owe. In that case, the taxpayer should contact the IRS as soon as possible, as there are a number of payment solutions the IRS may be able to offer to the taxpayer, including:

1. Installment agreements;

2. Delaying collection until the taxpayer's financial condition improves;

3. Offer in Compromise allowing taxpayers to settle their tax bill for less than the amount they owe.

If the taxpayer does not respond to the notice or subsequent notices, the account becomes delinquent, and may be turned over to the Automated Collection System (ACS), where IRS personnel will contact the taxpayer by telephone to work out an agreeable payment solution. If after several attempts the IRS is still unable to contact the taxpayer, or cannot work out a payment solution, the account may then be turned over to a revenue officer for collection. The revenue officer will again try to settle the account with the taxpayer.

ENFORCEMENT ACTIONS

If the IRS is still unable to work out a payment solution, it may, as a final resort, take enforcement action. These actions could include:

1. Filing a lien;

2. Serving a notice of levy; or

3. Seizure and sale of property.

Once the IRS takes collection action, the taxpayer still has options. As a result of the Taxpayer Bill of Rights, certain collection enforcement actions that a taxpayer disagrees with may now be appealed either before or after the action occurs. Normally, the IRS will stop the collection action until the appeal is settled.

An IRS Collection Appeal Request Form is set forth at Appendix 19.

IRS Tax Liens

Liens give the IRS a legal claim to the taxpayer's property as security or payment for their tax debt. A Notice of Federal Tax Lien may be filed only after:

1. The IRS assesses the tax liability;

2. The IRS sends the taxpayer a Notice and Demand for Payment—a bill that tells the taxpayer how much he or she owe in taxes; and

3. The taxpayer neglects or refuses to fully pay the debt within 10 days after being notified.

Once the above requirements are met, an IRS tax lien is created for the amount of the taxpayer's tax debt. By filing this notice, the taxpayer's creditors are publicly notified that the IRS has a claim against all of the taxpayer's property, including property the taxpayer acquires after the lien was filed.

The tax lien attaches to all the taxpayer's property, including their house and car, and to all their rights to property, such as their accounts receivable, if the taxpayer is an employer.

Lien Payoff Amount

The full amount of the taxpayer's lien will remain a matter of public record until it is paid in full. However, at any time, the taxpayer may request an updated lien payoff amount to show the remaining balance due. An IRS employee can issue a letter with the current amount due in order to release a lien.

The amount of the penalty is equal to the unpaid balance of the trust fund tax. The penalty is computed based on the unpaid income taxes withheld, plus the employee's portion of the withheld FICA taxes. For collected taxes, the penalty is based on the unpaid amount of collected excise taxes.

COLLECTION APPEAL RIGHTS

The taxpayer can appeal many IRS collection actions. If the taxpayer receives a Notice of Federal Tax Lien Filing; a Notice of Intent to Levy; or Notice of Jeopardy Levy and Right of Appeal, the taxpayer can appeal under

Due Process procedures. The taxpayer has 30 days to request a due process hearing with the IRS Office of Appeals.

A Request for a Collection Due Process Hearing Form is set forth at Appendix 20.

Lien and Levy Notices

The law provides the taxpayer the right to a fair hearing by the IRS Office of Appeals after a Notice of Federal Tax Lien is filed and before a levy on the taxpayer's property is issued. The taxpayer also has the right to contest the Office of Appeals' determination in Tax Court or U.S. District Court, as appropriate. Under Due Process, the taxpayer may request a hearing for each taxable period for one or both of the following IRS actions:

Lien Notice

The IRS is required to notify the taxpayer that a Notice of Federal Tax Lien has been filed within 5 days after filing. The taxpayer then has 30 days from the date of the lien notice to request a hearing with the IRS Office of Appeals.

Levy Notice

The IRS is required to notify the taxpayer of its intention to collect a tax liability by taking the taxpayer's property or rights to property. The IRS does this by sending the taxpayer a levy notice. No levy or seizure can occur within 30 days from the date of mailing of the levy notice or the date the levy notice is given to the taxpayer or left at the taxpayer's home or business. During that 30-day period, the taxpayer may request a hearing with the IRS Office of Appeals.

There are two exceptions to this levy or seizure notice provision:

1. When the collection of tax is in jeopardy; or

2. When the IRS issues a levy to collect from a state tax refund

In those instances, the IRS may issue a levy without sending a levy notice or waiting 30 days after it sends the notice.

THE DUE PROCESS HEARING

At the due process hearing, the taxpayer may raise any relevant issue relating to the unpaid tax including

1. Appropriateness of collection actions;

2. Collection alternatives such as installment agreement, offer in compromise, posting a bond or substitution of other assets;

3. Appropriate spousal defenses;

4. The existence or amount of the tax, but only if the taxpayer did not receive a notice of deficiency or did not have an opportunity to dispute the tax liability.

The taxpayer may not, however, raise an issue that was raised and considered at a prior administrative or judicial hearing, if he or she participated meaningfully in the prior hearing or proceeding.

Before filing a formal appeal of lien or levy notice, the taxpayer may be able to work out a solution with the Collection office that proposed the action. To do so, the taxpayer must contact the IRS employee whose name appears on the lien or levy notice and explain why they disagree with the action. The taxpayer should be aware, however, that this contact does not extend the 30 day period to request an appeal.

Once a due process hearing is requested with the Office of Appeals, unless the IRS has reason to believe that collection of the tax is in jeopardy, they will stop collection action during the 30 days after the levy notice and, if the appeal is timely, during the appeal process. The IRS will also suspend the collection statute of limitations—which is 10 years—from the date they receive a timely filed request for a hearing until the date the determination is final.

An appeal is timely if it is mailed on or before the 30th day after the date of the IRS lien or levy notice. If the appeal request is not timely, the taxpayer will be allowed a hearing, but there will be no statutory suspension of collection action and he or she cannot go to court if they disagree with the Office of Appeals' determination.

The Office of Appeals will contact the taxpayer to schedule a hearing, either in person or by telephone. At the conclusion of the hearing, the Office of Appeals will issue a written determination letter. If the taxpayer agrees with the decision, the taxpayer and the IRS are required to live up to the terms of the decision. If the taxpayer does not agree with the decision, he or she may request judicial review of the decision by initiating a case in a court of proper jurisdiction—i.e., the U.S. Tax Court or the U.S. District Court—on or before the 30th day after the date of the decision. Once the Court rules, its decision is binding on both the taxpayer and the IRS.

The IRS Office of Appeals will retain jurisdiction over its determinations and how they are carried out. The taxpayer may also return to the Office of Appeals if their circumstances change and impact the original decision. However, the taxpayer must first exhaust all administrative remedies.

A taxpayer may be represented by an attorney at the due process hearing if they so choose, however, retaining a lawyer is not a requirement. The taxpayer may also be represented by a certified public accountant or other person authorized to practice before the IRS.

CERTIFICATE OF RELEASE OF FEDERAL TAX LIEN

The IRS will issue a Release of the Notice of Federal Tax Lien under the following circumstances:

1. Within 30 days after the taxpayer satisfies the tax due, including interest and other additions, by paying the debt or by having it adjusted, or

2. Within 30 days after the IRS accepts a bond that the taxpayer submits, guaranteeing payment of the debt.

In addition, the taxpayer must pay all fees that a state or other jurisdiction charges to file and release the lien. These fees are added to the amount the taxpayer owes.

In general, 10 years after a tax is assessed, a lien releases automatically if the IRS has not filed it again. If the IRS knowingly or negligently does not release a Notice of Federal Tax Lien when it should be released, the taxpayer has the right to sue the federal government—but not IRS employees—for damages.

Section 6325(a) of the Internal Revenue Code directs the IRS to release a Federal Tax Lien after a tax liability becomes fully paid or legally unenforceable. The IRS also must release a lien when they accept a bond for payment of the tax. If the IRS hasn't released the lien within thirty days, the taxpayer can ask for a Certificate of Release of Lien by sending a written request with any required documents to the District Directory of the Internal Revenue Service, addressed to the District in which the lien was filed. The request must include:

1. The date of the request;

2. The name and address of the taxpayer;

3. One copy of each notice of Federal Tax Lien to be released; and

4. Why the taxpayer wants the IRS to release the lien.

If the tax has been paid, enclose a copy of either of the following:

1. An Internal Revenue Service receipt;

2. A canceled check; or

3. Any other acceptable proof.

For an immediate or urgent Certificate of Release of Federal Tax Lien, the taxpayer should visit or telephone the district office that filed the Notice of Federal Tax Lien and be prepared to show proof of payment. In order to receive an immediate release, unpaid taxes must be paid with a certified check, cashier's check, or money order.

Selected provisions of the Federal Tax Lien Act are set forth at Appendix 21.

APPENDIX 1:
TABLE OF STATE STATUTES GOVERNING DEBT COLLECTION

STATE	STATUTE
Alabama	Alabama Code §40-12-80
Alaska	Alaska Statutes §§8.24.0.011 et seq.
Arizona	Arizona Revised Statutes Annotated §§32-1001 et seq.
Arkansas	Arkansas Statutes Annotated §617-21-104 et seq.
California	California Civil Code §§1788 et seq.
Colorado	Colorado Revised Statutes §§5-10101 et seq; 12-14-101 et seq.
Connecticut	Connecticut General Statutes Annotated §§36-243.a et seq; 42-127 et seq.
Delaware	Delaware Code Annotated. Title 30. §2301(13).
District of Columbia	D.C. Code Annotated §§22-3423 et seq; 28-3814 et seq.
Florida	Florida Statutes §§559.55 et seq.
Georgia	Georgia Code Annotated §§7-3-1 et seq.
Hawaii	Hawaii Revised Statutes §§443-B-1 et seq.
Idaho	Idaho Code §§26-2222 et seq.
Illinois	Illinois Annotated Statutes. Chapter 111. §§2001 et seq.
Indiana	Indiana Code Annotated §§25-11-1-1 et seq.
Iowa	Iowa Code Annotated §§537.7101 et seq.
Kansas	Kansas Statutes Annotated §16a-5-107.

STATE	STATUTE
Kentucky	None.
Louisiana	Louisiana Revised Statutes Annotated §§9:3510 et seq.
Maine	Maine Revised Statutes Annotated. Title 32 §§11,001 et seq; Title 9-A §§1.101 et seq.
Maryland	Maryland Annotated Code. Article 56 §§323 et seq; Maryland Com. Law Code Annotated. §§14-201 et seq.
Massachusetts	Massachusetts General Laws Annotated. Chapter 93 §§24 et seq; §49.
Michigan	Michigan Compiled Laws Annotated §19.655; §18.425.
Minnesota	None.
Missouri	None.
Montana	None.
Nebraska	Nebraska Revised Statutes §§45-601 et seq; 45-175 et seq.
Nevada	Nevada Revised Statutes §§649.005 et seq.
New Hampshire	New Hampshire Revised Statutes Annotated §§358-C:1 et seq.
New Jersey	New Jersey Statutes Annotated §§45:18-1 et seq.
New Mexico	New Mexico Statutes Annotated §§61-18A-1 et seq.
New York	New York General Law §§600 et seq.
North Carolina	North Carolina General Statutes §§66-49.24 et seq; 75-50 et seq.
North Dakota	North Dakota Cent. Code §§13-05-01 et seq.
Ohio	None.
Oklahoma	None.
Oregon	Oregon Revised Statutes §§646.639 et seq; 697.010 et seq.
Pennsylvania	18 Pennsylvania Cons. Statutes Annotated §§7311; 201-1 et seq.
Rhode Island	None.
South Carolina	South Carolina Code Annotated §37-5-108.
South Dakota	None.
Tennessee	Tennessee Code Annotated §§62-20-101 et seq.

STATE	STATUTE
Texas	Texas Revised Civ. Statutes Annotated. Arts. 5069-11.01 et seq.
Utah	Utah Code Annotated §§12-1-1 et seq.
Vermont	Vermont Statutes Annotated. Title 9 §§2451a et seq.
Virginia	Virginia Code Annotated §§18.2 et seq.
Washington	Washington Revised Code Annotated §§19.16.100 et seq.
West Virginia	West Virginia Code §§47-16-1 §§18.2 et seq; 46A-2-101 et seq.
Wisconsin	Wisconsin Statutes Annotated §§218.04; 427.101 et seq.
Wyoming	Wyoming Statutes §§33-11-101 et seq.

APPENDIX 2:
APPLICATION FOR PROPERTY EXECUTION

PROPERTY EXECUTION PROCEEDINGS
APPLICATION AND EXECUTION
JD-CV-5EL Rev. 12-90
C.G.S. 52-356a

STATE OF CONNECTICUT
SUPERIOR COURT

NAME AND MAILING ADDRESS OF JUDGMENT CREDITOR OR ATTORNEY
(To be completed by Plaintiff)

TO:

┌   ┐

└   ┘

PLAINTIFF OR PLAINTIFF'S ATTORNEY: Type or print. Complete original and 4 copies of the "Application." If judgment debtor is a natural person, attach copy of form JD-CV-5b. Present original and 3 copies to clerk of court. Enter name and address of person to receive issued execution in the box above.

CLERK: Check the file to ensure that no stay of enforcement has been entered on the judgment, the time for filing an appeal of the judgment has expired, no appeal has been filed staying enforcement of the judgment and that the information provided on the application is correct. Sign original execution; original and copies to the applicant. Retain a copy for the file.

SHERIFF: Make execution as directed in the "Execution" section on page 2. Make return on signed original within four months from the date this execution issued. If judgment debtor is a natural person, attach exemption claim form (JD-CV-5b) to copy(ies) of execution served. Complete Section II on exemption claim form.

PERSON IN POSSESSION OF PROPERTY OF JUDGMENT DEBTOR WHO IS A NATURAL PERSON — Pursuant to Gen. Stat. 52-356a, you are required to mail to the judgment debtor indicated below at his last known address, postage prepaid, a copy of this property execution and the attached property execution exemption claim form. Complete Section III on exemption claim form before mailing it to judgment debtor. Twenty days from the date of the service of this property execution, you must deliver to the sheriff property owned by the judgment debtor in your possession or you must deliver to the sheriff payment of a debt owed by you to the judgment debtor. EXCEPT (1) If an exemption claim has been filed with the court you shall withhold delivery of the property or payment of the debt owed by you subject to the determination of the exemption claim by the court and (2) if the debt owed by you to the judgment debtor is not due at the expiration of the twenty days, you shall pay the amount to the sheriff when the debt becomes due if it becomes due within four months after the date of issuance of this execution.

PERSON IN POSSESSION OF PROPERTY OF JUDGMENT DEBTOR WHO IS NOT A NATURAL PERSON — Pursuant to Gen. Stat. 52-356a, you are required to deliver to the sheriff, property in your possession owned by the judgment debtor or pay to the sheriff the amount of a debt owed by you to the judgment debtor, provided, if the debt owed by you is not yet payable, payment shall be made to the sheriff when the debt becomes due if it becomes due within four months after the date of issuance of this execution.

APPLICATION

ADDRESS OF COURT *(Number, street, and town)* ☐ G.A. ☐ J.D. ☐ HOUSING	DATE OF JUDGMENT	DOCKET NUMBER

NAME(S) OF JUDGMENT CREDITOR(S) MAKING APPLICATION	OF *(Street and Town)*

NAME(S) OF JUDGMENT DEBTOR(S) *(Include any information necessary for identification)*	OF *(Street and Town)*

1. AMOUNT OF JUDGMENT *(including damages and, where applicable, prejudgment interest and atty. fees)*	2. AMOUNT OF COSTS IN OBTAINING JUDGMENT
3. TOTAL JUDGMENT AND COSTS *(Add 1 and 2 above)*	4. TOTAL PAID ON ACCOUNT
5. TOTAL UNPAID JUDGMENT *(Subtract 4 from 3 above)*	6. APPLICATION FOR PROPERTY EXECUTION *(If not waived by the court)*

7. TOTAL OF 5 AND 6 ABOVE	IS THIS A CONSUMER JUDGMENT? *("Consumer judgment" means a money judgment of less than $5,000 against a natural person resulting from a debt incurred primarily for personal, family or household purposes)* ☐ YES ☐ NO

IF THIS IS A CONSUMER JUDGMENT, HAS A STAY OF PROPERTY EXECUTIONS BEEN ENTERED PURSUANT TO AN INSTALMENT PAYMENT ORDER?
☐ YES ☐ NO

IF "YES", STATEMENT OF JUDGMENT CREDITOR OR JUDGMENT CREDITOR'S ATTORNEY OF DEFAULT ON INSTALMENT PAYMENT ORDER

SIGNED *(Plaintiff or attorney for plaintiff)*	DATE SIGNED	ADDRESS OF PERSON SIGNING	TELEPHONE NO.

PAGE 1 OF 2

APPLICATION FOR PROPERTY EXECUTION

EXECUTION

To Any Proper Officer:

Whereas on said date of judgment the Judgment Creditor(s) recovered judgment against the Judgment Debtor(s) before the court for the amount stated, as appears of record, whereof execution remains to be done. These are, therefore, BY AUTHORITY OF THE STATE OF CONNECTICUT TO COMMAND YOU: That of the nonexempt goods of said Judgment Debtor(s) within your precincts, you cause to be levied (the same being seized and sold as the law directs), paid and satisfied to said Judgment Creditor(s) the total unpaid amount of said judgment, plus your own fees in the following manner: You shall personally serve a copy of this execution on the judgment debtor, and if the judgment debtor is a natural person, a copy of the exemption claim form (JD-CV-5b), and make demand for payment by the judgment debtor of all sums due under the money judgment. On failure of the judgment debtor to make immediate payment you are commanded to levy on nonexempt personal property of the judgment debtor, other than debts due from a banking institution or earnings, sufficient to satisfy the judgment as follows: If such nonexempt personal property is in the possession of the judgment debtor, you shall take such personal property into your possession as is accessible without breach of peace. If the judgment debtor has left the state prior to service of this execution, or if he cannot be found with reasonable effort at his last known address in this state, you shall proceed with the levy after (1) making demand for payment at such last known address and on any agent or attorney of the judgment debtor of record with the clerk of the Superior Court and (2) making a reasonable effort to ascertain and provide notice of the execution at any forwarding address.

A. DEMAND ON THIRD PERSON
(If judgment debtor is a natural person)

On failure of the judgment debtor to make immediate payment of all sums due under the money judgment, and upon your being unable to levy on nonexempt personal property of the judgment debtor in the judgment debtor's possession and, if the judgment debtor has left the state prior to the service of this execution, upon your being unable to obtain payment sufficient to satisfy the judgment by making demand for payment at the judgment debtor's last known address in this state and on any agent or attorney of the judgment debtor of record with the clerk of the Superior Court, you are also commanded to make demand upon any third person having possession of nonexempt personal property of the judgment debtor for payment to you, or to levy on any nonexempt personal property or debt due said judgment debtor sufficient to satisfy the total amount of judgment unpaid pursuant to Gen. Stat. 52-356a(4)(c). After having made such demand you are directed to serve two true and attested copies of this execution, together with the exemption claim form, with your doings endorsed thereon, on the third person upon whom such demand was made.

B. DEMAND ON THIRD PERSON
(If judgment debtor is not a natural person)

On failure of the judgment debtor to make immediate payment of all sums due under the money judgment and upon your being unable to levy on nonexempt personal property of the judgment debtor in the judgment debtor's possession and, if the judgment debtor has left the state prior to the service of this execution, upon your being unable to obtain payment sufficient to satisfy the judgment by making demand for payment at the judgment debtor's last known address in this state and on any agent or attorney of the judgment debtor of record with the clerk of the Superior Court, you are also commanded to make demand upon any third person having possession of nonexempt personal property of the judgment debtor for payment to you or to levy on any nonexempt personal property or debt due said judgment debtor(s) sufficient to satisfy the total amount of the judgment unpaid pursuant to Gen. Stat. 52-356a(4)(c).

HEREOF FAIL NOT, AND MAKE DUE RETURN OF THIS WRIT WITH YOUR DOINGS THEREON, ACCORDING TO LAW, WITHIN FOUR MONTHS HEREOF.

NOTICE: THE JUDGMENT DEBTOR'S NONEXEMPT PERSONAL PROPERTY IS SUBJECT TO LEVY, SEIZURE, AND SALE BY THE SHERIFF PURSUANT TO THIS EXECUTION.

SIGNED *(Assistant Clerk)*

ON *(Date)*

RETURN OF SERVICE

STATE OF CONNECTICUT

....CONNECTICUT

ss.

....COUNTY

....19......

On the ....day of .... 19........, then and there I duly served the

foregoing

application, order and execution on

....

....the person(s) named therein, by leaving with or

ATTEST:

Proper Officer

JD-CV-5 (page 2) Rev. 12/90

PAGE 2 OF 2

....
Title

APPENDIX 3:
PROPERTY EXECUTION EXEMPTION
CLAIM FORM

EXEMPTION CLAIM FORM
PROPERTY EXECUTION
JD-CV-5bEL Rev. 1-96
C.G.S. 52-321a, 52-352b, 52-361a, 52-361b

STATE OF CONNECTICUT
SUPERIOR COURT

NAME AND MAILING ADDRESS OF JUDGMENT DEBTOR OR ATTORNEY
(To be completed by Plaintiff)

┌   ┐

└   ┘

INSTRUCTIONS
TO PLAINTIFF: *Complete section I below and follow*
instructions on form JD-CV-5.
TO SHERIFF: *Complete section II below and follow*
instructions on form JC-CV-5.
TO THIRD PERSON: *Complete section III below and*
follow instructions on form JD-CV-5.
TO JUDGMENT DEBTOR: *Read section IV below*

SECTION I *(To be completed by plaintiff)*

ADDRESS OF COURT *(Number, street, town, zip code)*   ☐ G.A.   ☐ J.D.   ☐ HOUSING SESSION

NAME OF JUDGMENT DEBTOR	DATE EXECUTION ISSUED	DOCKET NO.

NAME AND ADDRESS OF JUDGMENT CREDITOR	TELEPHONE NO.

SECTION II *(To be completed by sheriff)*

DATE OF SERVICE OF EXECUTION	NAME AND ADDRESS OF SHERIFF

NAME AND ADDRESS OF THIRD PERSON SERVED WITH EXECUTION *(if any)*	TELEPHONE NO. *(if known)*

SECTION III *(To be completed by third person served with execution (if any)*

DATE EXECUTION MAILED TO JUDGMENT DEBTOR

SECTION IV   **NOTICE TO JUDGMENT DEBTOR**

As a result of a judgment entered against you the attached execution has been issued against your personal property.
SOME OF YOUR PERSONAL PROPERTY MAY BE EXEMPT FROM EXECUTION -- Certain classes of personal property may be protected from execution by state statutes or other laws or regulations of this state or of the United States. A checklist and description of the most common classes of personal property of a natural person exempt from execution are set forth on page 2 of this form.
HOW TO CLAIM AN EXEMPTION ESTABLISHED BY LAW -- If you wish to claim that the property levied on by the sheriffis exempt by law from execution you must fill out and sign the Claim of Exemption on page 2 of this form and return this exemption claim form to the clerk of the Superior court at the above address. **The form must be received by the clerk of the Superior Court within 20 days after levy on the property.**
Upon receipt of this form, the court clerk will notify you and the judgment creditor of the date on which a hearing will be held by the court to determine the issues raised by your claim.
RIGHT TO REQUEST INSTALMENT PAYMENT ORDER -- Pursuant to section 52-356d of the general statutes, if you are a consumer judgment debtor, you may seek to have the court issue an instalment payment order with a provision that compliance with the order prevents a levy on your property. An instalment payment order is an order of the court that you pay a weekly amount to the judgment creditor until the judgment is satisfied.
"Consumer Judgment" means a money judgment of less than five thousand dollars against a natural person resulting from a debt or obligation incurred primarily for personal, family, or household purposes.
SETTING ASIDE THE JUDGMENT -- If the judgment was rendered against you because of your failure to appear in court, you may, pursuant to section 52-212 of the general statutes, within four months of the date judgment was rendered and upon belief that you have reasonable cause, move the court to set aside the judgment rendered against you.

PROPERTY EXECUTION EXEMPTION CLAIM FORM

SECTION V   CLAIM OF EXEMPTION ESTABLISHED BY LAW

I, the judgment debtor, hereby claim and certify under penalty of false statement that the property described below is exempt from execution as follows:

NAME AND ADDRESS OF PERSON HOLDING PROPERTY	TELEPHONE NO.
PROPERTY CLAIMED TO BE EXEMPT	
DESCRIBE BASIS FOR EXEMPTION AS ESTABLISHED BY LAW	

COMPLETE MAILING ADDRESS OF JUDGMENT DEBTOR	TELEPHONE NO.
SIGNED (Judgment debtor)	DATE SIGNED

SECTION VI   NOTICE OF HEARING ON EXEMPTION/MODIFICATION CLAIM

DATE AND TIME OF HEARING ___.M.	SIGNED (Assistant Clerk)

SECTION VII

ORDERED that the following item(s) are exempt from execution:

SIGNED (Assistant Clerk, Judge)		DATE SIGNED
	BY ORDER OF THE COURT	

CHECKLIST AND DESCRIPTION OF COMMON EXEMPTIONS ALLOWED BY LAW
(Gen. Stat. § 52-352b)

(a) Necessary apparel, bedding, foodstuffs, household furniture and appliances;

(b) Tools, books, instruments, farm animals and livestock feed, which are necessary to the judgment debtor in the course of his or her occupation, profession, farming operation or farming partnership;

(c) Burial plot for the judgment debtor and his or her immediate family;

(d) Public assistance payments and any wages earned by a public assistance recipient under an incentive earnings or similar program;

(e) Health and disability insurance payments;

(f) Health aids necessary to enable the judgment debtor to work or to sustain health;

(g) Worker's compensation, social security, veterans and unemployment benefits;

(h) Court approved payments for child support;

(i) Arms and military equipment, uniforms or musical instruments owned by any member of the militia or armed forces of the United States;

(j) One motor vehicle to the value of one thousand five hundred dollars, provided such value shall be determined as the fair market value of the motor vehicle less the amount of all liens and security interests which encumber it.

(k) Wedding and engagement rings;

(l) Residential utility deposits for one residence and one residential security deposit;

(m) Any assets or interests of a judgment debtor in, or payments received by the judgment debtor from, a plan or arrangement described in section 52-321a;

(n) Alimony and support, other than child support, but only to the extent that wages are exempt from execution under general statute section 52-361a;

(o) An award under a crime reparations act;

(p) All benefits allowed by any association of persons in this state towards the support of any of its members incapacitated by sickness or infirmity from attending to his usual business; and

(q) All moneys due the judgment debtor from any insurance company on any insurance policy issued on exempt property, to the same extent that the property was exempt;

(r) Irrevocable transfers of money to an account held by a bona fide nonprofit debt adjuster licensed pursuant to chapter 655 for the benefit of creditors of the exemptioner.

(s) Any interest of the judgment debtor in any property not to exceed in value one thousand dollars;

(t) Any interest of the judgment debtor not to exceed in value four thousand dollars in any accrued dividend or interest under, or loan value of, any unmatured life insurance contract owned by the judgment debtor under which the insured is the judgment debtor or an individual of whom the judgment debtor is a dependent; and

(u) The homestead of the judgment debtor to the value of seventy-five thousand dollars, provided value shall be determined as the fair market value of the real property less the amount of any statutory or consensual lien which encumbers it.

PAGE 2 OF 2

APPENDIX 4:
TABLE OF PROPERTY
EXEMPTIONS BY STATE

ALABAMA

ASSET	EXEMPT
Public Benefits	Real property to $5000; not in excess of 160 acres
Personal Property/ Household Goods	Books
	Church Pew
	Clothing
	Artwork/portraits
Insurance and Annuities	Annuity proceeds to $250 per month
	Disability proceeds to $250 per month
	Fraternal society benefits
	Proceeds from life insurance if beneficiary is insured's spouse or child
	Proceeds from life insurance if beneficiary is wife of insured
	Life insured proceeds if cannot be used to pay beneficiary's creditors
Pensions and Retirement Plans	Law enforcement officers
	State employees
	Teachers
Public Benefits and Entitlements	AFDC
	Coal miners' benefits
	Crime Victims' compensation
	Southeast Asian War POW's benefits
	Unemployment compensation
	Worker's compensation
Miscellaneous	Business partnership property

ALASKA

ASSET	EXEMPT
Public Benefits	$54,000 in property
Personal Property/ Household Goods	Motor vehicle to $3000
	Books, musical instruments, clothing, household goods to $3000
	Jewelry to $1000
	Building materials
	Burial place
	Pets to $1000
	Proceeds for damaged exempt property
	Wrongful death recoveries
	Recovery for personal injury
Insurance and Annuities	Disability benefits
	Benefits from fraternal society
	Insurance proceeds for personal injury or wrongful death
	Life insurance or annuity to $10,000
	Life insurance proceeds if beneficiary is insured's spouse or dependent
	Medical benefits
Pensions and Retirement Plans	ERISA
	Public employees
	Teachers; other pensions
Public Benefits and Entitlements	Unemployment compensation
	Worker's Compensation
	AFDC
	Adult assistance to elderly, blind, disabled
	Alaska longevity bonus
	Crime victims' compensation
	Federally exempt public benefits paid or due
	General relief assistance
	50% of permanent fund dividends
Miscellaneous	Alimony and child support
	Liquor licenses, books & tools of trade -$2800
	Business partnership property

ARIZONA

ASSET	EXEMPT
Real Estate	Real estate to $100,000. Sale proceeds exempt, 18 months after sale or until new home purchased

Personal Property/ Household Goods	Bible, bicycle, sewing machine, typewriter
	Burial plot to $500, books to $250, clothing to $500, furniture and furnishings
	Wedding and engagements rings to $1000
	Watch to $100, Pets, horses, cows and poultry to $500, Musical instruments to $250
	Prostheses, including wheelchair
	Motor vehicle to $1500-$4000 if disabled
	If homestead is not claimed, prepaid rent or security deposit to $1000 or 1 1/2 times your rent, whichever is less
	Bank deposit to $150 in one account
	Proceeds for sold or damaged exempt property
	Food, fuel and provisions for 6 months
Insurance and Annuities	Group life insurance policy or proceeds
	Health, accident or disability benefits
	Life insurance cash value to $1000 per
	Life insurance cash value to $2000 per dependent ($10,000 total)
	Life insurance proceeds to $20,000 if beneficiary is spouse or child
	Fraternal society benefits
Pensions and Retirement Plans	Board of Regents member
	Elected Officials
	ERISA
	Firefighters and police officers
	State employees
Public Benefits and Entitlements	Unemployment compensation
	Workers' compensation
	Welfare benefits
Miscellaneous	Minor child's earnings
	Business partnership property

ARKANSAS

ASSET	EXEMPTION
Public Benefits	Choose one or the other:
	1. For head of family; real or personal property used as a residence, to an unlimited value; property cannot exceed 1/4 acre, or 80 acres rural. No homestead may exceed 1 acre in city, town or village or 160 acres elsewhere.
	2. Real or personal property used as residence to $800 if single; $1250 if married
Personal Property/ Household Goods	Burial plot to 5 acres, in lieu of homestead option 2; clothing; motor vehicle to $1200

	Wedding rings with diamonds not exceeding 1/2 carat
Insurance and Annuities	Disability benefits; Group life insurance
	Life, health, accident or disability cash value or proceeds paid or due, to $500
	Life insurance proceeds if cannot be used to pay beneficiary's creditors
	Life insurance proceeds if beneficiary isn't the insurance; Annuity contract
	Fraternal society benefits
	Mutual assessment life or disability benefits to $1000
Pensions and Retirement Plans	Disabled firefighters and police officers
	Firefighters and police officers
	IRA deposits to $20,000, if deposited 1 year before attachment by creditor or bankruptcy
	School employees
Public Benefits and Entitlements	AFDC, Aid to blind, aged, disabled
	Crime victims' compensation
	Unemployment compensation
	Workers' compensation
Miscellaneous	Business partnership property
	Tools of trade to $750

CALIFORNIA—SYSTEM 1

ASSET	EXEMPT
Public Benefits	Real property, mobile home, coop or condo to $50,000 if single and not disabled; $75000 for families; $100,000 if 65 or older or disabled; $100,000 if 55 or older, single and earn under $15000 or married & earn under $20000. Sale proceeds exempt for 6 months
Personal Property/ Household Goods	Furnishings, clothing & food; burial place
	Bank deposits from SSA to $500; $750 if 2
	Building materials to $1000
	Jewelry, heirlooms & art to $2500 total
	Motor vehicles to $1200
	Personal injury claims or recoveries
	Proceeds from exempt property
Insurance and Annuities	Disability or health benefits, fidelity bonds
	Fraternal benefits—life insurance benefits to $4000 loan value, and unemployment benefits
	Homeowner's insurance proceeds for 6 mos. after received, to homestead amount
	Life insurance

Pensions and Retirement Plans	Private retirement benefits, IRAs & Keoghs
	Public employees
	Public retirement benefits
Public Benefits and Entitlements	Union benefits due to labor dispute
	Workers' compensation
	Aid to blind, aged, disabled, AFDC
	Financial aid to students, relocation benefits
	Unemployment benefits
Miscellaneous	Business or professional licenses, except liquor
	Inmates' trust funds to $1000
	Business partnership property
	County employees
	Tools, materials, uniforms, books, furnishings, equipment, motor vehicle to $2500, to $5000 if spouses are in same job. Motor vehicle cannot be claimed under both trade and personal

CALIFORNIA—SYSTEM 2

ASSET	EXEMPT
Public Benefits	Real property and coops, to $7500; unused homestead may be applied to other property
Personal Property/ Household Goods	Animals instruments & clothing to $200 per item
	Burial plot to $7500, if homestead not claimed
	Jewelry to $500
	Motor vehicle to $1200
	Personal injury recoveries to $7500
	Wrongful death recoveries
Insurance and Annuities	Disability benefits
	Fidelity bonds
	Life insurance proceeds
	Unmatured life insurance policy
Pensions and, ERISA, Retirements Plans, Public Benefits and Entitlements	Unemployment compensation
	Veterans' benefits
	Crime victims' compensation
	Public assistance
	Social Security
Miscellaneous	Business partnership property
	Alimony
	Business or professional licenses, except liquor
	Tools of trade to $750

COLORADO

ASSET	EXEMPT
Real Estate	Real property or a mobile home up to $20000,
Personal Property/ Household Goods	Pictures and books to $750; burial place
	Clothing to $750; Food & fuel to $300,
	Household goods to $1500
	Jewelry to $500 total; Motor vehicle to $1000
	Personal injury recoveries, unless debt related to injury
	Proceeds for damaged exempt property
Insurance and Annuities	Disability benefits to $200 per month; lump sum, exempt
	Fraternal society benefits
	Group life insurance
	Homeowner's insurance proceeds for 1 year after
	received, to $20,000
	Life insurance to $5000
	Life insurance if cannot be used to pay
Pensions and Retirement Plans	ERISA
	Firefighters and police
	Public employees and Teachers
Public Benefits and Entitlements	Veterans' benefits
	Workers' compensation
	AFDC, Aid to blind, aged, disabled
	Crime victims' compensation
	Unemployment compensation
Miscellaneous	Business partnership property
	Horses, machinery, harness & tools of farmer to $2000 total
	Library of professional to $1500 or stock in trade, supplies, fixtures, tools, equipment & books to $1500 total
	Livestock to $3000

CONNECTICUT

ASSET	EXEMPT
Public Benefits	None
Personal Property/ Household Goods	Security deposits for residence
	Appliances & furniture; burial place
	Motor vehicle to $1500
	Wedding & engagement rings
	Clothing
Insurance and Annuities	Benefits received under no-fault insurance law
	Disability benefits paid by association for its members

	Fraternal benefit society benefits
	Health or disability benefits
	Life insurance proceeds if cannot be used to pay beneficiary's creditors
Pensions and Retirement Plans	ERISA
	State employees
	Teachers
Public Benefits and Entitlements	Veterans' benefits
	Workers' compensation
	AFDC, Aid to blind, aged, disabled
	Crime victims' compensation
	Social Security
	Unemployment compensation
Miscellaneous	Alimony and child support
	Business partnership property
	Tools, books, instruments & farm animals

DELAWARE

ASSET	EXEMPT
Public Benefits	None. Property held as tenancy by the entirety exempt against debt of only one spouse
Personal Property/ Household Goods	Clothing, jewelry; burial place
	Church pew
	Pianos
	School books and family library
Insurance and Annuities	Annuity contract proceeds to $350 per month
	Employee life insurance
	Health or disability benefits
	Life insurance proceeds if cannot be used to pay beneficiary's creditors
	Fraternal society benefits
Pensions and Retirement Plans	Kent County employees
	Police officers and volunteer firefighters
	State employees
Public Benefits and Entitlements	Unemployment compensation
	Workers' compensation
	Aid to blind, aged, disabled, AFDC
Miscellaneous	Business partnership property
	Tools
	& Sussex Counties; to $50 in Kent County

DISTRICT OF COLUMBIA

ASSET	EXEMPT
Public Benefits	None. Exception, property held as tenancy by the entirety exempt against debt of only one spouse
Personal Property/ Household Goods	Cooking utensils, stoves, furniture, furnishings, radios, & sewing machines to $300
	Books to $400
	Clothing to $300
	Cooperative association holdings to $50
	Residential condominium deposit
	Food and fuel for 3 months
Insurance and Annuities	Fraternal society benefits
	Disability benefits
	Life insurance proceeds cannot be used to pay creditors
	Group life insurance
	Life insurance proceeds
	Other insurance proceeds to $200 per month, maximum 2 months, for head of family; else $60 per month
Pensions and Retirement Plans	Public school teachers
Public Benefits and Entitlements	Unemployment compensation
	Workers' compensation
	Aid to blind, aged, disabled, AFDC
	Crime victims' compensation
	General assistance
Miscellaneous	Business partnership property
	Library, furniture, tools of professional or artist to $300
	Mechanic's tools, tools of trade or business to $200
	Motor vehicle, cart, wagon and horse to $500
	Stock and materials to $200

FLORIDA

ASSET	EXEMPT
Public Benefits	Real property including mobile home to unlimited value; property cannot exceed 1/2 acre in municipality or 160 contiguous acres elsewhere
	Tenancy by the entirety property exempt against debt of only one spouse
Personal Property/ Household Goods	Personal property to $1000

Insurance and Annuities	Annuity contract proceeds
	Death benefits payable to a specific beneficiary the deceased's estate
	Disability or illness benefits
	Fraternal society benefits
	Cash surrender value of life insurance
Pensions and Retirement Plans	County officers
	ERISA
	Police officers and firefighters
	State officers, employees
	Teachers
Public Benefits and Entitlements	Veterans' benefits
	Workers' compensation
	Crime victims' compensation
	Public assistance
	Social Security
	Unemployment compensation
Miscellaneous	Alimony and child support
	Business partnership property

GEORGIA

ASSET	EXEMPT
Public Benefits	Real property, including coop, to $5000; unused homestead may be applied to any property
Personal Property/ Household Goods	Burial place
	Jewelry to $500; motor vehicles to $1000
	Personal injury recoveries to $7500
	Wrongful death recoveries
	Animals, crops, clothing, books, household goods, musical instruments to $200 per item; $3500 max
Insurance and Annuities	Annuity & endowment benefits
	Disability or health benefits to $250 per month
	Fraternal society benefits
	Life insurance proceeds if needed for support
	Life insurance proceeds if beneficiary not the insured
	Unmatured life insurance dividends value or cash value to $2000
Pensions and Retirement Plans	ERISA
	Public employees
	Any pension needed for support
Public Benefits and Entitlements	Veterans' benefits
	Workers' compensation

	Aid to blind and disabled
	Crime victims' compensation
	Local public assistance
	Social Security; old age assistance
	Unemployment compensation
Miscellaneous	Alimony and child support
	Books and tools of trade to $500

HAWAII

ASSET	EXEMPT
Public Benefits	Head of family or over 65 to $30,000. Others to $20,000; not to exceed 1 acre
Personal Property/ Household Goods	Burial place
	Clothing
	Jewelry to $1000
	Motor vehicle to $1000
	Furnishings
Insurance and Annuities	Annuity or endowment policy
	Disability benefits
	Fraternal society benefits
	Group life insurance
	Life or health insurance policy for spouse or child
Pensions and Retirement Plans	ERISA
	Police officers and firefighters
	Public officers and employees
Public Benefits and Entitlements	Workers' compensation
	Unemployment compensation
	Unemployment work relief funds to $60 per month
	Public assistance paid by DSSH
Miscellaneous	Business partnership property
	Tools, implements, books, instruments, uniforms, furnishings, motor vehicle and other personal property needed for livliehood

IDAHO

ASSET	EXEMPT
Public Benefits	$30,000; proceeds from sale exempt for 6 months
Personal Property/ Household Goods	Books, furnishings, clothing, musical instruments, family portraits and heirlooms to $500 per item,
	$4000 maximum
	Building materials
	Burial place

	Jewelry to $250; motor vehicle to $500
	Personal injury recoveries needed for support
	Wrongful death recoveries
	Crops to $1000
Insurance and Annuities	Annuity contract proceeds to $350 per month
	Death or disability benefits
	Fraternal society benefits
	Homeowner's insurance proceeds to $25,000
	Life insurance
	Medical benefits
Pensions and Retirement Plans	ERISA
	Firefighters and police officers
	Public employees
	Any pensions needed by support
Public Benefits and Entitlements	Veterans' benefits
	Workers' compensation
	Aid to blind, aged, disabled
	Crime victims' compensation
	Any type of government assistance
	General assistance; social security
	Unemployment compensation
Miscellaneous	Alimony, child support needed for support
	Liquor licenses
	Business partnership property
	Books and tools of trade to $1000

ILLINOIS

ASSET	EXEMPT
Public Benefits	Real property to $7500
Personal Property/ Household Goods	Family pictures, books, clothing, vehicles to $1200 personal injury recoveries to $7500; exempt property proceeds; wrongful death recoveries needed for support
Insurance and Annuities	Health or disability benefits
	Homeowners proceeds for destroyed home up to $7500
	Life insurance, annuity proceeds or cash value if beneficiary is insured's child, parent, spouse, or other dependent
	Fraternal society benefits
	Life insurance proceeds if cannot be used to pay beneficiary's creditors
	Life insurance proceeds needed for support

Pensions and Retirement Plans	Civil service employees; county employees
	Disabled firefighters; widows & children of firefighters
	ERISA; general assembly members
	Municipal employees
	Police officers and firefighters
	State university employees; teachers
Public Benefits and Entitlements	Veterans' benefits
	Workers' compensation
	Aid to aged, blind, disabled, AFDC
	Crime victims' compensation
	Social security
	Unemployment compensation
Miscellaneous	Alimony, child support
	Business partnership property
	Implements, books & tools of trade to $750

INDIANA

ASSET	EXEMPT
Public Benefits	Real property claimed as residence to $7500; in addition health aids) up to $10,000. Also, property held as tenancy by the entirety is exempt against debt of only one spouse.
Personal Property/ Household Goods	$4000 of tangible personal property; $100, any intangible personal property
Insurance and Annuities	Fraternal society benefits
	Life insurance
	Accident proceeds
Pensions and Retirement Plans	Firefighters, police, sheriffs
	Public employees
	State teachers
Public Benefits and Entitlements	Unemployment compensation
	Workers' compensation
	Crime Victims' compensation
Miscellaneous	Business partnership property
	National guard uniforms, arms & equipment
	State military personnel's uniforms equipment.

IOWA

ASSET	EXEMPT
Public Benefits	Real property unlimited value; property cannot exceed 1/2 acre in town or city, 40 acres elsewhere
Personal Property/ Household Goods	Furnishings & household goods to $2000
	Books, pictures & paintings to $1000

	Burial plot to 1 acre
	Clothing to $1000
	Motor vehicle & musical instruments to $5000
	Wedding or engagement rings
Insurance and Annuities	Accident, disability, health, illness or life proceeds to $15,000
	Employee group insurance
	Benefits from fraternal benefit society
	Life insurance proceeds to $10,000m paid to spouse child or other dependent
Pensions and Retirement Plans	Firefighters, police, public employees
	Other pensions needed for support
Public Benefits and Entitlements	Veterans' Benefits
	Workers' compensation
	Adopted child assistance
	AFDC
	Social Security
	Unemployment compensation
Miscellaneous	Alimony
	Liquor licenses
	Business partnership property
	Farming equipment; includes livestock, feed to $10,000; non-farming equipment to $10,000

KANSAS

ASSET	EXEMPT
Public Benefits	Real property & mobile home under 1 acre in town or city, 160 acres rural
Personal Property/ Household Goods	Burial place, funeral plan prepayments
	Clothing
	Food and fuel
	Furnishings & household equipment
	Jewelry to $1000
	Motor vehicle to $20,000
Insurance and Annuities	Life insurance
Pensions and Retirement Plans	Official in cities with populations between 120,000 & 200,000
	ERISA
	Police officers and firefighters
	Government employees
	State school employees

Public Benefits and Entitlements	Unemployment compensation
	Workers' compensation
	AFDC
	Crime victims' compensation
	Social welfare
	General assistance
Miscellaneous	Liquor licenses,
	Business partnership property
	Books, documents, furniture, instruments, equipment, to $7500 total

KENTUCKY

ASSET	EXEMPT
Public Benefits	Real or personal property claimed as residence to $5000
Personal Property/ Household Goods	Burial plot to $5000
	Clothing, jewelry, & furnishings to $3000 total
	Payments for lost earnings needed for support
	Medical expenses
	Reparation benefits
	Motor vehicle to $2500
	Personal injury recoveries to $7500(not to include pain & suffering)
	Wrongful death recoveries
Insurance and Annuities	Health or disability benefits
	Annuity contract proceeds to $350 per month
	Life insurance policy of spouse beneficiary
	Cooperative life or casualty insurance benefits
	Fraternal society benefits
	Life insurance proceeds if proceeds cannot be used to pay beneficiary's creditors
Pensions and Retirement Plans	Firefighters, police, teachers
	State employees; county government employees
	Other pensions needed for support
Public Benefits and Entitlements	Unemployment compensation
	Workers' compensation
	Aid to blind, aged, disabled, AFDC
	Crime victims' compensation
Miscellaneous	Alimony
	Business partnership property
	Furnishings of minister, attorney, physician, veterinarian or dentist to $2500

Motor vehicle of mechanic, minister, attorney, physician, veterinarian or dentist to $2500

Tools, equipment, livestock of farmer to $3000

Tools of non-farmer to $300

LOUISIANA

ASSET	EXEMPT
Public Benefits	$15,000; property cannot exceed 160 acres
Personal Property/ Household Goods	Furniture, utensils, clothing, family portraits, musical instruments, heating & cooling equipment, pressing irons, sewing machines, refrigerator, freezer, stove, washer & dryer
	Burial place
	Engagement & wedding rings to $5000
Insurance and Annuities	Fraternal society benefits
	Insurance policies or proceeds
	Health
Pensions and Retirement Plans	ERISA
Public Benefits and Entitlements	Unemployment compensation
	Workers' compensation
	Aid to blind, aged, disabled, AFDC
	Crime victims' compensation
Miscellaneous	Minor child's property
	Tools, instruments, books, truck (maximum tons) and trailer

MAINE

ASSET	EXEMPT
Public Benefits	Real or coop to $7500; if debtor over 60 or physically or mentally disabled, up to $60,000
Personal Property/ Household Goods	Animals, crops, musical instruments, books, to $200 per item.
	Clothing trade (above tools of trade exemption) & personal injury recoveries (above personal injury recovery exemption) to $4500 total; furnaces & stoves
	Jewelry (not wedding or engagement rings) to $500
	Payments for lost earnings needed for support
	Motor vehicle to $1200
	Personal injury recoveries to $7500 (not for pain and suffering)
	Farming tools & equipment
	Wrongful death recoveries

Insurance and Annuities	Life, endowment, annuity or accident policy proceed
	Annuity proceeds to $450 per month
	Disability or health proceeds, benefits or avails
	Group health or life policy or proceeds
	Fraternal society benefits
Pensions and Retirement Plans	ERISA
	Legislators
	State employees
Public Benefits and Entitlements	Veterans' benefits
	Workers' compensation
	AFDC
	Crime victims' compensation
	Social Security
	Unemployment compensation
Miscellaneous	Alimony and child support (50%)
	Business partnership property
	Boat used in commercial fishing up to 5 tons
	Materials & stock to $1000
	1 of each type of farm implement

MARYLAND

ASSET	EXEMPT
Public Benefits	None. Tenancy by the entirety property exempt against debt of one spouse.
Personal Property/ Household Goods	Appliances, furnishings, household goods, books, pets & clothing to $500 total
	Burial place
	Recovery for lost future earnings
Insurance and Annuities	Medical benefits deducted from wages
	Disability or health benefits
	Fraternal society benefits
	Life insurance
Pensions and Retirement Plans	ERISA (except IRAs)
	Deceased Baltimore police officers
	State employees
	Teachers
Public Benefits and Entitlements	Unemployment compensation
	Workers' compensation
	AFDC
	Crime victims' compensation
	General assistance

| Miscellaneous | Business partnership property |
| | Clothing, books, tools & appliances to $2500 |

MASSACHUSETTS

ASSET	EXEMPT
Public Benefits	$100,000; if over 65 or disabled, $150,000.
	Tenancy by the entirety property exempt against debt of only one spouse
Personal Property/ Household Goods	Bank deposits to $125
	Clothing
	Books to $200 total; sewing machine to $200
	Cash for fuel, heat, water or light to $75 per mo.
	Coop shares to $100
	Furniture to $3000; motor vehicle to $700
	Trust company, bank deposits to $500
	Burial place & church pew
Insurance and Annuities	Benefits from fraternal benefit society
	Life or endowment policy, proceeds or cash value
	Group annuity policy or proceeds
	Life insurance policy if beneficiary is married woman or cannot be used to pay beneficiary's creditors
	Disability benefits to $35 per week
	Group life insurance policy
Pensions and Retirement Plans	Private retirement benefits
	Savings bank employees
Public Benefits and Entitlements	Veterans' benefits
	Workers' compensation
	AFDC, aid to aged
	Unemployment compensation
Miscellaneous	Business partnership property
	Boats, fishing tackle of fisherman to $500
	Tools and fixtures to $500 total

MICHIGAN

ASSET	EXEMPT
Public Benefits	Real estate to $3500; property cannot exceed 1 lot or 40 acres rural. In addition, tenancy by the entirety property exempt against debt of only one spouse
Personal Property/ Household Goods	Building & loan association shares to $1000 par value, in lieu of homestead
	Burial place
	Church pew

Appliances, books, household goods to $1000 total

Food & fuel for 6 months

Insurance and Annuities

Life, endowment or annuity proceeds if cannot be used to pay beneficiary's creditors

Life or endowment proceeds if beneficiary is insured's spouse or child

Life insurance proceeds to $300 per year if beneficiary is a married woman or a husband

Benefits from fraternal benefit society

Disability, mutual life or health benefits

Pensions and Retirement Plans

Firefighters, police officers

IRAs

Legislators, public school employees, state employees

Public Benefits and Entitlements

Veterans' benefits for veterans

Workers' compensation

AFDC

Crime victims' compensation

Social welfare benefits

Unemployment compensation

Miscellaneous

Business partnership property

Tools, materials, stock, motor vehicle, horse & harness to $1000 total

MINNESOTA

ASSET	EXEMPT
Public Benefits	Real estate, cannot exceed 1/2 acre in city or
	160 acres rural
Personal Property/ Household Goods	Burial place
	Church pew; motor vehicle to $2000
	Appliances to $4500 total
	Clothing, food & utensils
	Personal injury and wrongful death recoveries
	Proceeds for damaged exempt property
	Books & musical instruments
Insurance and Annuities	Accident or disability proceeds
	Life insurance or endowment, proceeds if beneficiary isn't the insured or cannot be used to pay beneficiary's creditors
	Life insurance proceeds if beneficiary is spouse or child of insured to $20,000, plus $5000 per dependent
	Police
	Unmatured life insurance contract dividends, interest or loan value to $4000

	Fraternal society benefits
Pensions and Retirement Plans	ERISA
	$30,000 in present value
	Private retirement benefits
	Public employees and state employees
Public Benefits and Entitlements	Veteran's benefits
	Workers' compensation
	AFDC
	Crime victims' compensation
	Unemployment compensation
Miscellaneous	Minor child's earning
	Business partnership property
	Farm machines, livestock, crops of farmers to 13000
	School teacher materials
	Tools, machines, instruments.

MISSISSIPPI

ASSET	EXEMPT
Public Benefits	$30,000; property not above 160 acres
Personal Property/ Household Goods	Personal injury judgments to $10,000
	Tangible personal property $10,000
Insurance and Annuities	Disability benefits
	Homeowners' insurance to $30,000
	Life insurance to $50,000
	Fraternal society benefits
	Life insurance proceeds if cannot be used to pay beneficiary's creditors
Pensions and Retirement Plans	ERISA benefits deposited over 1 year before creditor attachment or filing bankruptcy
	IRAs and Keoghs
	Private retirement benefits
	Police officers, firefighters
	State employees
	Teachers
Public Benefits and Entitlements	Unemployment compensation
	Workers' compensation
	Aid to aged
	Social Security
Miscellaneous	Business partnership property

MISSOURI

ASSET	EXEMPT
Public Benefits	Real property to $8000, mobile home to $1000
Personal Property/ Household Goods	Appliances, household goods, clothing, books, crops, animals & musical instruments to $1000
	Jewelry to $500; motor vehicle to $500
	Wrongful death recoveries for person you depended
	Burial plot to $100
Insurance and Annuities	Insurance premium proceeds
	Death, disability or illness benefits
	Life insurance dividends, loan value or interest to $5000
	Life insurance
	Fraternal society benefits to $5000
Pensions and Retirement Plans	Employees of cities with 100,000 people
	ERISA
	Public officers & employees, police, highway & transportation, firefighters
	State employees
	Teachers
Public Benefits and Entitlements	Veterans' benefits
	Workers' compensation
	AFDC, Social Security
	Unemployment compensation
Miscellaneous	Alimony, child support to $500 per month
	Business partnership property
	Books & tools of trade to $2000

MONTANA

ASSET	EXEMPT
Public Benefits	Real estate; mobile home to $40,000
Personal Property/ Household Goods	Appliances, household furnishings, animals, crops, musical instruments, books, firearms, clothing & jewelry to $600 each, $4500 total
	Cooperative association shares to $500 value
	Motor vehicle to $1200
	Proceeds for damaged or lost exempt property for 6 months after received
	Burial place
	Food and provisions for 3 months

Insurance and Annuities	Annuity to $350 per month
	Disability or illness benefits; medical, surgical, or hospital benefits
	Group life insurance
	Life insurance proceeds if cannot be used to pay beneficiary's creditors
	Life insurance proceeds if annual premiums do not exceed $500
	Unmatured life insurance contracts to $4000
	Fraternal society benefits
Pensions and Retirement Plans	ERISA benefits deposited over 1 year before creditor attachment or bankruptcy
	Public employees
Public Benefits and Entitlements	Workers' compensation
	Veterans' benefits
	Aid to aged, disabled, AFDC
	Crime victims' compensation
	Social Security
	Unemployment compensation
	Vocational rehabilitation to the blind
Miscellaneous	Alimony
	Business partnership property
	Books & tools of trade to $3000

NEBRASKA

ASSET	EXEMPT
Public Benefits	$10,000; no more than 2 lots in city, 160 acres elsewhere; sale proceeds exempt for 6 months
Personal Property/ Household Goods	Burial place
	Clothing
	Furniture & kitchen utensils to $1500
	Perpetual care funds
	Recovery for personal injury
Insurance and Annuities	Disability benefits to $200 per month
	Fraternal society benefits to loan value of $10000
Pensions and Retirement Plans	County employees, state and school employees
	ERISA
	Military disability benefits to $2000
Public Benefits and Entitlements	Unemployment compensation
	Workers' compensation
	Aid to disabled, blind, aged, AFDC

| Miscellaneous | Business partnership property |
| | Equipment or tools to $1500 |

NEVADA

ASSET	EXEMPT
Public Benefits	Real property or trailer to $95,000
Personal Property/ Household Goods	Appliances, household goods, furniture, home & yard equipment to $3000 total
	Books to $1500
	Burial place
	Funeral service contract
	Motor vehicle to $1000
	Heirlooms
Insurance and Annuities	Group life or health policy or proceeds
	Benefits from fraternal society
	Annuity to $350 per month
	Health proceeds
	Life insurance proceeds if you're not the insured
	Life insurance policy or proceeds if annual premiums not over $1000
Pensions and Retirement Plans	Public employees
Public Benefits and Entitlements	Vocational rehabilitation benefits
	Unemployment compensation
	Aid to blind, aged, disabled, AFDC
Miscellaneous	Business partnership property
	Dwelling of miner or prospector; cars, equipment for mining & mining claim you work to 4500 total
	Farm trucks
	Library, equipment, supplies, tools & materials to $4500
	Uniforms, arms & equipment

NEW HAMPSHIRE

ASSET	EXEMPT
Public Benefits	Real property or portable housing to $5000
Personal Property/ Household Goods	Beds, bedsteads, bedding, furniture to $2000 sewing machine, cooking utensils needed, cooking & heating stoves, refrigerator
	Automobile to $1000
	Bibles & books to $800
	Burial place
	Jewelry to $500

	Proceeds for lost or destroyed exempt property
	Clothing, food & fuel to $400
	Cow, 6 sheep or fleece, 4 tons of hay
Insurance and Annuities	Homeowners' insurance proceeds to $5000
	Fraternal benefits
	Firefighters' aid benefits
	Life insurance if you're not the insured
	Life insurance or endowment proceeds if beneficiary is a married woman
Pensions and Retirement Plans	Police officers, firefighters
	Public employees
	Federal pension
Public Benefits and Entitlements	Workers' compensation
	Unemployment compensation
	Aid to blind, aged, disabled, AFDC
Miscellaneous	Child support
	Business partnership property
	Minor child's wages
	Tools of your occupation to $1200

NEW JERSEY

ASSET	EXEMPT
Public Benefits	None
Personal Property/ Household Goods	Personal property & corporation shares to $1000
	Burial place
	Clothing
	Furniture & household goods to $1000
Insurance and Annuities	Annuity to $500 per month
	Military disability or death benefits
	Disability, death, medical or hospital benefits for civil defense workers
	Life insurance proceeds if cannot be used to pay beneficiary's creditors
	Life insurance proceeds if another insured
	Fraternal society benefits
	Health or disability benefits
Pensions and Retirement Plans	Alcohol beverage control officers
	City boards of health employees
	County employees
	ERISA
	Public employees

Public Benefits and Entitlements	Workers' compensation
	Unemployment compensation
	Crime victims' compensation
	Old-age
Miscellaneous	Business partnership property

NEW MEXICO

ASSET	EXEMPT
Public Benefits	Up to $20,000 if married, widowed or supporting another
Personal Property/ Household Goods	Books, health equipment & furniture
	Building supplies
	Jewelry to $2500
	Materials
	Motor vehicle to $4000
	Clothing
	Cooperative shares
Insurance and Annuities	Benevolent association benefits to $5000
	Fraternal society benefits
	Life, accident, health or annuity benefits
Pensions and Retirement Plans	Pension or retirement benefits
	Public school employees
Public Benefits and Entitlements	Workers' compensation
	Unemployment compensation
	AFDC
	Crime victims' compensation
	General assistance
	Occupational disease disablement benefits
Miscellaneous	Ownership in unincorporated association
	Business partnership property
	$1500 in tools of the trade

NEW YORK

ASSET	EXEMPT
Public Benefits	Real estate condo, coop or mobile home to 10000
Personal Property/ Household Goods	Schoolbooks, books to $50, pictures, clothing, church pew, stoves, sewing machine, furniture refrigerator
	Burial place totals $5000
	Recovery for lost earnings needed for support
	Personal injury recoveries to $7500
	Security deposits, trust fund principal income you depended on needed for support

	Motor vehicles to $2400
	Food for 60 days
Insurance and Annuities	Annuity benefits, purchased within 6 months
	Disability or illness benefits to $400 per month
	Fraternal society benefits
	Insurance proceeds for damaged exempt property
	Life insurance proceeds that cannot pay beneficiary's creditors or if beneficiary is not the insured
Pensions and Retirement Plans	ERISA
Public Benefits and Entitlements	Workers' compensation
	Veterans' compensation
	Crime victims' compensation
	Aid to blind, aged, disabled, AFDC
	Home relief
	Social Security
	Unemployment compensation
Miscellaneous	Alimony, child support
	Business partnership property
	Farm machinery, team, professional furniture, books & instruments to $600 total
	Uniforms, arms of military

NORTH CAROLINA

ASSET	EXEMPT
Public Benefits	Real or personal property, claimed as residence to $7500. Tenancy by the entirety property exempt against debt of one spouse. $2500 of unused homestead may be applied to other property
Personal Property/ Household Goods	Crops, musical instruments, books, clothing, household goods to $2500 total, plus $500 per dependent (up to $2000)
	Burial plot to $7500, in lieu of homestead
	Motor vehicle to $1000
	Wrongful death or injury recoveries for person you depended on
Insurance and Annuities	Benefits from fraternal society
	Life insurance
Pensions and Retirement Plans	Legislators
	Municipal
Public Benefits and Entitlements	Unemployment compensation
	Workers' compensation
	AFDC

Miscellaneous	Aid to blind
	Crime victims' compensation
	Special adult compensation
	Business partnership property
	Books & tools of trade to $500

NORTH DAKOTA

ASSET	EXEMPT
Public Benefits	Real estate or trailer to $80,000
Personal Property/ Household Goods	Books to $100 & pictures, clothing
	Burial plots, church pew
	Cash to $7500, in lieu of homestead
	Crops raised to 160 acres
	Motor vehicle to $1200
	Personal injury recoveries to $7500
	Wrongful death recoveries to $7500
	Head of household not claiming crops may claim $5000 of any personal property or any of the following:
	Library & tools of professional to $1000
	Livestock & farm implements to $4500
	Tools & stock in trade to $1000
	Furniture to $1000
	Books & musical instruments to $1500
	Non-head of household not claiming crops, may claim $2500 of any personal property
Insurance and Annuities	Benefits from fraternal society
	Life insurance
Pensions and Retirement Plans	Annuities, pensions, IRAs, Keoghs & ERISA to $100,000 per plan, total cannot exceed $200,000
	Disabled veterans' benefits(not military retirement)
	Public employees
Public Benefits and Entitlements	Unemployment compensation
	Workers' compensation
	AFDC
	Crime victims' compensation
	Social Security
	Vietnam veterans' adjustment compensation
Miscellaneous	Business partnership property

OHIO

ASSET	EXEMPT
Public Benefits	Real or personal property claimed as residence to $5000, tenancy by the entirety property exempt against debt of only one spouse
Personal Property/ Household Goods	Animals, crops, books, musical instruments, jewelry to $400, appliances, household goods, furnishings, sporting equipment & firearms to $200 per item, $1500 total ($2000 if no homestead)
	Clothing to $200 per item
	Cash, money due within 90 days, bank & security deposits & tax refund to $400 total
	Personal injury recoveries to $5000
	Motor vehicle to $1000
	Wrongful death recoveries
	Stove & refrigerator to $300 each
	Burial place
Insurance and Annuities	Benevolent society benefits to $5000
	Disability benefits to $600 per month
	Benefits from fraternal benefit society
	Group life insurance policy or proceeds
	Life: child or dependent
	Life insurance proceeds for a spouse
	Life insurance proceeds if proceeds cannot be used to pay beneficiary's creditors
Pensions and Retirement Plans	ERISA
	Firefighters', police officers' death benefits and pensions Public employees
	State highway patrol employees
	Volunteer firefighters' dependents
Public Benefits and Entitlements	Unemployment compensation
	Workers' compensation
	AFDC
	Crime victims' compensation
	Vocational rehabilitation benefits

OKLAHOMA

ASSET	EXEMPT
Public Benefits	Real property to unlimited value
	Excess of 1/4 acre, may claim $5000 on 1 acre in city, town or village, or 160 acres rural

Personal Property/ Household Goods	Books, portraits, pictures
	Burial plots
	Clothing to $4000
	Furniture
	Motor vehicle to $3000
	Personal injury, wrongful death & workers' compensation recoveries to $50,000 total
Insurance and Annuities	Funeral benefits
	Life insurance policy or proceeds if another insured
	Limited stock insurance benefits
	Fraternal society benefits
Pensions and Retirement Plans	County employees
	Disabled veterans
	ERISA
	Law enforcement employees, police & firefighters
	Public employees and teachers
	Tax exempt benefits
Public Benefits and Entitlements	Unemployment compensation
	Workers' compensation
	AFDC
	Crime victims' compensation
	Social security
Miscellaneous	Alimony
	Business partnership property
	Farm tools to $5000 total

OREGON

ASSET	EXEMPT
Public Benefits	Residence to $15000($20000 for joint owners; if you don't own land then mobile home to 13000 18000 for joint owners
	Sale proceeds exempt 1 year from sale purchase another home
Personal Property/ Household Goods	Bank deposits to $7500
	Books, pictures & musical instruments to $300 Burial place
	Clothing, jewelry & other personal items to $900
	Domestic animals, poultry with food to last 60 days to $1000
	Furniture, household, items, utensils, radios & TV to $1400 total
	Payments for lost earnings, Motor vehicle to $1200

	Personal injury recoveries to $7500
Insurance and Annuities	Annuity contract benefits to $250 per month
	Fraternal society benefits
	Heath or disability proceeds
	Life insurance
Pensions and Retirement Plans	ERISA benefits; government employees
Public Benefits and Entitlements	Unemployment compensation
	Workers' compensation
	AFDC
	Aid to disabled, blind, old age
	Crime victims' compensation
	General assistance
	Medical assistance
	Vocational rehabilitation
Miscellaneous	Alimony, child support
	Liquor licenses
	Business partnership property
	Tools, library to $750

PENNSYLVANIA

ASSET	EXEMPT
Public Benefits	None. Tenancy by the entirety property exempt against debt of one spouse
Personal Property/ Household Goods	School books & sewing machine
	Clothing
Insurance and Annuities	Group life policy or proceeds
	Life insurance annuity contract payments, cash value or proceeds to $100 per month
	Life insurance annuity policy, cash value, proceeds
	Life insurance proceeds if proceeds cannot be used to pay beneficiary's creditors
	Fraternal society benefits
	No fault automobile insurance proceeds
	Accident or disability benefits
Pensions and Retirement Plans	County, municipal, and state employees
	Private retirement benefits
	Self employment benefits

RHODE ISLAND

ASSET	EXEMPT
Public Benefits	None
Personal Property/ Household Goods	Furniture to $1000 total
	Books to $300
	Burial place
	Clothing
	Debts due
	Certain animals
Insurance and Annuities	Accident or sickness proceeds or benefits,
	Fraternal society benefits
	Life insurance proceeds if beneficiary is not the insured
	Temporary disability insurance
Pensions and Retirement Plans	Private employees
	State & municipal employees
Public Benefits	Unemployment compensation,
	Workers' compensation
	Aid to blind, aged, disabled
	AFDC
	General assistance
	State disability benefits
	Veterans' disability or survivors' death benefits
Miscellaneous	A minor child's earnings
	Business partnership property
	Library
	Tools of trade to $500

SOUTH CAROLINA

ASSET	EXEMPT
Public Benefits	Real property to $5000
Personal Property/ Household Goods	Animals, crops, books, clothing, furnishings, musical instruments to $2500 total
	Burial place to $5000 if no homestead claimed
	Cash to $1000
	Jewelry to $500
	Motor vehicle to $1200
	Personal injury and wrongful death recoveries
Insurance and Annuities	Life insurance from person you depended to 4000
	Life insurance proceeds for spouse or child to $25000

	Life insurance proceeds if proceeds cannot be used to pay beneficiary's creditors
	Fraternal society benefits
	Disability or illness benefits
Pensions and Retirement Plans	ERISA
	Firefighters and police officers
	Public employees
Public Benefits and Entitlements	Unemployment compensation
	Workers' compensation
	AFDC
	Crime victims' compensation
	Aid to aged
	Social security
	Veterans' benefits
Miscellaneous	Alimony, child support
	Business partnership property
	Implements & tools of trade to $750

SOUTH DAKOTA

ASSET	EXEMPT
Public Benefits	Real property under 1 acre in town or 160 acres elsewhere. Sale proceeds to $30,000 (unlimited if over age 70 or an unmarried widow or widower) exempt for 1 year after sale
Personal Property/ Household Goods	Books to $200, pictures, burial plots, church pew, food, fuel & clothing
	Head of family may claim $4000 of any personal property
	Farming machinery to $1250 total
	Furniture to $200
	Professional library & tools to $300
	Tools of mechanics & stock in trade to $200
	None-head of family may claim $2000 of any personal property
Insurance and Annuities	Endowment, life insurance policy, proceeds or cash value to $20,000
	Health benefits to $20,000
	Fraternal society benefits
	Life insurance proceeds if proceeds cannot pay beneficiary's creditors
	Life insurance proceeds to $10,000, if beneficiary is surviving spouse or child
	Annuity to $250 per month

Pensions and Retirement Plans	Public employees
Public Benefits and Entitlements	Unemployment compensation
	Workers' compensation
	AFDC
Miscellaneous	Business partnership property

TENNESSEE

ASSET	EXEMPT
Public Benefits	$5000, $7500 for joint owners. Tenancy by the entirety property exempt against debt of 1 spouse
Personal Property/ Household Goods	School books, portraits
	Burial place
	Clothing
	Payments for lost earnings
	Personal injury recoveries to $7500
	Wrongful death recoveries to $7500
Insurance and Annuities	Fraternal society benefits
	Homeowners' insurance proceeds to $5000
	Life insurance
	Accident, health or disability benefits
Pensions and Retirement Plans	ERISA
	Public employees
	State & local government employees
	Teachers
Public Benefits and Entitlements	Unemployment compensation
	Workers' compensation
	AFDC
	Aid to blind, disabled,old age
	Crime victims' compensation to $5000
	General assistance
	Social security
	Veterans' benefits
Miscellaneous	Alimony owed for 30 days prior
	Business partnership property
	Tools of trade to $750

TEXAS

ASSET	EXEMPT
Public Benefits	Unlimited; to 1 acre in town, village, city or 100 acres (200 for families) elsewhere

Personal Property/ Household Goods	Sporting equipment; includes jewelry, heirlooms furnishings, food, cars, light trucks not for work, or any 2 of the following: auto, camper, truck, cab or trailer; bicycle or motorcycle to $15000 total ($30,000 for head of family). Total includes tools of trade, wages and life insurance cash value
Insurance and Annuities	Life, health, accident or annuity benefits & cash value
	Retired public school employees group insurance
	State employee uniform group insurance
	State college or university employee benefits
	Benefit from fraternal society
Pensions and Retirement Plans	County & district employees
	ERISA government or church benefits, Keoghs, and IRAs
	Firefighters, police and teachers
	Law enforcement officers' survivors
	Municipal employees
	State employees
Public Benefits and Entitlements	Unemployment compensation
	Workers' compensation
	Aid for dependent children
	Crime victims' compensation
	Medical assistance
Miscellaneous	Business partnership property
	Implements of farming or ranching needed to work; Tools, equipment & books

UTAH

ASSET	EXEMPT
Public Benefits	Real property or trailer to $8000; plus $2000 for spouse & $500 for dependent
Personal Property/ Household Goods	Animals, books & musical instruments to $500
	Burial place
	Bed, bedding, carpets, washer & dryer
	Clothing, not furs
	Furnishings & appliances to $500
	Heirloom to $500
	Proceeds for damaged exempt property
	Refrigerator, freezer, stove & sewing machine
	Personal injury recoveries
	Wrongful death recoveries
Insurance and Annuities	Fraternal society benefits
	Life insurance policy cash surrender value to $1500

	Life insurance proceeds if beneficiary is insured's spouse or dependent
	Disability, illness, medical or hospital benefits
Pensions and Retirement Plans	ERISA
	Public employees,
	Any pensions needed for support
Public Benefits and Entitlements	Unemployment compensation
	Workers' compensation
	AFDC
	Crime victims' compensation
	General assistance
	Occupational disease disability benefits
	Veterans' benefits
Miscellaneous	Alimony needed for support, child support
	Property of business partnership
	Books & tools of trade to $1500
	Military property
	Motor vehicle to $1500

VERMONT

ASSET	EXEMPT
Public Benefits	Real property or mobile home to $30,000, tenancy by the entirety property against debt of one spouse
Personal Property/ Household Goods	Furnishings, clothing, books, crops, animals, musical instruments to $2500 total
	Jewelry to $500, wedding ring unlimited
	Motor vehicles to $2500, bank deposits to $700
	Stove, refrigerator, water heater & sewing machine
	Wrongful death recoveries for person you depended
	Sidearms
	Personal injury recoveries
Insurance and Annuities	Group life or health benefits
	Fraternal society benefits
	Life insurance proceeds if beneficiary is not the insured
	Life insurance proceeds if proceeds cannot be used to pay beneficiary's creditors
	Annuity benefits to $350 per month
Pensions and Retirement Plans	Municipal employees
	IRAs, Keoghs to $10,000
	State employees & teachers
	Any pensions

Public Benefits and Entitlements	Unemployment compensation
	Workers' compensation
	Aid to blind, aged, disabled
	AFDC
	Crime victims' compensation
	General assistance
	Social security
	Veterans' benefits
Miscellaneous	Alimony, child support
	Business partnership property
	Books & tools of trade to $5000

VIRGINIA

ASSET	EXEMPT
Public Benefits	$5000, tenancy by the entirety property exempt against debt of one spouse
Personal Property/ Household Goods	Furniture, furnishings & utensil
	Burial place
	Wedding
Insurance and Annuities	Cooperative life insurance benefits
	Benefits from fraternal benefit society
	Group life insurance policy or proceeds
	Industrial sick benefits
	Life insurance cash values to $10,000
	Life insurance proceeds if beneficiary is not the insured
	Burial benefits
	Accident or disability benefits
Pensions and Retirement Plans	County & state employees
Public Benefits and Entitlements	Unemployment compensation
	Workers' compensation
	Aid to blind, aged, disabled
	AFDC
	Crime victims' compensation
	General assistance
Miscellaneous	Business partnership property
	Boat to $1500
	Tools of mechanic and farmer to $1000
	Uniforms, equipment of military

WASHINGTON

ASSET	EXEMPT
Public Benefits	Real property to $30,000
Personal Property/ Household Goods	Furniture, household goods to $1500 total
	Clothing (only $750 in furs & jewelry)
	Food & fuel
	Books to $1000
	Burial place
	Motor vehicle to $1200
Insurance and Annuities	Fire insurance proceeds for destroyed exemption
	Benefits from fraternal benefit society
	Life insurance proceeds if beneficiary is not the insured
	Disability proceeds or benefits
	Annuity to $250 per month
Pensions and Retirement Plans	Public employees
	ERISA, IRAs
	State patrol officers
	Volunteer firefighters
Public Benefits and Entitlements	Unemployment compensation
	Workers' compensation
	Child Welfare (AFDC)
	Crime victims' compensation
	General assistance
	Old-age assistance
Miscellaneous	Business partnership property
	Farm truck, stock, equipment of farmer to $3000
	Library, office furniture, equipment & supplies of professionals to $3000
	Tools & materials used in trade to $3000

WEST VIRGINIA

ASSET	EXEMPT
Public Benefits	Real or personal property claimed as residence to $7500, unused homestead may be applied to other property
Personal Property/ Household Goods	Crops, clothing, appliances, books, furnishings, musical instruments to $200 item, $1000 total
	Burial plot to $7500, if homestead is not claimed
	Payment for lost earnings
	Motor vehicle to $1200
	Jewelry to $500

	Personal injury recoveries to $7500
	Wrongful death recoveries needed for support
Insurance and Annuities	Benefits from fraternal society
	Group life insurance policy or proceeds
	Health or disability benefits
	Life insurance to $4000, from person you depended
	Life insurance proceeds unless you are both policy owner and beneficiary
	Life insurance proceeds or cash value if beneficiary is married woman
Pensions and Retirement Plans	ERISA
	Public employees
Public Benefits and Entitlements	Unemployment compensation
	Workers' compensation
	Aid to blind, aged, disabled
	AFDC
	Crime victims' compensation
	General assistance
	Social security
	Veterans' benefits
Miscellaneous	Alimony, child support
	Business partnership property
	Tools of trade to $750

WISCONSIN

ASSET	EXEMPT
Public Benefits	$40,000, Proceeds exempt for 2 years
Personal Property/ Household Goods	Automobile to $1000, food & fuel
	Bank deposits to $1000 is homestead not claimed
	US savings bonds to $200
	Beds & clothing
	Books, pictures, radio & TV
	Burial place, church pew, patents
	Cooking utensils & furniture to $200
	Jewelry to $400
Insurance and Annuities	Federal disability insurance
	Fire proceeds of destroyed exempt property
	Health, accident or disability benefits to $150/mo.
	Life insurance policy or proceeds to $5000, if beneficiary is a married woman
	Life insurance proceeds not used to pay beneficiary's creditors

Life insurance proceeds if beneficiary is not the insured

Benefits from fraternal society

Pensions and Retirement Plans	Public employees
	Firefighters, police officers
	Military pensions
	Private retirement benefits
Public Benefits and Entitlements	Workers' compensation
	Veterans' compensation
	AFDC, other social services payments
	Unemployment compensation
Miscellaneous	Business partnership property
	Farm utensils, small tools & implements to $300, tractor to $1500
	Printing materials of printer or publisher to $1500
	$400 for wages due workers
	Tools, implements, stock in trade of mechanic, miner, merchant or trader to $200
	Uniform, equipment, books

WYOMING

ASSET	EXEMPT
Public Benefits	Real property to $10,000(mobile trailer to $6000)
	Tenancy by the entirety property exempt against debt of one spouse
Personal Property/ Household Goods	Furniture, household articles & food to $2000 per person in the home
	Books
	Burial place, funeral contracts
	Clothing & wedding rings up to $1000
Insurance and Annuities	Benefits from fraternal society
	Group life or disability policy or proceeds
	Life insurance proceeds if beneficiary is not the insured
	Life insurance proceeds not used to pay beneficiary's expenses
	Disability benefits
	Annuity to $350 per month
Pensions and Retirement Plans	Firefighters, police officers
	Public employees
Public Benefits and Entitlements	Unemployment compensation
	Workers' compensation
	AFDC
	Crime victims' compensation

	General assistance
Miscellaneous	Liquor licenses
	Business partnership property
	Library & equipment of professional to $2000 tools, motor vehicle, implements in trade to $2000

APPENDIX 5:
APPLICATION FOR WAGE EXECUTION

WAGE EXECUTION PROCEEDINGS
APPLICATION, ORDER, EXECUTION
JD-CV-3 Rev. 1-91
Gen. Stat. § 31-58(j), 52-361a, 52-365d(e)
29 U.S.C. 206(a)(1)

STATE OF CONNECTICUT
SUPERIOR COURT

EMPLOYER: SEE PAGE 2 FOR INSTRUCTIONS

INSTRUCTIONS

JUDGMENT CREDITOR OR ATTORNEY

1. Prepare original and four copies.
2. Attach form JD-CV-3a to one copy of this form.
3. Present original and 3 copies to clerk of court.
4. Retain one copy for your file.

CLERK

1. Issue execution by signing original and 2 copies.
2. Retain one copy for court file
3. Enter any court ordered limitation at the bottom of section II on page 2.

SHERIFF

1. Leave 2 signed copies with employer.
2. Make return on signed original.
3. Leave 1 copy of Modification and Exemption Claim form (JD-CV-3a) with employer and fill in "Date of Service" on form.

NAME AND MAILING ADDRESS OF JUDGMENT CREDITOR OR ATTORNEY
(To be completed by Plaintiff)

(Fold)

ADDRESS OF COURT *(Number, street, and town,)*	☐ G.A.	☐ J.D.	☐ HOUSING	DATE OF JUDGMENT	DOCKET NUMBER

AMOUNT OF WEEKLY PAYMENTS ORDERED *(Employers must pay amount of execution calculated on page 2 of this form)* $	COMMENCEMENT DATE	TOTAL AMOUNT PAID TO DATE $	DATE OF LAST PAYMENT

NAME(S) OF JUDGMENT CREDITOR(S)	OF *(Street and Town)*	NAME(S) OF JUDGMENT DEBTOR(S)	OF *(Street and Town)*

EMPLOYER OF JUDGMENT DEBTOR *(If known)*	OF *(Street and Town)*	TELEPHONE NO.

APPLICATION

1. AMOUNT OF JUDGMENT *(In words) (Including damages and, where applicable, prejudgment interest and attorney fees)*	DOLLARS	$
2. AMOUNT OF COSTS IN OBTAINING JUDGMENT *(In words)*	DOLLARS	$
3. TOTAL JUDGMENT AND COSTS *(In words)(Add lines 1 and 2)*	DOLLARS	$
4. TOTAL PAID ON ACCOUNT *(In words)*	DOLLARS	$
5. TOTAL UNPAID JUDGMENT *(In words) (Subtract line 4 from line 3)*	DOLLARS	$
6. APPLICATION FEE FOR WAGE EXECUTION *(In words)(If not waived by the court)*	DOLLARS	$
7. TOTAL OF LINES 5 AND 6 *(in words)*	DOLLARS	$

SIGNED *(Judgment Creditor or Attorney)*	DATE APPLICATION SIGNED

ADDRESS OF PERSON SIGNING	TELEPHONE NO.

EXECUTION

To: Any Proper Officer
WHEREAS the above-named Judgment Creditor(s) recovered judgment against the above-named Judgment Debtor(s) for the above Amount of Judgment, as appears of record, whereof execution remains to be done on the Total Shown in line 7 above,
AND WHEREAS, pursuant to statute, the said court entered an order that said judgment be paid in weekly payments,
AND WHEREAS, the said Judgment Debtor(s) failed to comply with said order for weekly payments, as appears of record by application of said Judgment Creditor(s) moving that this execution issue on said Total in line 7 above.
These are, therefore, by authority of the State of Connecticut, to command you, that of any amount of any debt accruing by reason of personal services due any said Judgment Debtor as may not exceed the Amount of Execution calculated on the page 2 of this form, within your precincts, you cause to be levied, paid, and satisfied unto the said Judgment Creditor(s), with interest from the said Date of Judgment on the Total in line 5 above, to the date when this execution is satisfied, and your own fees.
Make service hereof within one year of this date, and due return hereof with your doings thereon, within thirty days from satisfaction hereof.

SIGNED *(Assistant Clerk of said court)* X	ON *(Date)*

PAGE 1 OF 2

The Law of Attachment and Garnishment

97

APPLICATION FOR WAGE EXECUTION

IMPORTANT NOTICE TO EMPLOYER

You are being served with a wage execution, a court order requiring you to withhold non-exempt wages from a person employed by you. This execution is being served upon you because your employee, the Judgment Debtor (on page 1), has had a judgment entered against him by the Superior Court requiring him to pay damages to the Judgment Creditor (on page 1) and has not made payment of the total amount of the judgment plus any court costs as shown on page 1. This notice is to inform you of the actions you must take in order to comply with the law regarding wage executions. Please read each section carefully.

I. YOU MUST NOTIFY THE EMPLOYEE — Your employee has certain legal rights which may allow him to request the court to change or stop this execution upon his wages. A notice of his rights and how to get a hearing in court is attached to the second copy of the wage execution given to you by the officer. You must complete your portion of the wage execution and your portion of the exemption and modification claim form and DELIVER OR MAIL, POSTAGE PREPAID, A COPY OF THESE PAPERS TO YOUR EMPLOYEE IMMEDIATELY so that your employee can make any claims allowed by law.

II. EXECUTION NOT EFFECTIVE FOR 20 DAYS —This execution is not effective until after 20 days from the day the officer served these papers on you. No money should be deducted from your employee's wages until the first wages you pay to your employee after the 20-day period ends.

If your employee elects within the 20-day period to make a claim to the court that his wages are partially or totally exempt from execution to pay this judgment or he seeks to have the amount of this execution changed, wages are not to be withheld from the employee until the court decides the claims or determines the rights of your employee in this case.

If you are not notified that your employee has filed papers with the court, the execution is to be enforced after 20 days from the date of service on you.

III. STAY OF EXECUTION — No earnings claimed to be exempt or subject to a claim for modification may be withheld from any employee until determination of the claim by the court.

IV. ONLY ONE EXECUTION ISSUED UNDER GEN. STAT. 52-361a TO BE SATISFIED AT A TIME — You must make deductions from your employee's wages and pay over the withheld money against only one execution issued under Gen. Stat. 52-361a at a time. If you are served with more than one execution issued under Gen. Stat. 52-361a against this employee's wages, the executions are to be satisfied

in the order in which you are served with them. (Wage executions and earnings assignments for support of a family, issued under C.G.S. § 52-362a or c, take precedence over this execution. Family support wage executions and earnings assignments are issued on Form JD-FM-1.)

V. MAXIMUM AMOUNT DEDUCTED — The maximum amount which can be legally withheld from your employee's wages is 25% of his disposable earnings for each week. The amount to be withheld to pay this execution may be less than 25%, but it can never be more. The computations you complete below will allow you to calculate the exact amount which should be withheld from this employee's wages.

Unless the court orders that this execution is to be for a smaller amount, you must withhold and pay over the maximum amount which you figure out using the computations below. Your employee has a right to request the court to reduce the amount withheld, but until you receive notice that the court has agreed to allow the amount to be reduced, you must withhold the maximum amount.

VI. YOUR DUTY TO COMPLY WITH THIS EXECUTION — You have a legal duty to make deductions from your employee's wages and pay any amounts deducted as required by this execution. If you do not, legal action may be taken against you. If you are found to be in contempt of a court order, you may be held liable to the Judgment Creditor for the amounts of wages which you did not withhold from your employee.

VII. DISCIPLINE AGAINST YOUR EMPLOYEE — You may not discipline, suspend or discharge your employee because this wage execution has been served upon you. If you do unlawfully take action against your employee, you may be liable to pay him all of his lost earnings and employment benefits from the time of your action to the time that the employee is reinstated

The law allows you to take disciplinary measures against the employee if you are served with more than 7 wage executions against his wages in any calendar year.

SECTION I — COMPUTATION OF EMPLOYEE'S DISPOSABLE EARNINGS

"DISPOSABLE EARNINGS" means that part of the earnings of an individual remaining after the deduction from those earnings of amounts to be withheld for payment of federal income and employment taxes, normal retirement contributions, union dues and initiation fees, group life insurance premiums, health insurance premiums, federal tax levies, and state income tax deductions authorized pursuant to section 12-34b (income tax deduction for out-of-state residents employed in Connecticut).

1. Employee's gross compensation per week...

2. Federal income tax withheld..

3. Federal employment tax..

4. Normal retirement contribution..

5. Union dues and initiation fees..

6. Group life insurance premium..

7. Health insurance premium..

8. Other federal tax levies..

9. State income tax withheld...

10. Total allowable deductions (Add lines 2-9)...

11. WEEKLY DISPOSABLE EARNINGS (Subtract line 10 from line 1)...................................

SECTION II — COMPUTATION OF AMOUNT OF EXECUTION

To be calculated by employer	COL. 1	COL. 2
A-1. Weekly disposable earnings (from line 11 above)	$	
A-2. 25% of disposable earnings for week		$
B-1. Weekly disposable earnings (from line 11 above)	$	
B-2. Forty times the HIGHER of the current federal minimum hourly wage OR state full minumum fair wage.	$	
Amount by which line B-1 exceeds B-2		$
AMOUNT OF EXECUTION (Lesser of the two amounts in column 2 subject to any court ordered limitation set forth in the box below if a lesser amount.)		$

COURT ORDERED LIMITATION (If any, to be entered by clerk)

JD-CV-3EL Rev. 1/91

PAGE 2 OF 2

APPENDIX 6:
INCOME EXECUTION FOR SUPPORT ENFORCEMENT

C.P.L.R 5241(b)

Form 4-8a
(Income Execution
Clerk of Court)
12/97

FAMILY COURT OF THE STATE OF NEW YORK
COUNTY OF

....

In the Matter of a Proceeding for Support
Under Article_____ of the Family Court Act

Docket No.

                          Petitioner

S.S.#

            -against-

                          Respondent.

S.S.#

INCOME
EXECUTION
FOR SUPPORT
ENFORCEMENT
(Clerk of Court)

....

TO: (employer) (income payor)

WHEREAS an order of support was entered in the   Court, County of
                 , of the State of   on the
day of   , 19   , directing that the amount of $ shall be paid
(bi-)(weekly)(semi)(monthly)(quarterly) by   (debtor) to
                                         (creditor); and

WHEREAS said payments have not been made and there is due and owing to said creditor
the amount of $ in arrears; and

WHEREAS, said debtor is (employed by   , whose address is
) (currently is receiving or will receive income from
                 , whose address is
).

NOW THEREFORE, YOU ARE DIRECTED to deduct from the amount payable to said debtor
now and henceforth, until further notice, the sum of $ (bi-) (weekly) (semi)
(monthly) (quarterly) to be applied to insure compliance with the direction in said order of support, and
a further sum of $ to be applied to the reduction of arrears until the amount of $
in arrears is paid in full; and to remit the amount so deducted to the following address:
within ten days of the date that Respondent is paid; and

YOU ARE FURTHER DIRECTED TO notify the undersigned promptly if and when the
debtor (ceases to be in your employ) (is no longer the recipient of income) and provide the
debtor's address (and the name and address of the new employer, if known).

Attached hereto is a NOTICE TO EMPLOYER OR INCOME PAYOR which is incorporated by reference and enforceable as if contained herein.

Dated: , 19

Clerk of the Family Court
of the State of New York
County of

Office and P.O. Address

Telephone Number

NOTICE TO CREDITOR

A copy of this Income Execution must be served upon the debtor by regular mail at the last known residence of said debtor, or such other place as the debtor is likely to receive notice, or in the same manner as a summons may be served.

You are also responsible for serving a copy of this Income Execution upon the employer or income payor 15 days after the date of service upon the debtor unless the debtor has asserted a mistake of fact as defined in C.P.L.R.5241.

NOTICE TO DEBTOR

Service of a copy of this Income Execution must be made upon you by the creditor by regular mail at your last known residence, or such other place as you are likely to receive notice, or in the same manner as a summons may be served.

NOTICE TO EMPLOYER OR INCOME PAYOR

TIMING, AMOUNT AND REMITTING OF DEDUCTIONS: Pursuant to the Civil Practice Law and Rules 5241, deductions must commence no later than the first pay period that occurs 14 days following the service of the Income Execution upon the employer or income payor, and payment must be sent within 7 business days of the date the debtor is paid. Each payment shall include the identity and social security number of the debtor and the date and amount of each withholding of the debtor's income included in the payment. "Date of withholding" means the date on which the income would otherwise have been paid or made available to the debtor were it not withheld by the employer or income payor.

Deductions from income shall not exceed the following: Where a debtor IS currently supporting a spouse or dependent child other than the creditor, the amount of the deductions to be withheld shall not exceed fifty percent of the earnings of the debtor remaining after the deduction therefrom of any amounts required by law to be withheld ("disposable earnings"), except that if any part of such deduction is to be applied to the reduction of arrears which shall have accrued more than twelve weeks prior to the beginning of the week for which such earnings are payable, the amount of such deduction shall not exceed fifty-five percent of disposable earnings.

Where a debtor IS NOT currently supporting a spouse or dependent child other than the creditor, the amount of the deductions to be withheld shall not exceed sixty percent of the earnings of the debtor remaining after the deductions therefrom of any amounts required by law to be withheld ("disposable earnings"), except that if any part of such deduction is to be applied to the reduction of arrears which shall have accrued more than twelve weeks prior to the beginning of the week for which such earnings are payable, the amount of such deduction shall not exceed sixty-five percent of disposable earnings.

An employer who receives an income execution issued by another state shall apply the income withholding law of the state of the debtor's principal place of employment in determining the above specifications concerning timing, amount and remitting of deductions.

FAILURE TO DEDUCT OR REMIT PAYMENTS: An employer or income payor served with an income execution who fails to deduct the amount specified shall be liable to the creditor, who may commence a proceeding against the employer or income payor for any accrued deductions, together with interest and reasonable attorney's fees. Upon an employer's failure to remit any amounts deducted pursuant to this income execution, either the creditor or the debtor may commence a proceeding against the employer or income payor for accrued deductions, and reasonable attorney's fees.

Additionally, upon a finding by the Family Court that the employer or income payor failed to deduct or remit deductions as specified in the income execution, the court shall issue an order directing compliance, and may direct the employer or income payor to pay a fine of up to $500.00 for the first such failure and $1,000.00 for each subsequent failure to deduct or remit.

DISCHARGE, LAYOFF, DISCIPLINING, REFUSAL TO PROMOTE OR REFUSAL TO HIRE BECAUSE OF THE EXISTENCE OF ONE OR MORE INCOME DEDUCTION ORDERS: Pursuant to Section 5252 of the Civil Practice Law and Rules, where an employer discharges, lays off, refuses to promote, or disciplines an employee, or refuses to hire a prospective employee, because of the existence of one or more income executions and/or income deduction orders, the court may direct the employer to pay a fine of up to $500.00 for the first and $1,000.00 for each subsequent instance of employer or income payor discrimination.

FURTHER: An employer must notify the creditor and issuer promptly when the debtor terminates employment and must provide the debtor's last address and the name and address of the debtor's new employer, if known.

An employer who complies with an income withholding notice that is regular on its face shall not be subject to civil liability to any individual or agency for conduct in compliance with the notice.

APPENDIX 7:
WAGE EXECUTION EXEMPTION CLAIM
FORM

EXEMPTION AND MODIFICATION CLAIM FORM
WAGE EXECUTION
JD-CV-3aEL Rev. 7-97
C.G.S. § 31-58(j), 52-212, 52-350a, 52-352b, 52-361a, 52-361b
29 U.S.C. 206(a)(1)

STATE OF CONNECTICUT
SUPERIOR COURT

NAME AND MAILING ADDRESS OF JUDGMENT DEBTOR OR ATTORNEY
(To be completed by Plaintiff)

TO:

INSTRUCTIONS

TO SHERIFF: Complete section II below and make service on employer in accordance with the instructions on form JD-CV-3.
TO EMPLOYER: Complete Section III below and

(Fold)

SECTION I *(Plaintiff to complete this section and attach to one copy of the wage execution application (JD-CV-3).)*

NAME AND ADDRESS OF COURT

NAME OF JUDGMENT DEBTOR	DOCKET NUMBER

NAME AND ADDRESS OF JUDGMENT CREDITOR OR ATTORNEY	TELEPHONE NO.

SECTION II *(To be completed by sheriff)*

DATE OF SERVICE OF WAGE EXECUTION ON EMPLOYER	NAME OF SHERIFF

SECTION III *(Employer to complete this section and immediately send one copy of this form and the Wage Execution form (JD-CV-3) to the judgment debtor pursuant to General Statutes section 52-361a(d).)*

NAME AND ADDRESS OF EMPLOYER	TELEPHONE NO. OF PAYROLL DEPT.

DATE OF DELIVERY OR MAILING TO JUDGMENT DEBTOR	TOTAL AMOUNT OF WAGE EXECUTION	AMOUNT TO BE TAKEN OUT FROM WEEKLY EARNINGS

SECTION IV   **NOTICE TO JUDGMENT DEBTOR**

As the result of a judgment entered against you, the attached execution has been issued against wages earned by you from the employer named above. In compliance with this execution, beginning 20 days from the Date of Service of Wage Execution on Employer indicated above, the employer will remove from your weekly earnings an amount of money which leaves you with the greater of seventy-five percent of your disposable earnings OR forty times the higher of the minimum hourly wage prescribed by federal law or state law. On page two of this form are those sections of the general statutes which your employer must follow in determining the weekly amount that may be taken out of your wages to satisfy the wage execution. If you determine that your employer has not calculated the weekly amount correctly, you should bring this to your employer's attention.

YOUR EARNINGS MAY BE EXEMPT FROM EXECUTION — Any wages earned by a public assistance recipient under an incentive earnings or similar program are exempt from execution. (Gen. Stat. § 52-353b(d))

HOW TO CLAIM AN EXEMPTION ALLOWED BY LAW — If you wish to claim that your earnings are exempt by law from execution you must fill out and sign the Claim of Exemption on page 2 of this form and return this exemption and modification claim form to the Superior Court at the above address.

Upon receipt of this form the clerk of the Superior Court will notify you and the judgment creditor of the date on which a hearing will be held by the court to determine the issues raised by your claim. If this form is received by the court no later than 20 days from the Date of Service of Wage Execution on Employer indicated above, the employer will not begin withholding your earnings until after your claim is determined by the court. A claim may also be filed after the 20 day period. No earnings claimed to be exempt may be withheld from any employee until determination of the claim.

MODIFICATION OF EXECUTION — If you have reasonable cause to believe that you are entitled to a modification of the wage execution and wish to have the execution so modified, you must fill out the Claim for Modification on page 2 of this form and return this exemption and modification claim form to the Superior Court at the above address.

Upon receipt of this form the clerk of Superior Court will notify you and the judgment creditor of the date on which a hearing will be held by the court to determine the issues raised by your claim. If this form is received by the court no later than 20 days from the Date of Service of Wage Execution on Employer indicated above, the employer will not begin withholding your earnings until after your claim is determined by the court. A claim may also be filed after the 20 day period. No earnings subject to a claim for modification may be withheld from any employee until determination of the claim.

SETTING ASIDE JUDGMENT — If the judgment was rendered against you because of your failure to appear in court, you may, pursuant to section 52-212 of the general statutes, within four months of the date judgment was rendered and upon belief that you have reasonable cause, move the court to set aside the judgment entered against you.

PAGE 1 OF 2

WAGE EXECUTION EXEMPTION CLAIM FORM

SECTION V   **CLAIM OF EXEMPTION ESTABLISHED BY LAW**

I, the Judgment Debtor hereby claim and certify under the penalty of false statement that my earnings are exempt from execution because:

☐ I am a public assistance recipient earning wages under an incentive earnings or similar program and my earnings are exempt from execution, or

☐ Other statutory exemption (state exemption and statutory citation) _____

_____

SIGNED *(Judgment Debtor)*	DATE SIGNED	NAME AND ADDRESS OF JUDGMENT DEBTOR	TELEPHONE NO.

SECTION VI   **CLAIM FOR MODIFICATION**

I, the Judgment Debtor hereby move for a modification of the wage execution issued against me as follows:

NEW AMOUNT REQUESTED /PER WEEK	DESCRIBE NATURE OF CLAIM FOR MODIFICATION

SIGNED *(Judgment Debtor)*	DATE SIGNED	NAME AND COMPLETE MAILING ADDRESS OF JUDGMENT DEBTOR	TELEPHONE NO.

SECTION VII   **STIPULATION TO MODIFICATION**

The Judgment Creditor(s) in this matter hereby agree to the modification of the Wage Execution claimed above.

SIGNED *(Judgment Creditor(s) or Attorney))*	DATE

SECTION VIII   **NOTICE OF HEARING ON EXEMPTION/MODIFICATION CLAIM**

DATE AND TIME OF HEARING	SIGNED *(Assistant Clerk)*

SECTION IX   **ORDER OF COURT**

ORDERED that the wage execution be modified as follows:

SIGNED *(Assistant Clerk)*	DATE SIGNED
BY ORDER OF THE COURT	

GENERAL STATUTES

1. The following is that part of General Statutes section 52-361a(f) which denotes what portion of your wages is subject to execution.

The maximum part of the aggregate weekly earnings of an individual which may be subject under this section to levy or other withholding for payment of a judgment is the lesser of (1) twenty-five percent of his disposable earnings for that week, or (2) the amount by which his disposable earnings for that week exceed forty times the higher of (A) the minimum hourly wage prescribed by section 6(a)(1) of the Fair Labor Standards Act of 1938, U.S.C. tit. 29, section 206(a)(1), or (B) the full minimum fair wage established by subsection (j) of section 31-58, in effect at the time the earnings are payable.

2. The following is that part of General Statutes section 52-350a(4) which defines disposable earnings and which defines portions of your wages which must be excluded from your total earnings when calculating the weekly amount which is subject to execution.

"Disposable earnings" means that part of the earnings of an individual remaining after the deduction from those earnings of amounts required to be withheld for payment of federal income and employment taxes, normal retirement contributions, union dues and initiation fees, group life insurance premiums, health insurance premiums, federal tax levies, and state income tax deductions authorized pursuant to C.G.S. 12-34b.

JD-CV-3aEL (page 2) Rev. 1/96   **PAGE 2 OF 2**

APPENDIX 8:
TABLE OF WAGE EXEMPTIONS BY STATE

STATE	EXEMPT
Alabama	Judgment creditor—greater of 75% of your weekly net earnings or $114 per week
Alaska	Weekly net earnings to $350; sole wage earner in household $2200
Arizona	Minimum 75% of earned but unpaid wages, pension payment. Judgment creditor—greater of 75% of your weekly net earnings or $114 per week
Arkansas	Earned but unpaid wages due for 60 days, but not under $25 per week
California—System 1	Public employees vacation credits 75% of wages paid 30 days before being sought by creditor
California—System 2	None
Colorado	Judgment Creditor—greater of 75% of your weekly net earnings or $114 per week
Connecticut	Judgment Creditor—greater of 75% of your weekly net earnings or $114 per week
Delaware	85% of earned but unpaid wages
District of Columbia	Judgment Creditor—greater of 75% of your weekly net earnings or $114 per week; non-wage and non-pension earnings for 60 days to $200 per month for head of family; else $60 per month
Florida	Earned but unpaid wages, or wages in bank account; federal government employees pension payments needed for support & received 3 months before being attached by creditor

STATE	EXEMPT
Georgia	Judgment Creditor—greater of 75% of your weekly net earnings or $114 per week
Hawaii	Unpaid wages due for services of past 31 days; 95% of 1st $100; 90% of 2nd $100; 80% of balance; Prisoner's wages held by DSSH
Idaho	Judgment Creditor—greater of 75% of your weekly net earnings or $114 per week
Illinois	Judgment Creditor—greater of 75% of your weekly net earnings or $114 per week
Indiana	Judgment Creditor—greater of 75% of your weekly net earnings or $114 per week
Iowa	Minimum 75% of earned but unpaid wages, pension payments
Kansas	Judgment Creditor—greater of 75% of your weekly net earnings or $114 per week
Kentucky	Judgment Creditor—greater of 75% of your weekly net earnings or $114 per week
Louisiana	Judgment Creditor—greater of 75% of your weekly net earnings or $114 per week
Maine	Judgment Creditor—greater of 75% of your weekly net earnings or $114 per week only
Maryland	Earned but unpaid wages; greater of 75% or $145 per week, in Kent Worcester Counties; Greater of 75% of actual wages or $114 per week
Massachusetts	Earned but unpaid wages to $125 per week Payment (wage or pension) up to $100 per week
Michigan	60% of earned but unpaid wages for head of household; else 40%. Head of household may keep at least $15 per week + $2 per week per non-spouse dependent; others may keep at least $10 per week
Minnesota	Judgment Creditor—greater of 75% of your weekly net earnings or $114 per week; wages deposited into bank accounts for 20 days after depositing; Wages of released inmates paid within 6 months of release
Mississippi	Judgment Creditor—100% first 30 days; after 30 days—greater of 75% of your weekly net earnings or $114 per week

STATE	EXEMPT
Missouri	Judgment Creditor—greater of 75% of your weekly net earnings or $114 per week Wages of servant or common laborer to $90
Montana	Judgment Creditor—greater of 75% of your weekly net earnings or $114 per week
Nebraska	Judgment Creditor—greater of 85% (for head of family; all others 75%) of weekly net earnings or $114 per week
Nevada	Judgment Creditor—greater of 75% of weekly net earnings or $114 per week
New Hampshire	Court decides amount exempt
New Jersey	90% of earned but unpaid wages if income under $7500; if income over $7500, court decides amount Wages or allowances of military personnel
New Mexico	Judgment Creditor—greater of 75% of your weekly net earnings or $114 per week
New York	90% of earned but unpaid wages received 60 days before creditor attachment
North Carolina	Earned but unpaid wages received 60 days
North Dakota	Judgment Creditor—greater of 75% of your weekly net earnings or $114 per week
Ohio	Judgment Creditor—greater of 75% of your weekly net earnings or $114 per week
Oklahoma	75% of wages earned 90 days before creditor attachment
Oregon	Judgment Creditor—greater of 75% of your weekly net earnings or $114 per week Wages withheld in an employees bond savings account
Pennsylvania	Earned but unpaid wages
Rhode Island	Wages to $50; wages due military member or survivor on active duty; Wages of spouse
South Carolina	None
South Dakota	Earned wages owed 60 days before being sought by creditor, needed for support of family
Tennessee	Judgment Creditor—greater of 75% of your weekly net earnings or $114 per week (plus $2.50 per week per child)

STATE	EXEMPT
Texas	Earned but unpaid wages
Utah	Judgment Creditor—greater of 75% of your weekly net earnings or $114 per week
Vermont	Judgment Creditor—greater of 75% of your weekly net earnings or $114 per week
Virginia	Judgment Creditor—greater of 75% of your weekly net earnings or $114 per week
Washington	Judgment Creditor—greater of 75% of your weekly net earnings or $114 per week
West Virginia	Judgment Creditor—greater of 80% of your weekly net earnings or $114 per week
Wisconsin	Wages for 30 days; if you have dependents, $120 plus $20 per dependent, not to exceed 75% of your wages. No dependents, no less than $75 nor more than $100
Wyoming	Judgment Creditor—greater of 75% of your weekly net earnings or $114 per week

APPENDIX 9:
APPLICATION FOR BANK EXECUTION

BANK EXECUTION PROCEEDINGS
APPLICATION AND EXECUTION
JD-CV-24EL Rev. 6-96
C.G.S. 52-367a, 52-367b

STATE OF CONNECTICUT
SUPERIOR COURT
(See page 2 for instructions to banking institution)
INSTRUCTIONS

APFEABA
EXISSUE

JUDGMENT CREDITOR OR ATTORNEY	*CLERK*
1. Prepare on typewriter.	1. Check the file to ensure that the information
2. Complete the application section; make original and 4 copies.	provided on the application is correct.
3. Put an "X" in the appropriate box of the "execution" section below.	2. Sign original execution.
If box A is chosen, complete section 1 of the Exemption Claim	3. Return original and 2 copies to applicant.
Form, JD-CV-24a and attach to this form.	4. Retain a copy for file.
4. Present original and 3 copies to clerk of court.	

APPLICATION / Fold

ADDRESS OF COURT

☐ JUDICIAL DISTRICT
☐ HOUSING SESSION   ☐ G.A. _____   DOCKET NO.

NAME AND MAILING ADDRESS OF JUDGMENT CREDITOR OR ATTORNEY *(To be completed by Judgment Creditor)*

NAME(S) OF JUDGMENT CREDITOR(S)   OF *(Town)*   NAME(S) AND ADDRESS(ES) OF JUDGMENT DEBTOR(S)

DATE OF JUDGMENT   AMOUNT OF DAMAGES   AMOUNT OF COSTS   AMOUNT OF DAMAGES AND COSTS ALREADY PAID *(if any)*

TOTAL UNPAID DAMAGES AND COSTS   TOTAL UNPAID DAMAGES AND COSTS *(in words)*

SIGNED *(Judgment Creditor or Attorney)*   DATE SIGNED

ADDRESS OF PERSON SIGNING   TELEPHONE NO.

EXECUTION

TO ANY PROPER OFFICER,

Whereas on said Date of Judgment the above-named Judgment Creditor(s) recovered judgment against the above-named Judgment Debtor(s) before the above-named court for the amount of damages and costs stated above, as appears of record, whereof execution remains to be done. These are, therefore, BY AUTHORITY OF THE STATE OF CONNECTICUT TO COMMAND YOU:

☐ **A. IF JUDGMENT DEBTOR IS A NATURAL PERSON**

Within seven days from your receipt of this execution, make demand upon the main office of any banking institution having its main office within your county, or if such main office is not within your county and such banking institution has one or more branch offices within your county, upon an employee of such a branch office, such employee and such branch office having been designated by the banking institution in accordance with regulations adopted by the banking commissioner, for payment to you pursuant to section 52-367b(b) of the general statutes of any nonexempt debt due said Judgment Debtor(s), which sum shall not exceed the total unpaid damages and costs on said judgment as stated above, plus interest on the unpaid amount of said judgment from its date until the time when this execution shall be satisfied, plus your own fee. After having made such demand you are directed to serve a true and attested copy of this execution, together with the attached affidavit and exemption claim form, with your doings endorsed thereon, with the banking institution officer upon whom such demand was made. Said sum shall be received by you and applied on this execution in accordance with the provisions of section 52-367b of the general statutes.

☐ **B. OTHER**

Make demand upon the main office of any banking institution having its main office within your county, or if such main office is not within your county and such banking institution has one or more branch offices within your county, upon an employee of such a branch office, such employee and such branch office having been designated by the banking institution in accordance with regulations adopted by the banking commissioner, for payment to you of any debt due said Judgment Debtor(s), which sum shall not exceed the total unpaid damages and costs on said judgment as stated above, plus interest on the unpaid amount of said judgment, from its date until the time when this execution shall be satisfied, plus your own fees. Said sum shall be received by you and applied on this execution. After having made such demand you are directed to serve a true and attested copy hereof, with your doings thereon endorsed, with the banking institution officer upon whom such demand was made.

HEREOF FAIL NOT, AND MAKE DUE RETURN OF THIS WRIT WITH YOUR DOINGS THEREON, ACCORDING TO LAW.

SIGNED *(Assistant Clerk)*   DATE SIGNED

PAGE 1 OF 2

The Law of Attachment and Garnishment

APPLICATION FOR BANK EXECUTION

INSTRUCTIONS TO BANKING INSTITUTION UPON RECEIPT OF
BANK EXECUTION WHEN JUDGMENT DEBTOR IS A NATURAL PERSON

1. Complete section II of the accompanying Exemption Claim Form (JD-CV-24a) and send, forthwith, 2 copies of both this form and the Exemption Claim Form to the judgment debtor, postage pre-paid, at his last known address with respect to the affected accounts on the records of your institution.

2. Remove from the judgment debtor's account the amount of any debts due from you to the judgment debtor not exceeding the Total Unpaid Damages and Costs as appears on page 1 of this form plus interest and the sheriff's fee, before your midnight deadline, as defined in section 42a-4-104 of the general statutes.

3. You must hold the amount removed from the judgment debtor's account pursuant to this execution for fifteen days from the date you mail the copies of this form and the Exemption Claim Form to the judgment debtor. During such fifteen day period you must not pay the officer serving this execution.

4. If the judgment debtor returns the Exemption Claim Form or other written notice that an exemption is being claimed you must, within two business days of receipt of such notice, send a copy of such notice to the clerk of the court which issued the execution. You must continue to hold the amount removed from the judgment debtor's account for forty-five days or until a court order is received regarding disposition of the funds, whichever occurs earlier. If no order is received within forty-five days of the date you send a copy of the Exemption Claim Form or notice to the clerk of the court, you must return the funds to the judgment debtor's account.

5. If you do not receive a claim of exemption within fifteen days of the mailing to the judgment debtor of the execution and Exemption Claim Form you must, upon demand, forthwith pay the serving officer the amount removed from the judgment debtor's account.

6. If no exemption claim is filed or if the court orders you to pay the serving officer an amount removed from the judgment debtor's account not exceeding the amount due on the execution and you fail or refuse to do so, you shall be liable in an action therefor to the judgment creditor(s) named in the execution for the amount of nonexempt monies which you fail or refuse to pay over.

7. If you pay exempt monies from the account of the judgment debtor contrary to these instructions, or the provisions of section 52-367b of the general statutes, you shall be liable in an action therefor to the judgment debtor for any exempt monies so paid. The provisions of section 52-367b, as amended from time to time, take precedence over these instructions.

INSTRUCTIONS TO BANKING INSTITUTION UPON RECEIPT OF
BANK EXECUTION WHEN JUDGMENT DEBTOR IS NOT A NATURAL PERSON

1. You must pay the officer serving this execution the amount of any debts due from you to the judgment debtor not exceeding the Total Unpaid Damages and Costs as appears on page 1 of this form, plus interest and the sheriff's fee.

2. You must act on this execution according to section 42a-4-303 of the general statutes, before your midnight deadline, as defined in section 42a-4-104 of the general statutes.

APPENDIX 10:
BANK EXECUTION EXEMPTION
CLAIM FORM

EXEMPTION CLAIM FORM
BANK EXECUTION
JD-CV-24a Rev. 4-97
C.G.S. 31-58(j), 52-321a, 52-350a, 52-352b, 52-361a,
52-367b, 29 U.S.C. 206(a)(1)

STATE OF CONNECTICUT
SUPERIOR COURT

NAME AND ADDRESS OF JUDGMENT DEBTOR OR ATTORNEY *(To be completed by plaintiff)*

TO: ⌐   ¬

      L   ⌐

SECTION I *(To be completed by plaintiff)*

☐ Judicial District	☐ Housing Session	☐ G.A. No.	NAME AND ADDRESS OF COURT *(No., Street, Town and Zip Code)*
NAME OF JUDGMENT DEBTOR			DOCKET NO.

SECTION II *(To be completed by banking institution - see instructions on page 2)*

NAME AND ADDRESS OF BANKING INSTITUTION TO WHICH EXEMPTION CLAIM *(IF ANY)* IS TO BE RETURNED	DATE OF MAILING TO JUDGMENT DEBTOR

DESCRIPTION OF ACCOUNT(S) AND AMOUNT(S) REMOVED PURSUANT TO EXECUTION

SECTION III NOTICE TO JUDGMENT DEBTOR

As a result of a judgment entered against you, the attached execution has been issued against funds deposited by you in the banking institution named above. In compliance with this execution, the banking institution has removed from the account(s) enumerated above the amount of money indicated above.

THE MONEY IN YOUR ACCOUNT(S) MAY BE EXEMPT FROM EXECUTION - The money in your account(s) may be protected from execution by state statutes or by other laws or regulations of this state or of the United States. A checklist and a description of the exemptions established by law are set forth on the page 2.

HOW TO CLAIM AN EXEMPTION ESTABLISHED BY LAW - If you wish to claim that the money in your account(s) is exempt by law from execution, you must fill out and sign before a proper official the Affidavit of Claim of Exemption below and mail or deliver this exemption claim form to the banking institution at the above address. This form must be received by the banking institution no later than 15 days from the DATE OF MAILING TO THE JUDGMENT DEBTOR indicated above.

Upon receipt of this form the bank will forward it to the Superior Court and the court clerk will notify you and the judgment creditor of the date on which a hearing will be held by the court to determine the issues raised by your claim.

SECTION IV AFFIDAVIT OF CLAIM OF EXEMPTION ESTABLISHED BY LAW

I, the judgment debtor named above, hereby claim and certify under the penalty of false statement that the money in the above account(s) is exempt by law from execution as follows:

ACCOUNT NUMBER	DESCRIBE CLAIMED EXEMPTION ESTABLISHED BY LAW
AMOUNT CLAIMED TO BE EXEMPT	

ACCOUNT NUMBER	DESCRIBE CLAIMED EXEMPTION ESTABLISHED BY LAW
AMOUNT CLAIMED TO BE EXEMPT	

☐ Additional sheet(s) attached hereto and made a part hereof *(if necessary)*.

SIGNED *(Individual attorney or pro se party)*	DATE SIGNED	STATE OF CONNECTICUT, COUNTY OF
X		} SS
COMPLETE MAILING ADDRESS OF JUDGMENT DEBTOR		SUBSCRIBED AND SWORN TO BEFORE ME THIS
		_____ DAY OF _____ , 19 ___
		SIGNED *(Notary Public, Commissioner of Superior Court)*
TELEPHONE NO.		X

Page 1 of 2

BANK EXECUTION EXEMPTION CLAIM FORM

1. Public Assistance payments and any wages earned by a public assistance recipient under an incentive earnings or similar program. (C.G.S. 52-352b(d))
2. Health and disability insurance payments. (C.G.S. 52-352b(e))
3. Worker's Compensation, social security, veterans and unemployment benefits. (C.G.S. 52-352b(g))
4. Court approved payments for child support. (C.G.S. 52-352b(h))
5. Any assets or interests of a judgment debtor in, or payments received by the judgment debtor from, a plan or arrangement described in C.G.S. 52-321a. (C.G.S. 52-352b(m))
6. Alimony and support, other than child support, but only to the extent that wages are exempt from execution under section 52-361a*. (C.G.S. 52-352b(n))
7. An award under a crime reparations act. (C.G.S. 52-352b(o))
8. All benefits allowed by any association of persons in this state towards the support of any of its members incapacitated by sickness or infirmity from attending to his usual business; and all monies due the debtor from any insurance company upon any insurance policy issued on exempt property, to the same extent that the property was exempt. (C.G.S. 52-352b(p), (q))
9. Any interest of the judgment debtor in any property not to exceed in value one thousand dollars. (C.G.S. § 52-352b(r))
10. Irrevocable transfers of money to an account held by a bona fide nonprofit debt adjuster licensed pursuant to sections 36a-655 to 36a-665, inclusive, of the general statutes for the benefit of creditors of the judgment debtor. (C.G.S. 52-352b(u))
11. There may be other laws or regulations of this state or of the United States which set forth additional exemptions.

*The following is that part of C.G.S. 52-361a which denotes what portion of wages is exempt from execution:

   The maximum part of the aggregate weekly earnings of an individual which may be subject to levy or other withholding for payment of a judgment is the lesser of (1) twenty-five per cent of his disposable earnings for that week, or (2) the amount by which his disposable earnings for that week exceed forty times the higher of (A) the minimum hourly wage prescribed by Section 6(a)(1) of the Fair Labor Standards Act of 1938, U.S.C. tit. 29, Section 206(a)(1), or (B), the full minimum fair wage established by subsection (j) of Section 31-58, in effect at the time the earnings are payable.

   C.G.S. 52-350a(4) defines "disposable earnings" as that part of the earnings of an individual remaining after the deduction from those earnings of amounts required to be withheld for payment of federal income and employment taxes, normal retirement contributions, union dues and initiation fees, group life insurance premiums, health insurance premiums, federal tax levies, and state income tax deductions authorized pursuant to C.G.S. 12-34b.

TO BANKING INSTITUTION

1. Complete section II of this form and send 2 copies of this form and the bank execution form to the judgment debtor pursuant to section 52-367b of the General Statutes.

2. If this claim of exemption is returned completed, fill out section V of this form and mail, within two business days, to the issuing clerk's office at the address of court indicated on the front side. See additional instructions on the bank execution, form.

TO CLERK

1. Attach this form to each bank execution issued in a civil or family matter against a judgment debtor that is a natural person.
2. Deliver the execution along with this form to the judgment creditor requesting the execution.
3. If judgment debtor completes and returns this form claiming an exemption, enter the appearance of the judgment debtor with address set forth on page 1.
4. Set matter down for short calendar hearing.
5. Complete section VI below.
6. Send file-stamped copy of this form to judgment debtor and judgment creditor.
7. After hearing, send copy of any order entered to the banking institution.

SECTION V *(To be completed by banking institution upon return of exemption claim form)*

DATE CLAIM RECEIVED	DATE MAILED TO COURT	NAME OF BANK OFFICER	TELEPHONE NO.

SECTION VI   NOTICE TO JUDGMENT DEBTOR AND JUDGMENT CREDITOR

The assets in dispute are being held for (1) forty-five days from the date the exemption claim form was received by the banking institution designated on the front of this form or (2) until disposition is ordered by the court at a hearing to be held at short calendar on the date set forth below, whichever occurs earlier.

DATE OF HEARING	TIME OF HEARING ☐ A.M. ☐ P.M.	SIGNED *(Assistant Clerk)*	DATE SIGNED

ORDER AFTER HEARING

The Court/Magistrate, having held a hearing to determine the issues raised by this claim, hereby orders that:

SIGNED *(Judge/Magistrate)*	DATE SIGNED

JD-CV-24a(EL) (page 2) Rev. 4-97   **Page 2 of 2**

APPENDIX 11:
SAMPLE CONSTRUCTION LIEN
CLAIM FORM

CONSTRUCTION LIEN CLAIM

TO THE CLERK, COUNTY OF _____ :

In accordance with the terms and provisions of the [applicable statute], notice is hereby given that:

1. (Name of claimant) of (address of claimant) has on (date) claimed a construction lien against the below stated real property of (owner against whose property the lien is claimed), in the amount of ($), for the value of the work, services, material or equipment provided in accordance with a contract with (name of contracting party with whom claimant has a contract) for the following work, services, materials or equipment:

[Details of work, services, material or equipment]

2. The amount due for work, services, materials or equipment delivery provided by claimant in connection with the improvement of the real property, and upon which this lien claim is based, is as follows:

Total contract amount: $

Amendments to contract: $

Total contract amount and amendments to contract: $

Less:

Agreed upon credits: $

Contract amount paid to date: $

Amendments to contract amount paid to date: $

TOTAL REDUCTIONS FROM CONTRACT AMOUNT AND AMENDMENTS TO CONTRACT: $

TOTAL LIEN CLAIM AMOUNT: $

Notice of Unpaid Balance and Right to File Lien (if any) was previously filed with the County Clerk of County on [Date] as #____ in Book#____ Page#____.

3. This construction lien is claimed against the interest of (name) as (check one):

Owner

Lessee

Other (describe):

in that certain tract or parcel of land and premises described as Block#___, Lot#___, on the tax map of the _____ County, State of _____, for the improvement of which property the aforementioned work, services, materials or equipment was provided.

4. The work, services, materials or equipment was provided pursuant to the terms of a written contract (or, in the case of a supplier, a delivery or order slip signed by the owner, contractor, or subcontractor having a direct contractual relation with a contractor, or an authorized agent of any of them), dated, between (claimant) and (name of other contracting party) of (address).

5. The date of the provision of the last work, services, material or equipment for which payment is claimed is (date).

NOTICE TO OWNER OF REAL PROPERTY

Your real estate may be subject to sale to satisfy the amount asserted by this claim. However, your real estate cannot be sold until the facts and issues which form the basis of this claim are decided in a legal proceeding before a court of law. The lien claimant is required by law to commence suit to enforce this claim.

The claimant filing this lien claim shall forfeit all rights to enforce the lien and shall be required to discharge the lien of record, if the claimant fails to bring an action in the Superior Court, in the county in which the real property is situated, to establish the lien claim:

1. Within one year of the date of the last provision of work, services, material or equipment, payment for which the lien claim was filed; or

2. Within 30 days following receipt of written notice, by personal service or certified mail, return receipt requested, from the owner requiring the claimant to commence an action to establish the lien claim. You will be given proper notice of the proceeding and an opportunity to challenge this claim and set forth your position. If, after you (and/or your contractor or subcontractor) have had the opportunity to challenge this lien claim, the court of law enters a judgment against you and in favor of the claimant filing this lien claim, and thereafter you fail to pay that judgment, your real estate may then be sold to satisfy the judgment.

You may choose to avoid subjecting your real estate to sale by doing either of the following:

1. You (or your contractor or subcontractor) can pay the claimant and obtain a discharge of lien claim from the claimant; or

2. You (or your contractor or subcontractor) can cause the lien claim to be discharged by filing a surety bond or making a deposit of funds as provided for in [cite applicable law]).

If you (or your contractor or subcontractor) choose to pay the claimant under 1. above, you will lose your right to challenge this lien claim in a legal proceeding before a court of law.

If you (or your contractor or subcontractor) choose to discharge the lien claim by filing a surety bond or making a deposit of funds as provided in [cite applicable law], you will retain your right to challenge this lien claim in a legal proceeding before a court of law.

NOTICE TO SUBCONTRACTOR OR CONTRACTOR:

This lien has been filed with the county clerk and served upon the owner of the real estate. This lien places the owner on notice that the real estate may be sold to satisfy this claim unless the owner pays the claimed sum to this claimant.

[Date and Signature Lines]

CLAIMANT'S REPRESENTATION AND VERIFICATION

Claimant represents and verifies that:

1. The amount claimed herein is due and owing at the date of filing, pursuant to claimant's contract described in the construction lien claim.

2. The work, services, material or equipment for which this lien claim is filed was provided exclusively in connection with the improvement of the real property which is the subject of this claim.

3. This claim has been filed within 90 days from the last date upon which the work, services, materials or equipment for which payment is claimed was provided.

4. The foregoing statements made by me are true, to the best of my knowledge. I am aware that if any of the foregoing statements made by me are false, this construction lien claim will be void and that I will be liable for damages to the owner or any other person injured as a consequence of the filing of this lien claim.

[Name and Signature Line for Claimant]

[Date]

APPENDIX 12:
SAMPLE SATISFACTION OF JUDGMENT
AND RELEASE OF LIEN

BE IT KNOWN, that [Name of Lienholder] ("Lienholder"), of [Address] contracted with [Name of Contracting Party] on [Date of Contract] to furnish labor and/or materials for construction on the premises owned by [Name of Property Owner] located at [Address] .

On [Date of Filing] , the lienholder filed a notice of lien against the above property in the Office of the County Clerk, County of [Name of County] in the State of [Name of State]. Said lien was duly recorded in [Set forth recording information] of the Lien Records of the County.

In consideration of [Dollar Amount ($xxx)] Dollars, receipt of which is acknowledged, lienholder releases the above described property and the owner personally from all liability arising from the labor performed and/or materials furnished by lienholder under the terms of the above-mentioned contract, and authorizes and directs that the above-mentioned lien be discharged of record.

DATED:

    BY:

    [SIGNATURE LINE—LIENHOLDER]

ACKNOWLEDGMENT

STATE OF   )

COUNTY OF   )

On the ___ day of _____, 20__, before me personally came [Name of Lienholder] , to me known to be the individual described in and who executed the foregoing instrument, and acknowledged that he/she executed the same.

NOTARY PUBLIC

APPENDIX 13:
APPLICABLE SECTIONS—UCC ARTICLE 9—SECURED TRANSACTIONS

Section 9-102. Policy and Subject Matter of Article

(1) Except as otherwise provided in Section 9-104 on excluded transactions, this Article applies

(a) to any transaction (regardless of its form) which is intended to create a security interest in personal property or fixtures including goods, documents, instruments, general intangibles, chattel paper or accounts; and also

(b) to any sale of accounts or chattel paper.

(2) This Article applies to security interests created by contract including pledge, assignment, chattel mortgage, chattel trust, trust deed, factor's lien, equipment trust, conditional sale, trust receipt, other lien or title retention contract and lease or consignment intended as security. This Article does not apply to statutory liens except as provided in Section 9-310.

Section 9-104. Transactions Excluded from Article

This Article does not apply

(a) to a security interest subject to any statute of the United States, to the extent that such statute governs the rights of parties to and third parties affected by transactions in particular types of property; or

(b) to a landlord's lien; or

(c) to a lien given by statute or other rule of law for services or materials except as provided in Section 9-310 on priority of such liens; or

(d) to a transfer of a claim for wages, salary or other compensation of an employee; or

(e) to a transfer by a government or governmental subdivision or agency; or

(f) to a sale of accounts or chattel paper as part of a sale of the business out of which they arose, or an assignment of accounts or chattel paper which is for the purpose of collection only, or a transfer of a right to payment under a contract to an assignee who is also to do the performance under the contract or a transfer of a single account to an assignee in whole or partial satisfaction of a preexisting indebtedness; or

(g) to a transfer of an interest in or claim in or under any policy of insurance, except as provided with respect to proceeds (Section 9-306) and priorities in proceeds (Section 9-312); or

(h) to a right represented by a judgment (other than a judgment taken on a right to payment which was collateral); or

(i) to any right of set-off; or

(j) except to the extent that provision is made for fixtures in Section 9-313, to the creation or transfer of an interest in or lien on real estate, including a lease or rents thereunder; or

(k) to a transfer in whole or in part of any claim arising out of tort; or

(l) to a transfer of an interest in any deposit account (subsection (1) of Section 9-105), except as provided with respect to proceeds (Section 9-306) and priorities in proceeds (Section 9-312).

Section 9-112. Where Collateral is Not Owned by Debtor

Unless otherwise agreed, when a secured party knows that collateral is owned by a person who is not the debtor, the owner of the collateral is entitled to receive from the secured party any surplus under Section 9-502(2) or under Section 9-504(1), and is not liable for the debt or for any deficiency after resale, and he has the same right as the debtor

(a) to receive statements under Section 9-208;

(b) to receive notice of and to object to a secured party's proposal to retain the collateral in satisfaction of the indebtedness under Section 9-505;

(c) to redeem the collateral under Section 9-506;

(d) to obtain injunctive or other relief under Section 9-507(1); and

(e) to recover losses caused to him under Section 9-208(2).

Section 9-203. Attachment and Enforceability of Security Interest; Proceeds; Formal Requisites

(1) Subject to the provisions of Section 4-208 on the security interest of a collecting bank, Section 8-321 on security interests in securities and Section 9-113 on a security interest arising under the Article on Sales, a security interest is not enforceable against the debtor or third parties with respect to the collateral and does not attach unless:

(a) the collateral is in the possession of the secured party pursuant to agreement, or the debtor has signed a security agreement which contains a description of the collateral and in addition, when the security interest covers crops growing or to be grown or timber to be cut, a description of the land concerned;

(b) value has been given; and

(c) the debtor has rights in the collateral.

Section 9-207. Rights and Duties When Collateral is in Secured Party's Possession

(1) A secured party must use reasonable care in the custody and preservation of collateral in his possession. In the case of an instrument or chattel paper reasonable care includes taking necessary steps to preserve rights against prior parties unless otherwise agreed.

(2) Unless otherwise agreed, when collateral is in the secured party's possession

(a) reasonable expenses (including the cost of any insurance and payment of taxes or other charges) incurred in the custody, preservation, use or operation of the collateral are chargeable to the debtor and are secured by the collateral;

(b) the risk of accidental loss or damage is on the debtor to the extent of any deficiency in any effective insurance coverage;

(c) the secured party may hold as additional security any increase or profits (except money) received from the collateral, but money so received, unless remitted to the debtor, shall be applied in reduction of the secured obligation;

(d) the secured party must keep the collateral identifiable but fungible collateral may be commingled;

(e) the secured party may repledge the collateral upon terms which do not impair the debtor's right to redeem it.

(3) A secured party is liable for any loss caused by his failure to meet any obligation imposed by the preceding subsections but does not lose his security interest.

(4) A secured party may use or operate the collateral for the purpose of preserving the collateral or its value or pursuant to the order of a court of appropriate jurisdiction or, except in the case of consumer goods, in the manner and to the extent provided in the security agreement.

Section 9-302. When Filing is Required to Perfect Security Interest; Security Interests to Which Filing Provisions of This Article Do Not Apply

(1) A financing statement must be filed to perfect all security interests except the following:

(a) a security interest in collateral in possession of the secured party under Section 9-305;

(b) a security interest temporarily perfected in instruments or documents without delivery under Section 9-304 or in proceeds for a 10 day period under Section 9-306;

(c) a security interest created by an assignment of a beneficial interest in a trust or a decedent's estate;

(d) a purchase money security interest in consumer goods; but filing is required for a motor vehicle required to be registered; and fixture filing is required for priority over conflicting interests in fixtures to the extent provided in Section 9-313;

(e) an assignment of accounts which does not alone or in conjunction with other assignments to the same assignee transfer a significant part of the outstanding accounts of the assignor;

(f) a security interest of a collecting bank (Section 4-208) or in securities (Section 8-321) or arising under the Article on Sales (see Section 9-113) or covered in subsection (3) of this section;

(g) an assignment for the benefit of all the creditors of the transferor, and subsequent transfers by the assignee thereunder.

(2) If a secured party assigns a perfected security interest, no filing under this Article is required in order to continue the perfected status of the security interest against creditors of and transferees from the original debtor.

(3) The filing of a financing statement otherwise required by this Article is not necessary or effective to perfect a security interest in property subject to

(a) a statute or treaty of the United States which provides for a national or international registration or a national or international certificate of title or which specifies a place of filing different from that specified in this Article for filing of the security interest; or

(b) the following statutes of this state; [list any certificate of title statute covering automobiles, trailers, mobile homes, boats, farm tractors, or the like, and any central filing statute .]; but during any period in which collateral is inventory held for sale by a person who is in the business of selling goods of that kind, the filing provisions of this Article (Part 4) apply to a security interest in that collateral created by him as debtor; or

(c) a certificate of title statute of another jurisdiction under the law of which indication of a security interest on the certificate is required as a condition of perfection (subsection (2) of Section 9-103).

(4) Compliance with a statute or treaty described in subsection (3) is equivalent to the filing of a financing statement under this Article, and a security interest in property subject to the statute or treaty can be perfected only by compliance therewith except as provided in Section 9-103 on multiple state transactions. Duration and renewal of perfection of a security interest perfected by compliance with the statute or treaty are governed by the provisions of the statute or treaty; in other respects the security interest is subject to this Article.

Section 9-304. Perfection of Security Interest in Instruments, Documents, and Goods Covered By Documents; Perfection By Permissive Filing; Temporary Perfection Without Filing or Transfer of Possession

(1) A security interest in chattel paper or negotiable documents may be perfected by filing. A security interest in money or instruments (other than certificated securities or instruments which constitute part of chattel paper) can be perfected only by the secured party's taking possession, except as provided in subsections (4) and (5) of this section and subsections (2) and (3) of Section 9-306 on proceeds.

(2) During the period that goods are in the possession of the issuer of a negotiable document therefor, a security interest in the goods is perfected by perfecting a security interest in the document, and any security interest in the goods otherwise perfected during such period is subject thereto.

(3) A security interest in goods in the possession of a bailee other than one who has issued a negotiable document therefor is perfected by issuance of a document in the name of the secured party or by the bailee's receipt of notification of the secured party's interest or by filing as to the goods.

(4) A security interest in instruments (other than certificated securities) or negotiable documents is perfected without filing or the taking of possession for a period of 21 days from the time it attaches to the extent that it arises for new value given under a written security agreement.

(5) A security interest remains perfected for a period of 21 days without filing where a secured party having a perfected security interest in an instrument (other than a certificated security), a negotiable document or goods in possession of a bailee other than one who has issued a negotiable document therefor

(a) makes available to the debtor the goods or documents representing the goods for the purpose of ultimate sale or exchange or for the purpose of loading, unloading, storing, shipping, transshipping, manufacturing, processing or otherwise dealing with them in a manner preliminary to their sale or exchange, but priority between conflicting security interests in the goods is subject to subsection (3) of Section 9-312; or

(b) delivers the instrument to the debtor for the purpose of ultimate sale or exchange or of presentation, collection, renewal or registration of transfer.

(6) After the 21 day period in subsections (4) and (5) perfection depends upon compliance with applicable provisions of this Article.

Section 9-305. When Possession By Secured Party Perfects Security Interest Without Filing

A security interest in letters of credit and advices of credit (subsection (2)(a) of Section 5-116), goods, instruments (other than certificated securities), money, negotiable documents, or chattel paper may be perfected by the secured party's taking possession of the collateral. If such collateral other than goods covered by a negotiable document is held by a bailee, the secured party is deemed to have possession from the time the bailee receives notification of the secured party's interest. A security interest is perfected by possession from the time possession is taken without a relation back and continues only so long as possession is retained, unless otherwise specified in this Article. The security interest may be otherwise perfected as provided in this Article before or after the period of possession by the secured party.

Section 9-402. Formal Requisites of Financing Statement; Amendments; Mortgage as Financing Statement

(1) A financing statement is sufficient if it gives the names of the debtor and the secured party, is signed by the debtor, gives an address of the secured party from which information concerning the security interest may be obtained, gives a mailing address of the debtor and contains a statement indicating the types, or describing the items, of collateral. A financing statement may be filed before a security agreement is made or a security interest otherwise attaches. When the financing statement covers crops growing or to be grown, the statement must also contain a description of the real estate concerned. When the financing statement covers timber to be cut or covers minerals or the like (including oil and gas) or accounts subject to subsection (5) of Section 9-103, or when the financing statement is filed as a fixture filing (Section 9-313) and the collateral is goods which are or are to become fixtures, the statement must also comply with subsection (5). A copy of the security agreement is sufficient as a financing statement if it contains the above information and is signed by the debtor. A carbon, photographic or other reproduction of a security agreement or a financing statement is sufficient as a financing statement if the security agreement so provides or if the original has been filed in this state.

(2) A financing statement which otherwise complies with subsection (1) is sufficient when it is signed by the secured party instead of the debtor if it is filed to perfect a security interest in

(a) collateral already subject to a security interest in another jurisdiction when it is brought into this state, or when the debtor's location is changed to this state. Such a financing statement must state that the collateral was brought into this state or that the debtor's location was changed to this state under such circumstances; or

(b) proceeds under Section 9-306 if the security interest in the original collateral was perfected. Such a financing statement must describe the original collateral; or

(c) collateral as to which the filing has lapsed; or

(d) collateral acquired after a change of name, identity or corporate structure of the debtor (subsection (7)).

Section 9-406. Release of Collateral

A secured party of record may by his signed statement release all or a part of any collateral described in a filed financing statement. The statement of release is sufficient if it contains a description of the collateral being released, the name and address of the debtor, the name and address of the secured party, and the file number of the financing statement. . .

Section 9-501. Default; Procedure When Security Agreement Covers Both Real and Personal Property

(1) When a debtor is in default under a security agreement, a secured party has the rights and remedies provided in this Part and except as limited by subsection (3) those provided in the security agreement. He may reduce his claim to judgment, foreclose or otherwise enforce the security interest by any available judicial procedure. If the collateral is documents the secured party may proceed either as to the documents or as to the goods covered thereby. A secured party in possession has the rights, remedies and duties provided in Section 9-207. The rights and remedies referred to in this subsection are cumulative.

(2) After default, the debtor has the rights and remedies provided in this Part, those provided in the security agreement and those provided in Section 9-207.

(3) To the extent that they give rights to the debtor and impose duties on the secured party, the rules stated in the subsections referred to below may not be waived or varied except as provided with respect to compulsory disposition of collateral (subsection (3) of Section 9-504 and Section 9-505) and with respect to redemption of collateral (Section 9-506) but the parties may by agreement determine the standards by which the fulfillment of these rights and duties is to be measured if such standards are not manifestly unreasonable:

(a) subsection (2) of Section 9-502 and subsection (2) of Section 9-504 insofar as they require accounting for surplus proceeds of collateral;

(b) subsection (3) of Section 9-504 and subsection (1) of Section 9-505 which deal with disposition of collateral;

(c) subsection (2) of Section 9-505 which deals with acceptance of collateral as discharge of obligation;

(d) Section 9-506 which deals with redemption of collateral; and

(e) subsection (1) of Section 9-507 which deals with the secured party's liability for failure to comply with this Part.

(4) If the security agreement covers both real and personal property, the secured party may proceed under this Part as to the personal property or he may proceed as to both the real and the personal property in accordance with his rights and remedies in respect of the real property in which case the provisions of this Part do not apply.

(5) When a secured party has reduced his claim to judgment the lien of any levy which may be made upon his collateral by virtue of any execution based upon the judgment shall relate back to the date of the perfection of the security interest in such collateral. A judicial sale, pursuant to such execution, is a foreclosure of the security interest by judicial procedure within the meaning of this section, and the secured party may purchase at the sale and thereafter hold the collateral free of any other requirements of this Article.

APPENDIX 14:
NOTICE OF APPLICATION FOR PREJUDGMENT REMEDY/CLAIM FOR HEARING TO CONTEST APPLICATION OR CLAIM FOR EXEMPTION

NOTICE OF APPLICATION FOR PREJUDGMENT REMEDY/CLAIM FOR HEARING TO CONTEST APPLICATION OR CLAIM EXEMPTION
JD-CV-53 Rev. 2-98
C.G.S. §§ 52-278c et seq.

STATE OF CONNECTICUT
SUPERIOR COURT
INSTRUCTIONS TO PLAINTIFF/APPLICANT

1. Complete section I in connection with all prejudgment remedies EXCEPT ex parte prejudgment remedies and submit to the Clerk along with your application and other required documents.
2. Upon receipt of signed order for hearing from clerk, serve this form on defendant(s) with other required documents.

| | CLP/JRA Application For PJR | CLP/JHRG Contest PJR Application (If Section II Completed) |

SECTION I - CASE INFORMATION (to be completed by Plaintiff/Applicant)

☐ Judicial District ☐ Housing Session ☐ G.A. No. ____

COURT ADDRESS

Has a temporary restraining order been requested? ☐ YES ☐ NO

AMOUNT, LEGAL INTEREST, OR PROPERTY IN DEMAND, EXCLUSIVE OF INTEREST AND COSTS IS ("X" one of the following)

NAME OF CASE (First-named plaintiff vs. First-named defendant)

☐ LESS THAN $2500
☐ $2500 THROUGH $14,999.99
☐ $15,000 OR MORE
("X" if applicable)

☐ SEE ATTACHED FORM JD-CV-67 FOR CONTINUATION OF PARTIES

☐ CLAIMING OTHER RELIEF IN ADDITION TO OR IN LIEU OF MONEY DAMAGES

CASE TYPE (From Judicial Branch code list) NO. COUNTS
MAJOR: MINOR:

NAME AND ADDRESS OF PLAINTIFF/APPLICANT (Person making application for Prejudgment Remedy) (No., street, town and zip code)

NAME(S) AND ADDRESS(ES) OF DEFENDANT(S) AGAINST WHOM PREJUDGMENT REMEDY IS SOUGHT (No., street, town and zip code) (Attach additional sheet if necessary)

NAME AND ADDRESS OF ANY THIRD PERSON HOLDING PROPERTY OF DEFENDANT WHO IS TO BE MADE A GARNISHEE BY PROCESS PREVENTING DISSIPATION OF SUCH PROPERTY

FOR THE PLAINTIFF(S) ENTER THE APPEARANCE OF:

NAME AND ADDRESS OF ATTORNEY, LAW FIRM OR PLAINTIFF IF PRO SE (No., street, town and zip code)

| TELEPHONE NO. | JURIS NO. (If atty. or law firm) | SIGNED | DATE SIGNED |

SECTION II - NOTICE TO DEFENDANT

You have rights specified in the Connecticut General Statutes, including Chapter 903a, that you may wish to exercise concerning this application for a prejudgment remedy. These rights include the right to a hearing:
(1) to object to the proposed prejudgment remedy because you have a defense to or set-off against the action or a counterclaim against the plaintiff or because the amount sought in the application for the prejudgment remedy is unreasonably high or because payment of any judgment that may be rendered against you is covered by any insurance that may be available to you;
(2) to request that the plaintiff post a bond in accordance with section 52-278d of the General Statutes to secure you against any damages that may result from the prejudgment remedy;
(3) to request that you be allowed to substitute a bond for the prejudgment remedy sought; and
(4) to show that the property sought to be subjected to the prejudgment remedy is exempt from such a prejudgment remedy.

You may request a hearing to contest the application for a prejudgment remedy, assert any exemption or make a request concerning the posting or substitution of a bond in connection with the prejudgment remedy. The hearing may be requested by any proper motion or by completing section III below and returning this form to the superior court at the Court Address listed above.

You have a right to appear and be heard at the hearing on the application to be held at the above court location on:

| DATE | TIME M. | COURTROOM |

SECTION III - DEFENDANT'S CLAIM AND REQUEST FOR HEARING (to be completed by Defendant)

I, the defendant named below, request a hearing to contest the application for prejudgment remedy, claim an exemption or

☐ that the amount sought in the application for prejudgment remedy is unreasonably high.
☐ a defense, counterclaim, set-off, or exemption.
☐ that any judgment that may be rendered is adequately secured by insurance.
☐ that I be allowed to substitute a bond for the prejudgment remedy.
☐ that the plaintiff be required to post a bond to secure me against any damages that may result from the prejudgment remedy.

FOR COURT USE ONLY

I certify that a copy of the above claim was mailed/delivered to the Plaintiff or the Plaintiff's attorney on the Date Mailed shown below:

| DATE COPY(IES) MAILED/DELIVERED | SIGNED (Defendant) | DATE SIGNED |

TYPE OR PRINT NAME AND ADDRESS OF DEFENDANT

DOCKET NO
PJR CV

| NAME OF EACH PARTY SERVED* | ADDRESS AT WHICH SERVICE WAS MADE* |

*If necessary, attach additional sheet with names of each party served and the address at which service was made

---

APPENDIX 15:
SELECTED PROVISIONS OF THE
CONSUMER CREDIT PROTECTION ACT
(15 U.S.C. 1671-1677)

Subchapter II. Restrictions on Garnishment

Sec. 1671. Congressional findings and declaration of purpose

(a) Disadvantages of garnishment

The Congress finds:

(1) The unrestricted garnishment of compensation due for personal services encourages the making of predatory extensions of credit. Such extensions of credit divert money into excessive credit payments and thereby hinder the production and flow of goods in interstate commerce.

(2) The application of garnishment as a creditors' remedy frequently results in loss of employment by the debtor, and the resulting disruption of employment, production, and consumption constitutes a substantial burden on interstate commerce.

(3) The great disparities among the laws of the several States relating to garnishment have, in effect, destroyed the uniformity of the bankruptcy laws and frustrated the purposes thereof in many areas of the country.

(b) Necessity for regulation

On the basis of the findings stated in subsection (a) of this section, the Congress determines that the provisions of this subchapter are necessary and proper for the purpose of carrying into execution the powers of the Congress to regulate commerce and to establish uniform bankruptcy laws.

Sec. 1672. Definitions

For the purposes of this subchapter:

(a) The term "earnings" means compensation paid or payable for personal services, whether denominated as wages, salary, commission, bonus, or otherwise, and includes periodic payments pursuant to a pension or retirement program.

(b) The term "disposable earnings" means that part of the earnings of any individual remaining after the deduction from those earnings of any amounts required by law to be withheld.

(c) The term "garnishment" means any legal or equitable procedure through which the earnings of any individual are required to be withheld for payment of any debt.

Sec. 1673. Restriction on garnishment

(a) Maximum allowable garnishment

Except as provided in subsection (b) of this section and in section 1675 of this title, the maximum part of the aggregate disposable earnings of an individual for any workweek which is subjected to garnishment may not exceed:

(1) 25 per centum of his disposable earnings for that week, or

(2) the amount by which his disposable earnings for that week exceed thirty times the Federal minimum hourly wage prescribed by section 206(a)(1) of title 29 in effect at the time the earnings are payable, whichever is less. In the case of earnings for any pay period other than a week, the Secretary of Labor shall by regulation prescribe a multiple of the Federal minimum hourly wage equivalent in effect to that set forth in paragraph (2).

(b) Exceptions

(1) The restrictions of subsection (a) of this section do not apply in the case of

(A) any order for the support of any person issued by a court of competent jurisdiction or in accordance with an administrative procedure, which is established by State law, which affords substantial due process, and which is subject to judicial review.

(B) any order of any court of the United States having jurisdiction over cases under chapter 13 of title 11.

(C) any debt due for any State or Federal tax.

(2) The maximum part of the aggregate disposable earnings of an individual for any workweek which is subject to garnishment to enforce any order for the support of any person shall not exceed:

(A) where such individual is supporting his spouse or dependent child (other than a spouse or child with respect to whose support such order is used), 50 per centum of such individual's disposable earnings for that week; and

(B) where such individual is not supporting such a spouse or dependent child described in clause (A), 60 per centum of such individual's disposable earnings for that week; except that, with respect to the disposable earnings of any individual for any workweek, the 50 per centum specified in clause (A) shall be deemed to be 55 per centum and the 60 per centum specified in clause (B) shall be deemed to be 65 per centum, if and to the extent that such earnings are subject to garnishment to enforce a support order with respect to a period which is prior to the twelve-week period which ends with the beginning of such workweek.

(c) Execution or enforcement of garnishment order or process prohibited

No court of the United States or any State, and no State (or officer or agency thereof), may make, execute, or enforce any order or process in violation of this section.

Sec. 1674. Restriction on discharge from employment by reason of garnishment

(a) Termination of employment

No employer may discharge any employee by reason of the fact that his earnings have been subjected to garnishment for any one indebtedness.

(b) Penalties

Whoever willfully violates subsection (a) of this section shall be fined not more than $1,000, or imprisoned not more than one year, or both.

Sec. 1675. Exemption for State-regulated garnishments

The Secretary of Labor may by regulation exempt from the provisions of section 1673(a) and (b)(2) of this title garnishments issued under the laws of any State if he determines that the laws of that State provide restrictions on garnishment which are substantially similar to those provided in section 1673(a) and (b)(2) of this title.

Sec. 1676. Enforcement by Secretary of Labor

The Secretary of Labor, acting through the Wage and Hour Division of the Department of Labor, shall enforce the provisions of this subchapter.

Sec. 1677. Effect on State laws

This subchapter does not annul, alter, or affect, or exempt any person from complying with, the laws of any State

(1) prohibiting garnishments or providing for more limited garnishment than are allowed under this subchapter, or

(2) prohibiting the discharge of any employee by reason of the fact that his earnings have been subjected to garnishment for more than one indebtedness.

APPENDIX 16:
POST-JUDGMENT INTERROGATORIES

POST JUDGMENT REMEDIES
INTERROGATORIES

JD-CV-23 Rev. 12-98 Gen. Stat. §§ 52-321a,
52-351b, 52-352b, 52-361a, 52-361b, 52-400a, 52-400c
P.A. 97-86

STATE OF CONNECTICUT
SUPERIOR COURT

FORM JD-CV-23a MUST BE ATTACHED TO THIS FORM

COURT USE ONLY
POSTJRI

Judicial District ☐	Housing Session ☐	☐ G.A. No. _____ AT	DOCKET NO.

ADDRESS OF COURT *(No., street, town, and zip code)*

DATE OF JUDGMENT	ORIGINAL AMOUNT OF JUDGMENT	AMOUNT DUE THEREON

NAME OF JUDGMENT CREDITOR	OF *(Street and town)*

NAME OF JUDGMENT DEBTOR	OF *(Street and town)*

NAME AND ADDRESS OF PERSON BELIEVED TO HAVE ASSETS OF JUDGMENT DEBTOR *(if applicable)*

DATE OF SERVICE OF INTERROGATORIES	NAME AND ADDRESS OF PERSON TO WHOM INTERROGATORIES SHALL BE RETURNED

INSTRUCTIONS

JUDGMENT CREDITOR: Put an "X" in the box next to the questions to be answered on form JD-CV-23a attached hereto.
PERSON SERVED WITH INTERROGATORIES: Answer the questions indicated by "X" on form JD-CV-23a attached hereto. You must disclose assets of the judgment debtor up to an amount clearly sufficient to satisfy the judgment indicated by the "Amount Due Thereon" above. Place answers in space provided on form. If you need more room to answer these questions, use the space on the reverse side of form JD-CV-23a or attach additional sheets.

NOTICE

Neither the interrogatories themselves, notice thereof nor objections thereto shall be filed with the court.

The person served with these interrogatories must answer and return them within thirty days of the date of their service to the person named above.

If the person served with these interrogatories fails, within thirty days, to return a sufficient answer or disclose sufficient assets for execution, or on objection by that person to the interrogatories, the judgment creditor may move the court for such supplemental discovery orders as may be necessary to ensure disclosure including (1) an order for compliance with the interrogatories or (2) an order authorizing additional interrogatories. The judgment creditor may obtain discovery, including the taking of depositions, from any person served with interrogatories in accordance with procedures for discovery in civil actions without further order of the court. The court may order such additional discovery as justice requires. Failure to comply with a discovery order may subject the person served to being held in contempt of court. Attorney's fees may be allowed for counsel at a contempt hearing necessary to enforce such a court order and for counsel at any discovery hearing required because of the failure to answer these interrogatories.

NOTICE OF RIGHTS TO PERSON SERVED

1. Pursuant to Gen. Stat. § 52-351b, you must reveal information concerning the amount, nature and location of the judgment debtor's assets up to an amount clearly sufficient in value to ensure full satisfaction of the judgment with interests and costs.

2. Pursuant to subsection (d) of Gen. Stat. § 52-351b, any party from whom discovery is sought may apply to the court for protection from annoyance, embarrassment, oppression or undue burden or expense.

3. Certain personal property is exempt from execution. The following list is a description of common classes of property exempt from execution from a judgment debtor who is a natural person. (Gen. Stat. § 52-352b).
   (a) Necessary apparel, bedding, foodstuffs, household furniture and appliances;
   (b) Tools, books, instruments, farm animals and livestock feed which are necessary to the judgment debtor in the course   of his or her occupation, or profession, farming operation or farming partnership;
   (c) Public assistance payments and any wages earned by a public assistance recipient under an incentive earnings or similar program;
   (d) Health and disability insurance payments;
   (e) Health aids necessary to enable the judgment debtor to work or to sustain health;
   (f) Worker's compensation, social security, veterans and unemployment benefits;
   (g) Court approved payments for child support;
   (h) Arms and military equipment, uniforms or musical instruments owned by any member of the militia or armed forces of
       the United States;

(continued on page 2)

(i) One motor vehicle to the value of one thousand five hundred dollars, provided such value shall be determined as the fair market value of the motor vehicle less the amount of all liens and security interests which encumber it;

(j) Wedding and engagement rings;

(k) Residential utility deposits for one residence and one residential security deposit;

(l) Any assets or interests of a judgment debtor in, or payments received by the judgment debtor from, a plan or arrangement described in Gen. Stat. § 52-321a;

(m) Alimony and support, other than child support, but only to the extent that wages are exempt from execution under Gen. Stat. § 52-361a;

(n) An award under a crime reparations act;

(o) All benefits allowed by any association of persons in this state towards the support of any of its members incapacitated by sickness or infirmity from attending to his usual business;

(p) All moneys due the judgment debtor from any insurance company on any insurance policy issued on exempt property, to the same extent that the property was exempt;

(q) Burial plot for the judgment debtor and his or her immediate family;

(r) Irrevocable transfers of money to an account held by a bona fide nonprofit debt adjuster licensed pursuant to chapter 655 of the general statutes for the benefit of creditors of the judgment debtor; --

(s) Any interest of the judgment debtor in any property not to exceed in value one thousand dollars;

(t) Any interest of the judgment debtor not to exceed in value four thousand dollars in any accrued dividend or interest under, or loan value of, any unmatured life insurance contract owned by the judgment debtor under which the insured is the judgment debtor or an individual of whom the judgment debtor is a dependent; and

(u) The homestead of the judgment debtor to the value of seventy-five thousand dollars, provided value shall be determined as the fair market value of the real property less the amount of any statutory or consensual lien which encumbers it.

APPENDIX 17:
PETITION FOR EXAMINATION OF JUDGMENT DEBTOR AND NOTICE OF HEARING

PETITION FOR EXAMINATION OF JUDGMENT DEBTOR AND NOTICE OF HEARING JD-CV-54 Rev. 12-99 C.G.S. § 52-397	STATE OF CONNECTICUT **SUPERIOR COURT** www.jud.state.ct.us INSTRUCTIONS TO JUDGMENT CREDITOR	COURT USE ONLY **QUIZ** COURT USE ONLY **PEJD**

1. *Prepare and present original and two copies to the clerk for review and signature.*
2. *Attach completed "Subpoena" form JD-CL-43, if applicable.*
3. *Present original and one copy of signed petition to proper officer for service.*
4. *Make copy for your file.*
5. *Original petition must be returned to court after service at least six days prior to the court hearing.*
6. *Attend court hearing.*

TO: The Superior Court

			DOCKET NO.

☐ Judicial District	☐ Housing Session	☐ G.A. No. ____	At _____	☐ Small Claims Area At _____

ADDRESS OF COURT *(No., street, town and zip code)*

NAME(S) OF JUDGMENT CREDITOR(S)	ADDRESS(ES) *(No., street, town and zip code)*

NAME OF JUDGMENT DEBTOR	ADDRESS *(No., street, town and zip code)*

DATE OF JUDGMENT	AMOUNT OF DAMAGES AWARDED	AMOUNT OF COSTS AWARDED	TOTAL DAMAGES AND COSTS AWARDED

NAME AND ADDRESS OF JUDGMENT CREDITOR'S ATTORNEY *(If applicable)*

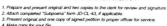

PETITION FOR EXAMINATION OF JUDGMENT DEBTOR

A judgment was recovered against the above-named judgment debtor in the Superior Court on the date and for the amount of damages and costs indicated above. *("X" one or both)*

☐ An execution was issued on this judgment which has been returned unsatisfied in whole or in part.

☐ Postjudgment interrogatories were served on the judgment debtor in accordance with the Connecticut General Statutes, but the judgment debtor has failed to respond within thirty days of the date of service.

The judgment creditor(s) requests that the judgment debtor be ordered to appear before the Superior Court where the judgment was entered, to be examined under oath concerning any property and means of paying this judgment.

SIGNED *(Judgment creditor or attorney)*	DATE SIGNED	TELEPHONE NO.

ORDER FOR EXAMINATION AND NOTICE OF HEARING

The Petition for Examination of Judgment Debtor having been presented to the court, **IT IS ORDERED THAT THE ABOVE-NAMED JUDGMENT DEBTOR APPEAR** before the Superior Court **AT THE COURT LOCATION SHOWN ABOVE**, to be examined under oath concerning the judgment debtor's property and means of paying the judgment described in the above Petiton for Examination of Judgment Debtor **ON THE DATE AND TIME SET FOR THE HEARING SHOWN BELOW.**

COURT HEARING DATE AND TIME		
DATE OF HEARING	COURTROOM	TIME OF HEARING ____ . M.

TO ANY PROPER OFFICER:

By authority of the State of Connecticut, you are commanded to give notice of the pendency of this Petition and to summon the judgment debtor to appear at the place, date, and time set for the examination by serving on said judgment debtor, as prescribed by law for the service of civil process, a true and attested copy of the foregoing Petition and of this order **at least twelve days** prior to the hearing date shown above.

Make service and return this Petition to the court **at least six days** prior to the hearing date shown above.

SIGNED *(Judge/Clerk)* _____   DATE SIGNED _____

APPENDIX 18:
UNIFORM FRAUDULENT TRANSFER ACT

Section 1. Definitions.

As used in this [Act]:

(1) "Affiliate" means:

(i) a person who directly or indirectly owns, controls, or holds with power to vote, 20 percent or more of the outstanding voting securities of the debtor, other than a person who holds the securities,

(A) as a fiduciary or agent without sole discretionary power to vote the securities; or

(B) solely to secure a debt, if the person has not exercised the power to vote;

(ii) a corporation 20 percent or more of whose outstanding voting securities are directly or indirectly owned, controlled, or held with power to vote, by the debtor or a person who directly or indirectly owns, controls, or holds with power to vote, 20 percent or more of the outstanding voting securities of the debtor, other than a person who holds the securities,

(A) as a fiduciary or agent without sole power to vote the securities; or

(B) solely to secure a debt, if the person has not in fact exercised the power to vote;

(iii) a person whose business is operated by the debtor under a lease or other agreement, or a person substantially all of whose assets are controlled by the debtor; or

(iv) a person who operates the debtor's business under a lease or other agreement or controls substantially all of the debtor's assets.

(2) "Asset" means property of a debtor, but the term does not include:

(i) property to the extent it is encumbered by a valid lien;

(ii) property to the extent it is generally exempt under nonbankruptcy law; or

(iii) an interest in property held in tenancy by the entireties to the extent it is not subject to process by a creditor holding a claim against only one tenant.

(3) "Claim" means a right to payment, whether or not the right is reduced to judgment, liquidated, unliquidated, fixed, contingent, matured, unmatured, disputed, undisputed, legal, equitable, secured, or unsecured.

(4) "Creditor" means a person who has a claim.

(5) "Debt" means liability on a claim.

(6) "Debtor" means a person who is liable on a claim.

(7) "Insider" includes:

(i) if the debtor is an individual,

(A) a relative of the debtor or of a general partner of the debtor;

(B) a partnership in which the debtor is a general partner;

(C) a general partner in a partnership described in clause (B); or

(D) a corporation of which the debtor is a director, officer, or person in control;

(ii) if the debtor is a corporation,

(A) a director of the debtor;

(B) an officer of the debtor;

(C) a person in control of the debtor;

(D) a partnership in which the debtor is a general partner;

(E) a general partner in a partnership described in clause (D); or

(F) a relative of a general partner, director, officer, or person in control of the debtor;

(iii) if the debtor is a partnership,

(A) a general partner in the debtor;

(B) a relative of a general partner in, or a general partner of, or a person in control of the debtor;

(C) another partnership in which the debtor is a general partner;

(D) a general partner in a partnership described in clause (C); or

(E) a person in control of the debtor;

(iv) an affiliate, or an insider of an affiliate as if the affiliate were the debtor; and

(v) a managing agent of the debtor.

(8) "Lien" means a charge against or an interest in property to secure payment of a debt or performance of an obligation, and includes a security interest created by agreement, a judicial lien obtained by legal or equitable process or proceedings, a common-law lien, or a statutory lien.

(9) "Person" means an individual, partnership, corporation, association, organization, government or governmental subdivision or agency, business trust, estate, trust, or any other legal or commercial entity.

(10) "Property" means anything that may be the subject of ownership.

(11) "Relative" means an individual related by consanguinity within the third degree as determined by the common law, a spouse, or an individual related to a spouse within the third degree as so determined, and includes an individual in an adoptive relationship within the third degree.

(12) "Transfer" means every mode, direct or indirect, absolute or conditional, voluntary or involuntary, of disposing of or parting with an asset or an interest in an asset, and includes payment of money, release, lease, and creation of a lien or other encumbrance.

(13) "Valid lien" means a lien that is effective against the holder of a judicial lien subsequently obtained by legal or equitable process or proceedings.

COMMENTS:

(1) The definition of "affiliate" is derived from § 101(2) of the Bankruptcy Code.

(2) The definition of "asset" is substantially to the same effect as the definition of "assets" in § 1 of the Uniform Fraudulent Conveyance Act. The definition in this Act, unlike that in the earlier Act, does not, however require a determination that the property is liable for the debts of the debtor. Thus, an unliquidated claim for damages resulting from personal injury or a contingent claim of a surety for reimbursement, contribution, or subrogation may be counted as an asset for the purpose of determining whether the holder of the claim is solvent as a debtor under § 2 of this Act, although applicable law may not allow such an asset to be levied on and sold by a creditor. Cf. Manufacturers &

Traders Trust Co. v. Goldman (In re Ollag Construction Equipment Corp.), 578 F.2d 904, 907-09 (2d Cir. 1978).

Subparagraphs (i), (ii), and (iii) provide clarification by excluding from the term not only generally exempt property but also an interest in a tenancy by the entirety in many states and an interest that is generally beyond reach by unsecured creditors because subject to a valid lien. This Act, like its predecessor and the Statute of 13 Elizabeth, declares rights and provides remedies for unsecured creditors against transfers that impede them in the collection of their claims. The laws protecting valid liens against impairment by levying creditors, exemption statutes, and the rules restricting levyability of interest in entireties property are limitations on the rights and remedies of unsecured creditors, and it is therefore appropriate to exclude property interests that are beyond the reach of unsecured creditors from the definition of "asset" for the purposes of this Act.

A creditor of a joint tenant or tenant in common may ordinarily collect a judgment by process against the tenant's interest, and in some states a creditor of a tenant by the entirety may likewise collect a judgment by process against the tenant's interest. See 2 American Law of Property 10, 22, 28-32 (1952); Craig, An Analysis of Estates by the Entirety in Bankruptcy, 48 Am.Bankr.L.J. 255, 258-59 (1974). The levyable interest of such a tenant is included as an asset under this Act.

The definition of "assets" in the Uniform Fraudulent Conveyance Act excluded property that is exempt from liability for debts. The definition did not, however, exclude all property that cannot be reached by a creditor through judicial proceedings to collect a debt. Thus, it included the interest of a tenant by the entirety although in nearly half the states such an interest cannot be subjected to liability for a debt unless it is an obligation owed jointly by the debtor with his or her cotenant by the entirety. See 2 American Law of Property 29 (1952); Craig, An Analysis of Estates by the Entirety in Bankruptcy, 48 Am.Bankr.L.J. 255, 258 (1974). The definition in this Act requires exclusion of interests in property held by tenants by the entirety that are not subject to collection process by a creditor without a right to proceed against both tenants by the entirety as joint debtors.

The reference to "generally exempt" property in § 1(2)(ii) recognizes that all exemptions are subject to exceptions. Creditors having special rights against generally exempt property typically include claimants for alimony, taxes, wages, the purchase price of the property, and labor or materials that improve the property. See Uniform Exemptions Act § 10 and the accompanying Comment. The fact that a particular creditor may reach generally exempt property by resorting to judicial process does not warrant its inclusion as an asset in determining whether the debtor is insolvent.

Since this Act is not an exclusive law on the subject of voidable transfers and obligations (see Comment (8) to § 4 infra), it does not preclude the holder of a claim that may be collected by process against property generally exempt as to other creditors from obtaining relief from a transfer of such property that hinders, delays, or defrauds the holder of such a claim. Likewise the holder of an unsecured claim enforceable against tenants by the entirety is not precluded by the Act from pursuing a remedy against a transfer of property held by the entirety that hinders, delays, or defrauds the holder of such a claim.

Nonbankruptcy law is the law of a state or federal law that is not part of the Bankruptcy Code, Title 11 of the United States Code. The definition of an "asset" thus does not include property that would be subject to administration for the benefit of creditors under the Bankruptcy Code unless it is subject under other applicable law, state or federal, to process for the collection of a creditor's claim against a single debtor.

(3) The definition of "claim" is derived from § 101(4) of the Bankruptcy Code. Since the purpose of this Act is primarily to protect unsecured creditors against transfers and obligations injurious to their rights, the words "claim" and "debt" as used in the Act generally have reference to an unsecured claim and debt. As the context may indicate, however, usage of the terms is not so restricted. See, e.g. §§ 1(1)(i)(B) and 1(8).

(4) The definition of "creditor" in combination with the definition of "claim" has substantially the same effect as the definition of "creditor" under § 1 of the Uniform Fraudulent Conveyance Act. As under that Act, the holder of an unliquidated tort claim or a contingent claim may be a creditor protected by this Act.

(5) The definition of "debt" is derived from § 101(11) of the Bankruptcy Code.

(6) The definition of "debtor" is new.

(7) The definition of "insider" is derived from § 101(28) of the Bankruptcy Code. The definition has been restricted in clauses (i)(C), (ii)(E), and (iii)(D) to make clear that a partner is not an insider of an individual, corporation, or partnership if any of these latter three persons is only a limited partner. The definition of "insider" in the Bankruptcy Code does not purport to make a limited partner an insider of the partners or of the partnership with which the limited partner is associated, but it is susceptible of a contrary interpretation and one which would extend unduly the scope of the defined relationship when the limited partner is not a person in control of the partnership. The definition of

"insider" in this Act also differs from the definition in the Bankruptcy Code in omitting the reference in 11 U.S.C. § 101(28)(D) to an elected official or relative of such an official as an insider of a municipality. As in the Bankruptcy Code (see 11 U.S.C. § 102(3)), the word "includes" is not limiting, however. Thus, a court may find a person living with an individual for an extended time in the same household or as a permanent companion to have the kind of close relationship intended to be covered by the term "insider." Likewise, a trust may be found to be an insider of a beneficiary.

(8) The definition of "lien" is derived from paragraphs (30), (31), (43), and (45) of § 101 of the Bankruptcy Code, which define "judicial lien," "lien," "security interest," and "statutory lien" respectively.

(9) The definition of "person" is adapted from paragraphs (28) and (30) of § 1-201 of the Uniform Commercial Code, defining "organization" and "person" respectively.

(10) The definition of "property" is derived from § 1-201(33) of the Uniform Probate Code. Property includes both real and personal property, whether tangible or intangible, and any interest in property, whether legal or equitable.

(11) The definition of "relative" is derived from § 101(37) of the Bankruptcy Code but is explicit in its references to the spouse of a debtor in view of uncertainty as to whether the common law determines degrees of relationship by affinity.

(12) The definition of "transfer" is derived principally from § 101(48) of the Bankruptcy Code. The definition of "conveyance" in § 1 of the Uniform Fraudulent Conveyance Act was similarly comprehensive, and the references in this Act to "payment of money, release, lease, and the creation of a lien or incumbrance" are derived from the Uniform Fraudulent Conveyance Act. While the definition in the Uniform Fraudulent Conveyance Act did not explicitly refer to an involuntary transfer, the decisions under that Act were generally consistent with an interpretation that covered such a transfer. See, e.g., Hearn 45 St. Corp. v. Jano, 283 N.Y. 139, 27 N.E.2d 814, 128 A.L.R. 1285 (1940) (execution and foreclosure sales); Lefkowitz v. Finkelstein Trading Corp., 14 F.Supp. 898, 899 (S.D.N.Y. 1936) (execution sale); Langan v. First Trust & Deposit Co., 277 App.Div. 1090, 101 N.Y.S.2d 36 (4th Dept. 1950), aff'd, 302 N.Y. 932, 100 N.E.2d 189 (1951) (mortgage foreclosure); Catabene v. Wallner, 16 N.J.Super. 597, 602, 85 A.2d 300, 302 (1951) (mortgage foreclosure).

(13) The definition of "valid lien" is new. A valid lien includes an equitable lien that may not be defeated by a judicial lien creditor. See, e.g.,

Pearlman v. Reliance Insurance Co., 371 U.S. 132, 136 (1962) (upholding a surety's equitable lien in respect to a fund owing a bankrupt contractor).

Section 2. Insolvency.

(a) A debtor is insolvent if the sum of the debtor's debts is greater than all of the debtor's assets, at a fair valuation.

(b) A debtor who is generally not paying his [or her] debts as they become due is presumed to be insolvent.

(c) A partnership is insolvent under subsection (a) if the sum of the partnership's debts is greater than the aggregate of all of the partnership's assets, at a fair valuation, and the sum of the excess of the value of each general partner's nonpartnership assets over the partner's nonpartnership debts.

(d) Assets under this section do not include property that has been transferred, concealed, or removed with intent to hinder, delay, or defraud creditors or that has been transferred in a manner making the transfer voidable under this [Act].

(e) Debts under this section do not include an obligation to the extent it is secured by a valid lien on property of the debtor not included as an asset.

COMMENTS:

(1) Subsection (a) is derived from the definition of "insolvent" in § 101(29)(A) of the Bankruptcy Code. The definition in subsection (a) and the correlated definition of partnership insolvency in subsection (c) contemplate a fair valuation of the debts as well as the assets of the debtor. As under the definition of the same term in § 2 of the Uniform Fraudulent Conveyance Act exempt property is excluded from the computation of the value of the assets. See § 1(2) supra. For similar reasons interests in valid spendthrift trusts and interests in tenancies by the entireties that cannot be severed by a creditor of only one tenant are not included. See the Comment to § 1(2) supra. Since a valid lien also precludes an unsecured creditor from collecting the creditor's claim from the encumbered interest in a debtor's property, both the encumbered interest and the debt secured thereby are excluded from the computation of insolvency under this Act. See § 1(2) supra and subsection (e) of this section.

The requirement of § 550(b)(1) of the Bankruptcy Code that a transferee be "without knowledge of the voidability of the transfer" in order to be protected has been omitted as inappropriate. Knowledge of the facts rendering the transfer voidable would be inconsistent with the good faith that is required of a protected transferee. Knowledge of the voidability of a transfer would seem to involve a legal conclusion. Determination of the voidability of the transfer ought not to require the court to inquire into the legal sophistication of the transferee.

(2) Section 2(b) establishes a rebuttable presumption of insolvency from the fact of general nonpayment of debts as they become due. Such general nonpayment is a ground for the filing of an involuntary petition under § 303(h)(1) of the Bankruptcy Code. See also U.C.C. § 1-201(23), which declares a person to be "insolvent" who "has ceased to pay his debts in the ordinary course of business." The presumption imposes on the party against whom the presumption is directed the burden of proving that the nonexistence of insolvency as defined in § 2(a) is more probable than its existence. See Uniform Rules of Evidence (1974 Act), Rule 301(a). The 1974 Uniform Rule 301(a) conforms to the Final Draft of Federal Rule 301 as submitted to the United States Supreme Court by the Advisory Committee on Federal Rules of Evidence. "The so-called 'bursting bubble' theory, under which a presumption vanishes upon the introduction of evidence which would support a finding of the nonexistence of the presumed fact, even though not believed, is rejected as according presumptions too 'slight and evanescent' an effect." Advisory Committee's Note to Rule 301. See also 1 J.Weinstein & M.Berger, Evidence ¶ 301 [01] (1982).

The presumption is established in recognition of the difficulties typically imposed on a creditor in proving insolvency in the bankruptcy sense, as provided in subsection (a). See generally Levit, The Archaic Concept of Balance-Sheet Insolvency, 47 Am.Bankr.L.J. 215 (1973). Not only is the relevant information in the possession of a noncooperative debtor but the debtor's records are more often than not incomplete and inaccurate. As a practical matter, insolvency is most cogently evidenced by a general cessation of payment of debts, as has long been recognized by the laws of other countries and is now reflected in the Bankruptcy Code. See Honsberger, Failure to Pay One's Debts Generally as They Become Due: The Experience of France and Canada, 54 Am.Bankr.L.J. 153 (1980); J. MacLachlan, Bankruptcy 13, 63-64, 436 (1956). In determining whether a debtor is paying its debts generally as they become due, the court should look at more than the amount and due dates of the indebtedness. The court should also take into account such factors as the number of the debtor's debts, the proportion of those debts not being paid, the duration of the nonpayment, and the existence of bona fide disputes or other special circumstances alleged to constitute an explanation for the stoppage of payments. The court's determination may be affected by a consideration of the debtor's payment practices prior to the period of alleged nonpayment and the payment practices of the trade or industry in which the debtor is engaged. The case law that has developed under § 303(h)(1) of the Bankruptcy Code has not required a showing that a debtor has failed or refused to pay a majority in number and amount of his or her debts in order to prove general nonpayment of debts as they become due. See, e.g., Hill v. Cargill, Inc. (In re Hill), 8 B.R. 779, 3 C.B.C.2d 920 (Bk.D.Minn. 1981) (nonpayment of three largest debts held to constitute general nonpayment, although small debts were being paid); In re All Media Properties, Inc., 5 B.R. 126, 6 B.C.D. 586, 2 C.B.C.2d 449 (Bk.S.D.Tex. 1980) (missing significant number of payments or regularly missing payments significant in amount said to constitute general nonpayment; missing payments on more than 50% of aggregate of claims said not to be required to show general nonpayment; nonpayment for more than 30 days after billing held to establish nonpayment of a debt when it is due); In re Kreidler Import Corp., 4 B.R. 256, 6 B.C.D. 608, 2 C.B.C.2d 159 (Bk.D.Md. 1980) (nonpayment of one debt constituting 97% of debtor's total indebtedness held to constitute general nonpayment). A presumption of insolvency does not arise from nonpayment of a debt as to which there is a genuine bona fide dispute, even though the debt is a substantial part of the debtor's indebtedness. Cf. 11 U.S.C. § 303(h)(1), as amended by § 426(b) of Public Law No. 98-882, the Bankruptcy Amendments and Federal Judgeship Act of 1984.

(3) Subsection (c) is derived from the definition of partnership insolvency in § 101(29)(B) of the Bankruptcy Code. The definition conforms generally to the definition of the same term in § 2(2) of the Uniform Fraudulent Conveyance Act.

(4) Subsection (d) follows the approach of the definition of "insolvency" in § 101(29) of the Bankruptcy Code by excluding from the computation of the value of the debtor's assets any value that can be realized only by avoiding a transfer of an interest formerly held by the debtor or by discovery or pursuit of property that has been fraudulently concealed or removed.

(5) Subsection (e) is new. It makes clear the purpose not to render a person insolvent under this section by counting as a debt an obligation secured by property of the debtor that is not counted as an asset. See also Comments to §§ 1(2) and 2(a) supra.

Section 3. Value.

(a) Value is given for a transfer or an obligation if, in exchange for the transfer or obligation, property is transferred or an antecedent debt is secured or satisfied, but value does not include an unperformed promise made otherwise than in the ordinary course of the promisor's business to furnish support to the debtor or another person.

(b) For the purposes of Sections 4(a)(2) and 5, a person gives a reasonably equivalent value if the person acquires an interest of the debtor in an asset pursuant to a regularly conducted, noncollusive foreclosure sale or execution of a power of sale for the acquisition or disposition of the interest of the debtor upon default under a mortgage, deed of trust, or security agreement.

(c) A transfer is made for present value if the exchange between the debtor and the transferee is intended by them to be contemporaneous and is in fact substantially contemporaneous.

COMMENTS:

(1) This section defines "value" as used in various contexts in this Act, frequently with a qualifying adjective. The word appears in the following sections:

4(a)(2) ("reasonably equivalent value");

4(b)(8) ("value . . . reasonably equivalent);

5(a) ("reasonably equivalent value");

5(b) ("present, reasonably equivalent value");

8(a) ("reasonably equivalent value");

8(b), (c), (d), and (e) ("value");

8(f)(1) ("new value"); and

8(f)(3) ("present value").

(2) Section 3(a) is adapted from § 548(d)(2)(A) of the Bankruptcy Code. See also § 3(a) of the Uniform Fraudulent Conveyance Act. The definition in Section 3 is not exclusive. "Value" is to be determined in light of the purpose of the Act to protect a debtor's estate from being depleted to the prejudice of the debtor's unsecured creditors. Consideration having no utility from a creditor's viewpoint does not satisfy the statutory definition. The definition does not specify all the kinds of consideration that do not constitute value for the purposes of this Act—e.g., love and affection. See, e.g., United States v. West, 299 F.Supp. 661, 666 (D.Del. 1969).

(3) Section 3(a) does not indicate what is "reasonably equivalent value" for a transfer or obligation. Under this Act, as under § 548(a)(2) of the Bankruptcy Code, a transfer for security is ordinarily for a reasonably equivalent value notwithstanding a discrepancy between the

value of the asset transferred and the debt secured, since the amount of the debt is the measure of the value of the interest in the asset that is transferred. See, e.g., Peoples-Pittsburgh Trust Co. v. Holy Family Polish Nat'l Catholic Church, Carnegie, Pa., 341 Pa. 390, 19 A.2d 360 (1941). If, however, a transfer purports to secure more than the debt actually incurred or to be incurred, it may be found to be for less than a reasonably equivalent value. See e.g., In re Peoria Braumeister Co., 138 F.2d 520, 523 (7th Cir. 1943) (chattel mortgage securing a $3,000 note held to be fraudulent when the debt secured was only $2,500); Hartford Acc. & Indemnity Co. v. Jirasek, 254 Mich. 131, 140, 235 N.W. 836, 839 (1931) (quitclaim deed given as mortgage held to be fraudulent to the extent the value of the property transferred exceeded the indebtedness secured). If the debt is a fraudulent obligation under this Act, a transfer to secure it as well as the obligation would be vulnerable to attack as fraudulent. A transfer to satisfy or secure an antecedent debt owed an insider is also subject to avoidance under the conditions specified in Section 5(b).

(4) Section 3(a) of the Uniform Fraudulent Conveyance Act has been thought not to recognize that an unperformed promise could constitute fair consideration. See McLaughlin, Application of the Uniform Fraudulent Conveyance Act, 46 Harv.L.Rev. 404, 414 (1933). Courts construing these provisions of the prior law nevertheless have held unperformed promises to constitute value in a variety of circumstances. See, e.g., Harper v. Lloyd's Factors, Inc., 214 F.2d 662 (2d Cir. 1954) (transfer of money for promise of factor to discount transferor's purchase-money notes given to fur dealer); Schlecht v. Schlecht, 168 Minn. 168, 176-77, 209 N.W. 883, 886-87 (1926) (transfer for promise to make repairs and improvements on transferor's homestead); Farmer's Exchange Bank v. Oneida Motor Truck Co., 202 Wis. 266, 232 N.W. 536 (1930) (transfer in consideration of assumption of certain of transferor's liabilities); see also Hummel v. Cernocky, 161 F.2d 685 (7th Cir. 1947) (transfer in consideration of cash, assumption of a mortgage, payment of certain debts, and agreement to pay other debts). Likewise a transfer in consideration of a negotiable note discountable at a commercial bank, or the purchase from an established, solvent institution of an insurance policy, annuity, or contract to provide care and accommodations clearly appears to be for value. On the other hand, a transfer for an unperformed promise by an individual to support a parent or other transferor has generally been held voidable as a fraud on creditors of the transferor. See, e.g., Springfield Ins. Co. v. Fry, 267 F.Supp. 693 (N.D.Okla. 1967); Sandler v. Parlapiano, 236 App.Div. 70, 258 N.Y.Supp. 88 (1st Dep't 1932); Warwick Municipal Employees Credit Union v. Higham, 106 R.E. 363, 259 A.2d 852 (1969); Hulsether v. Sanders, 54 S.D. 412, 223 N.W. 335 (1929); Cooper v. Cooper, 22

Tenn.App. 473, 477, 124 S.W.2d 264, 267 (1939); Note, Rights of Creditors in Property Conveyed in Consideration of Future Support, 45 Iowa L.Rev. 546, 550-62 (1960). This Act adopts the view taken in the cases cited in determining whether an unperformed promise is value.

(5) Subsection (b) rejects the rule of such cases as Durrett v. Washington Nat. Ins. Co., 621 F.2d 201 (5th Cir. 1980) (nonjudicial foreclosure of a mortgage avoided as a fraudulent transfer when the property of an insolvent mortgagor was sold for less than 70% of its fair value); and Abramson v. Lakewood Bank & Trust Co., 647 F.2d 547 (5th Cir. 1981), cert. denied, 454 U.S. 1164 (1982) (nonjudicial foreclosure held to be fraudulent transfer if made without fair consideration). Subsection (b) adopts the view taken in Lawyers Title Ins. Corp. v. Madrid (In re Madrid), 21 B.R. 424 (B.A.P. 9th Cir. 1982), aff'd on another ground, 725 F.2d 1197 (9th Cir. 1984), that the price bid at a public foreclosure sale determines the fair value of the property sold. Subsection (b) prescribes the effect of a sale meeting its requirements, whether the asset sold is personal or real property. The rule of this subsection applies to a foreclosure by sale of the interest of a vendee under an installment land contract in accordance with applicable law that requires or permits the foreclosure to be effected by a sale in the same manner as the foreclosure of a mortgage. See G.Osborne, G.Nelson, & D.Whitman, Real Estate Finance Law 83-84, 95-97 (1979). The premise of the subsection is that "a sale of the collateral by the secured party as the normal consequence of default . . . [is] the safest way of establishing the fair value of the collateral . . . ." 2 G.Gilmore, Security Interests in Personal Property, 1227 (1965).

If a lien given an insider for a present consideration is not perfected as against a subsequent bona fide purchaser or is so perfected after a delay following an extension of credit secured by the lien, foreclosure of the lien may result in a transfer for an antecedent debt that is voidable under Section 5(b) infra. Subsection (b) does not apply to an action under Section 4(a)(1) to avoid a transfer or obligation because made or incurred with actual intent to hinder, delay, or defraud any creditor.

(6) Subsection (c) is an adaptation of § 547(c)(1) of the Bankruptcy Code. A transfer to an insider for an antecedent debt may be voidable under § 5(b) infra.

Section 4. Transfers Fraudulent as to Present And Future Creditors.

(a) A transfer made or obligation incurred by a debtor is fraudulent as to a creditor, whether the creditor's claim arose before or after the transfer was made or the obligation was incurred, if the debtor made the transfer or incurred the obligation:

(1) with actual intent to hinder, delay, or defraud any creditor of the debtor; or

(2) without receiving a reasonably equivalent value in exchange for the transfer or obligation, and the debtor:

(i) was engaged or was about to engage in a business or a transaction for which the remaining assets of the debtor were unreasonably small in relation to the business or transaction; or

(ii) intended to incur, or believed or reasonably should have believed that he [or she] would incur, debts beyond his [or her] ability to pay as they became due.

(b) In determining actual intent under subsection (a)(1), consideration may be given, among other factors, to whether:

(1) the transfer or obligation was to an insider;

(2) the debtor retained possession or control of the property transferred after the transfer;

(3) the transfer or obligation was disclosed or concealed;

(4) before the transfer was made or obligation was incurred, the debtor had been sued or threatened with suit;

(5) the transfer was of substantially all the debtor's assets;

(6) the debtor absconded;

(7) the debtor removed or concealed assets;

(8) the value of the consideration received by the debtor was reasonably equivalent to the value of the asset transferred or the amount of the obligation incurred;

(9) the debtor was insolvent or became insolvent shortly after the transfer was made or the obligation was incurred;

(10) the transfer occurred shortly before or shortly after a substantial debt was incurred; and

(11) the debtor transferred the essential assets of the business to a lienor who transferred the assets to an insider of the debtor.

Comments"

(1) Section 4(a)(1) is derived from § 7 of the Uniform Fraudulent Conveyance Act. Factors appropriate for consideration in determining actual intent under paragraph (1) are specified in subsection (b).

(2) Section 4(a)(2) is derived from §§ 5 and 6 of the Uniform Fraudulent Conveyance Act but substitutes "reasonably equivalent value" for "fair consideration." The transferee's good faith was an element of "fair consideration" as defined in § 3 of the Uniform Fraudulent Conveyance Act, and lack of fair consideration was one of the elements of a fraudulent transfer as defined in four sections of the Uniform Act. The transferee's good faith is irrelevant to a determination of the adequacy of the consideration under this Act, but lack of good faith may be a basis for withholding protection of a transferee or obligee under § 8 infra.

(3) Unlike the Uniform Fraudulent Conveyance Act as originally promulgated, this Act does not prescribe different tests when a transfer is made for the purpose of security and when it is intended to be absolute. The premise of this Act is that when a transfer is for security only, the equity or value of the asset that exceeds the amount of the debt secured remains available to unsecured creditors and thus cannot be regarded as the subject of a fraudulent transfer merely because of the encumbrance resulting from an otherwise valid security transfer. Disproportion between the value of the asset securing the debt and the size of the debt secured does not, in the absence of circumstances indicating a purpose to hinder, delay, or defraud creditors, constitute an impermissible hindrance to the enforcement of other creditors' rights against the debtor-transferor. Cf. U.C.C. § 9-311.

(4) Subparagraph (i) of § 4(a)(2) is an adaptation of § 5 of the Uniform Fraudulent Conveyance Act but substitutes "unreasonably small [assets] in relation to the business or transaction" for "unreasonably small capital." The reference to "capital" in the Uniform Act is ambiguous in that it may refer to net worth or to the par value of stock or to the consideration received for stock issued. The special meanings of "capital" in corporation law have no relevance in the law of fraudulent transfers. The subparagraph focuses attention on whether the amount of all the assets retained by the debtor was inadequate, i.e., unreasonably small, in light of the needs of the business or transaction in which the debtor was engaged or about to engage.

(5) Subsection (b) is a nonexclusive catalogue of factors appropriate for consideration by the court in determining whether the debtor had an actual intent to hinder, delay, or defraud one or more creditors. Proof of the existence of any one or more of the factors enumerated in subsection (b) may be relevant evidence as to the debtor's actual intent but

does not create a presumption that the debtor has made a fraudulent transfer or incurred a fraudulent obligation. The list of factors includes most of the badges of fraud that have been recognized by the courts in construing and applying the Statute of 13 Elizabeth and § 7 of the Uniform Fraudulent Conveyance Act. Proof of the presence of certain badges in combination establishes fraud conclusively—i.e., without regard to the actual intent of the parties—when they concur as provided in § 4(a)(2) or in § 5. The fact that a transfer has been made to a relative or to an affiliated corporation has not been regarded as a badge of fraud sufficient to warrant avoidance when unaccompanied by any other evidence of fraud. The courts have uniformly recognized, however, that a transfer to a closely related person warrants close scrutiny of the other circumstances, including the nature and extent of the consideration exchanged. See 1 G. Glenn, Fraudulent Conveyances and Preferences § 307 (Rev. ed. 1940). The second, third, fourth, and fifth factors listed are all adapted from the classic catalogue of badges of fraud provided by Lord Coke in Twyne's Case, 3 Coke 80b, 76 Eng.Rep. 809 (Star Chamber 1601). Lord Coke also included the use of a trust and the recitation in the instrument of transfer that it "was made honestly, truly, and bona fide," but the use of the trust is fraudulent only when accompanied by elements or badges specified in this Act, and recitals of "good faith" can no longer be regarded as significant evidence of a fraudulent intent.

(6) In considering the factors listed in § 4(b) a court should evaluate all the relevant circumstances involving a challenged transfer or obligation. Thus the court may appropriately take into account all indicia negativing as well as those suggesting fraud, as illustrated in the following reported cases:

(a) Whether the transfer or obligation was to an insider: Salomon v. Kaiser (In re Kaiser), 722 F.2d 1574, 1582-83 (2d Cir. 1983) (insolvent debtor's purchase of two residences in the name of his spouse and the creation of a dummy corporation for the purpose of concealing assets held to evidence fraudulent intent); Banner Construction Corp. v. Arnold, 128 So.2d 893 (Fla.Dist.App. 1961) (assignment by one corporation to another having identical directors and stockholders constituted a badge of fraud); Travelers Indemnity Co. v. Cormaney, 258 Iowa 237, 138 N.W.2d 50 (1965) (transfer between spouses said to be a circumstance that shed suspicion on the transfer and that with other circumstances warranted avoidance); Hatheway v. Hanson, 230 Iowa 386, 297 N.W. 824 (1941) (transfer from parent to child said to require a critical examination of surrounding circumstances, which, together with other indicia of fraud, warranted avoidance); Lumpkins v. McPhee, 59 N.M. 442,

286 P.2d 299 (1955) (transfer from daughter to mother said to be indicative of fraud but transfer held not to be fraudulent due to adequacy of consideration and delivery of possession by transferor).

(b) Whether the transferor retained possession or control of the property after the transfer: Harris v. Shaw, 224 Ark. 150, 272 S.W.2d 53 (1954) (retention of property by transferor said to be a badge of fraud and, together with other badges, to warrant avoidance of transfer); Stephens v. Reginstein, 89 Ala. 561, 8 So. 68 (1890) (transferor's retention of control and management of property and business after transfer held material in determining transfer to be fraudulent); Allen v. Massey, 84 U.S. (17 Wall.) 351 (1872) (joint possession of furniture by transferor and transferee considered in holding transfer to be fraudulent); Warner v. Norton, 61 U.S. (20 How.) 448 (1857) (surrender of possession by transferor deemed to negate allegations of fraud).

(c) Whether the transfer or obligation was concealed or disclosed: Walton v. First National Bank, 13 Colo. 265, 22 P. 440 (1889) (agreement between parties to conceal the transfer from the public said to be one of the strongest badges of fraud); Warner v. Norton, 61 U.S. (20 How.) 448 (1857) (although secrecy said to be a circumstance from which, when coupled with other badges, fraud may be inferred, transfer was held not to be fraudulent when made in good faith and transferor surrendered possession); W.T. Raleigh Co. v. Barnett, 253 Ala. 433, 44 So.2d 585 (1950) (failure to record a deed in itself said not to evidence fraud, and transfer held not to be fraudulent).

(d) Whether, before the transfer was made or obligation was incurred, a creditor sued or threatened to sue the debtor: Harris v. Shaw, 224 Ark. 150, 272 S.W. 2d 53 (1954) (transfer held to be fraudulent when causally connected to pendency of litigation and accompanied by other badges of fraud); Pergrem v. Smith, 255 S.W.2d 42 (Ky.App. 1953) (transfer in anticipation of suit deemed to be a badge of fraud; transfer held fraudulent when accompanied by insolvency of transferor who was related to transferee); Bank of Sun Prairie v. Hovig, 218 F.Supp. 769 (W.D.Ark. 1963) (although threat or pendency of litigation said to be an indicator of fraud, transfer was held not to be fraudulent when adequate consideration and good faith were shown).

(e) Whether the transfer was of substantially all the debtor's assets: Walbrun v. Babbitt, 83 U.S. (16 Wall.) 577 (1872) (sale by insolvent retail shop owner of all of his inventory in a single transaction held to be fraudulent); Cole v. Mercantile Trust Co., 133 N.Y. 164, 30 N.E.

847 (1892) (transfer of all property before plaintiff could obtain a judgment held to be fraudulent); Lumpkins v. McPhee, 59 N.M. 442, 286 P.2d 299 (1955) (although transfer of all assets said to indicate fraud, transfer held not to be fraudulent because full consideration was paid and transferor surrendered possession).

(f) Whether the debtor had absconded: In re Thomas, 199 F. 214 (N.D.N.Y. 1912) (when debtor collected all of his money and property with the intent to abscond, fraudulent intent was held to be shown).

(g) Whether the debtor had removed or concealed assets: Bentley v. Young, 210 F. 202 (S.D.N.Y 1914), aff'd, 223 F. 536 (2d Cir. 1915) (debtor's removal of goods from store to conceal their whereabouts and to sell them held to render sale fraudulent); Cioli v. Kenourgios, 59 Cal.App. 690, 211 P. 838 (1922) (debtor's sale of all assets and shipment of proceeds out of the country held to be fraudulent notwithstanding adequacy of consideration).

(h) Whether the value of the consideration received by the debtor was reasonably equivalent to the value of the asset transferred or the amount of the obligation incurred: Toomay v. Graham, 151 S.W.2d 119 (Mo.App. 1941) (although mere inadequacy of consideration said not to be a badge of fraud, transfer held to be fraudulent when accompanied by badges of fraud); Texas Sand Co. v. Shield, 381 S.W.2d 48 (Tex. 1964) (inadequate consideration said to be an indicator of fraud, and transfer held to be fraudulent because of inadequate consideration, pendency of suit, family relationship of transferee, and fact that all nonexempt property was transferred); Weigel v. Wood, 355 Mo. 11, 194 S.W.2d 40 (1946) (although inadequate consideration said to be a badge of fraud, transfer held not to be fraudulent when inadequacy not gross and not accompanied by any other badge; fact that transfer was from father to son held not sufficient to establish fraud).

(i) Whether the debtor was insolvent or became insolvent shortly after the transfer was made or obligation was incurred: Harris v. Shaw, 224 Ark. 150, 272 S.W. 2d 53 (1954) (insolvency of transferor said to be a badge of fraud and transfer held fraudulent when accompanied by other badges of fraud); Bank of Sun Prairie v. Hovig, 218 F.Supp. 769 (W.D. Ark. 1963) (although the insolvency of the debtor said to be a badge of fraud, transfer held not fraudulent when debtor was shown to be solvent, adequate consideration was paid, and good faith was shown, despite the pendency of suit); Wareheim v. Bayliss, 149 Md. 103, 131 A. 27 (1925) (although insolvency of debtor acknowledged to be an indicator of fraud, transfer held not to be fraudulent when adequate consideration was paid and whether debtor was insolvent in fact was doubtful).

(j) Whether the transfer occurred shortly before or shortly after a substantial debt was incurred: Commerce Bank of Lebanon v. Halladale A Corp., 618 S.W. 2d 288, 292 (Mo.App. 1981) (when transferors incurred substantial debts near in time to the transfer, transfer was held to be fraudulent due to inadequate consideration, close family relationship, the debtor's retention of possession, and the fact that almost all the debtor's property was transferred).

(7) The effect of the two transfers described in § 4(b)(11), if not avoided, may be to permit a debtor and a lienor to deprive the debtor's unsecured creditors of access to the debtor's assets for the purpose of collecting their claims while the debtor, the debtor's affiliate or insider, and the lienor arrange for the beneficial use or disposition of the assets in accordance with their interests. The kind of disposition sought to be reached here is exemplified by that found in Northern Pacific Co. v. Boyd, 228 U.S. 482 (1913), the leading case in establishing the absolute priority doctrine in reorganization law. There the Court held that a reorganization whereby the secured creditors and the management-owners retained their economic interests in a railroad through a foreclosure that cut off claims of unsecured creditors against its assets was in effect a fraudulent disposition (id. at 502-05). See Frank, Some Realistic Reflections on Some Aspects of Corporate Reorganization, 19 Va. L.Rev. 541, 693 (1933). For cases in which an analogous injury to unsecured creditors was inflicted by a lienor and a debtor, see Jackson v. Star Sprinkler Corp. of Florida, 575 F.2d 1223, 1231-34 (8th Cir. 1978); Heath v. Helmick, 173 F.2d 157, 161-62 (9th Cir. 1949); Toner v. Nuss, 234 F.S. 457, 461-62 (E.D.Pa. 1964); and see In re Spotless Tavern Co., Inc., 4 F.Supp. 752, 753, 755 (D.Md. 1933).

(8) Nothing in § 4(b) is intended to affect the application of § 2-402(2), 9-205, 9-301, or 6-105 of the Uniform Commercial Code. Section 2-402(2) recognizes the generally prevailing rule that retention of possession of goods by a seller may be fraudulent but limits the application of the rule by negating any imputation of fraud from "retention of possession in good faith and current course of trade by a merchant-seller for a commercially reasonable time after a sale or identification." Section 9-205 explicitly negates any imputation of fraud from the grant of liberty by a secured creditor to a debtor to use, commingle, or dispose of personal property collateral or to account for its proceeds. The section recognizes that it does not relax prevailing requirements for delivery of possession by a pledgor. Moreover, the section does not mitigate the general requirement of § 9-301(1)(b) that a nonpossessory security interest in personal property must be accompanied by no-

tice-filing to be effective against a levying creditor. Finally, like the Uniform Fraudulent Conveyance Act this Act does not pre-empt the statutes governing bulk transfers, such as Article 6 of the Uniform Commercial Code. Compliance with the cited sections of the Uniform Commercial Code does not, however, insulate a transfer or obligation from avoidance. Thus a sale by an insolvent debtor for less than a reasonably equivalent value would be voidable under this Act notwithstanding compliance with the Uniform Commercial Code.

Section 5. Transfers Fraudulent as to Present Creditors.

(a) A transfer made or obligation incurred by a debtor is fraudulent as to a creditor whose claim arose before the transfer was made or the obligation was incurred if the debtor made the transfer or incurred the obligation without receiving a reasonably equivalent value in exchange for the transfer or obligation and the debtor was insolvent at that time or the debtor became insolvent as a result of the transfer or obligation.

(b) A transfer made by a debtor is fraudulent as to a creditor whose claim arose before the transfer was made if the transfer was made to an insider for an antecedent debt, the debtor was insolvent at that time, and the insider had reasonable cause to believe that the debtor was insolvent.

COMMENTS:

> (1) Subsection (a) is derived from § 4 of the Uniform Fraudulent Conveyance Act. It adheres to the limitation of the protection of that section to a creditor who extended credit before the transfer or obligation described. As pointed out in Comment (2) accompanying § 4, this Act substitutes "reasonably equivalent value" for "fair consideration."

> (2) Subsection (b) renders a preferential transfer—i.e., a transfer by an insolvent debtor for or on account of an antecedent debt—to an insider vulnerable as a fraudulent transfer when the insider had reasonable cause to believe that the debtor was insolvent. This subsection adopts for general application the rule of such cases as Jackson Sound Studios, Inc. v. Travis, 473 F.2d 503 (5th Cir. 1973) (security transfer of corporation's equipment to corporate principal's mother perfected on eve of bankruptcy of corporation held to be fraudulent); In re Lamie Chemical Co., 296 F. 24 (4th Cir. 1924) (corporate preference to corporate officers and directors held voidable by receiver when corporation was insolvent or nearly so and directors had already voted for liquidation); Stuart v. Larson, 298 F. 223 (8th Cir. 1924), noted 38 Harv.L.Rev. 521 (1925) (corporate preference to director held voidable). See generally 2 G. Glenn, Fraudulent Conveyances and Preferences 386 (rev. ed. 1940). Subsection (b) overrules such cases as Epstein v. Goldstein, 107

F.2d 755, 757 (2d Cir. 1939) (transfer by insolvent husband to wife to secure his debt to her sustained against attack by husband's trustee); Hartford Accident & Indemnity Co. v. Jirasek, 254 Mich. 131, 139, 235 N.W. 836, 389 (1931) (mortgage given by debtor to his brother to secure an antecedent debt owed the brother sustained as not fraudulent).

(3) Subsection (b) does not extend as far as § 8(a) of the Uniform Fraudulent Conveyance Act and § 548(b) of the Bankruptcy Code in rendering voidable a transfer or obligation incurred by an insolvent partnership to a partner, who is an insider of the partnership. The transfer to the partner is not vulnerable to avoidance under § 4(b) unless the transfer was for an antecedent debt and the partner had reasonable cause to believe that the partnership was insolvent. The cited provisions of the Uniform Fraudulent Conveyance Act and the Bankruptcy Act make any transfer by an insolvent partnership to a partner voidable. Avoidance of the partnership transfer without reference to the partner's state of mind and the nature of the consideration exchanged would be unduly harsh treatment of the creditors of the partner and unduly favorable to the creditors of the partnership.

Section 6. When Transfer is Made or Obligation is Incurred.

For the purposes of this [Act]:

(1) a transfer is made:

(i) with respect to an asset that is real property other than a fixture, but including the interest of a seller or purchaser under a contract for the sale of the asset, when the transfer is so far perfected that a good-faith purchaser of the asset from the debtor against whom applicable law permits the transfer to be perfected cannot acquire an interest in the asset that is superior to the interest of the transferee; and

(ii) with respect to an asset that is not real property or that is a fixture, when the transfer is so far perfected that a creditor on a simple contract cannot acquire a judicial lien otherwise than under this [Act] that is superior to the interest of the transferee;

(2) if applicable law permits the transfer to be perfected as provided in paragraph (1) and the transfer is not so perfected before the commencement of an action for relief under this [Act], the transfer is deemed made immediately before the commencement of the action;

(3) if applicable law does not permit the transfer to be perfected as provided in paragraph (1), the transfer is made when it becomes effective between the debtor and the transferee;

(4) a transfer is not made until the debtor has acquired rights in the asset transferred;

(5) an obligation is incurred:

(i) if oral, when it becomes effective between the parties; or

(ii) if evidenced by a writing, when the writing executed by the obligor is delivered to or for the benefit of the obligee.

COMMENTS:

(1) One of the uncertainties in the law governing the avoidance of fraudulent transfers and obligations is the difficulty of determining when the cause of action arises. Subsection (b) clarifies this point in time. For transfers of real estate Section 6(1) fixes the time as the date of perfection against a good faith purchaser from the transferor and for transfers of fixtures and assets constituting personalty, the time is fixed as the date of perfection against a judicial lien creditor not asserting rights under this Act. Perfection typically is effected by notice-filing, recordation, or delivery of unequivocal possession. See U.C.C. §§ 9-302, 9-304, and 9-305 (security interest in personal property perfected by notice-filing or delivery of possession to transferee); 4 American Law of Property § 17.10-17.12 (1952) (recordation of transfer or delivery of possession to grantee required for perfection against bona fide purchaser from grantor). The provision for postponing the time a transfer is made until its perfection is an adaptation of § 548(d)(1) of the Bankruptcy Code. When no steps are taken to perfect a transfer that applicable law permits to be perfected, the transfer is deemed by paragraph (2) to be perfected immediately before the filing of an action to avoid it; without such a provision to cover that eventuality, an unperfected transfer would arguably be immune to attack. Some transfers—e.g., an assignment of a bank account, creation of a security interest in money, or execution of a marital or premarital agreement for the disposition of property owned by the parties to the agreement—may not be amenable to perfection as against a bona fide purchaser or judicial lien creditor. When a transfer is not perfectible as provided in paragraph (11), the transfer occurs for the purpose of this Act when the transferor effectively parts with an interest in the asset as provided in § 1(12) supra.

(2) Paragraph (4) requires the transferor to have rights in the asset transferred before the transfer is made for the purpose of this section. This provision makes clear that its purpose may not be circumvented by notice-filing or recordation of a document evidencing an interest in an asset to be acquired in the future. Cf. Bankruptcy Code § 547(e); U.C.C. § 9-203(1)(c).

(3) Paragraph (5) is new. It is intended to resolve uncertainty arising from Rubin v. Manufacturers Hanover Trust Co., 661 F.2d 979, 989-91, 997 (2d Cir. 1981), insofar as that case holds that an obligation of guaranty may be deemed to be incurred when advances covered by the guaranty are made rather than when the guaranty first became effective between the parties. Compare Rosenberg, Intercorporate Guaranties and the Law of Fraudulent Conveyances: Lender Beware, 125 U.Pa.L.Rev. 235, 256-57 (1976).

An obligation may be avoided as fraudulent under this Act if it is incurred under the circumstances specified in § 4(a) or § 5(a). The debtor may receive reasonably equivalent value in exchange for an obligation incurred even though the benefit to the debtor is indirect. See Rubin v. Manufacturers Hanover Trust Co., 661 F.2d at 991-92; Williams v. Twin City Co., 251 F.2d 678, 681 (9th Cir. 1958); Rosenberg, supra at 243-46.

Section 7. Remedies of Creditors.

(a) In an action for relief against a transfer or obligation under this [Act], a creditor, subject to the limitations in Section 8, may obtain:

(1) avoidance of the transfer or obligation to the extent necessary to satisfy the creditor's claim;

(2) an attachment or other provisional remedy against the asset transferred or other property of the transferee in accordance with the procedure prescribed by [ ];]

(3) subject to applicable principles of equity and in accordance with applicable rules of civil procedure,

(i) an injunction against further disposition by the debtor or a transferee, or both, of the asset transferred or of other property;

(ii) appointment of a receiver to take charge of the asset transferred or of other property of the transferee; or

(iii) any other relief the circumstances may require.

(b) If a creditor has obtained a judgment on a claim against the debtor, the creditor, if the court so orders, may levy execution on the asset transferred or its proceeds.

COMMENTS:

(1) This section is derived from §§ 9 and 10 of the Uniform Fraudulent Conveyance Act. Section 9 of that Act specified the remedies of creditors whose claims have matured, and § 10 enumerated the remedies avail-

able to creditors whose claims have not matured. A creditor holding an unmatured claim may be denied the right to receive payment for the proceeds of a sale on execution until his claim has matured, but the proceeds may be deposited in court or in an interest-bearing account pending the maturity of the creditor's claim. The remedies specified in this section are not exclusive.

(2) The availability of an attachment or other provisional remedy has been restricted by amendments of statutes and rules of procedure to reflect views of the Supreme Court expressed in Sniadach v. Family Finance Corp. of Bay View, 395 U.S. 337 (1969), and its progeny. This judicial development and the procedural changes that followed in its wake do not preclude resort to attachment by a creditor in seeking avoidance of a fraudulent transfer or obligation. See, e.g., Britton v. Howard Sav. Bank, 727 F.2d 315, 317-20 (3d Cir. 1984); Computer Sciences Corp. v. Sci-Tek Inc., 367 A.2d 658, 661 (Del. Super. 1976); Great Lakes Carbon Corp. v. Fontana, 54 A.D.2d 548, 387 N.Y.S. 2d 115 (1st Dep't 1976). Section 7(a)(2) continues the authorization for the use of attachment contained in § 9(b) of the Uniform Fraudulent Conveyance Act, or of a similar provisional remedy, when the state's procedure provides therefor, subject to the constraints imposed by the due process clauses of the United States and state constitutions.

(3) Subsections (a) and (b) of § 10 of the Uniform Fraudulent Conveyance Act authorized the court, in an action on a fraudulent transfer or obligation, to restrain the defendant from disposing of his property, to appoint a receiver to take charge of his property, or to make any order the circumstances may require. Section 10, however, applied only to a creditor whose claim was unmatured. There is no reason to restrict the availability of these remedies to such a creditor, and the courts have not so restricted them. See, e.g., Lipskey v. Voloshen, 155 Md. 139, 143-45, 141 Atl. 402, 404-05 (1928) (judgment creditor granted injunction against disposition of property by transferee, but appointment of receiver denied for lack of sufficient showing of need for such relief); Matthews v. Schusheim, 36 Misc. 2d 918, 922-23, 235 N.Y.S.2d 973, 976-77, 991-92 (Sup.Ct. 1962) (injunction and appointment of receiver granted to holder of claims for fraud, breach of contract, and alimony arrearages; whether creditor's claim was mature said to be immaterial); Oliphant v. Moore, 155 Tenn. 359, 362-63, 293 S.W. 541, 542 (1927) (tort creditor granted injunction restraining alleged tortfeasor's disposition of property).

(4) As under the Uniform Fraudulent Conveyance Act, a creditor is not required to obtain a judgment against the debtor-transferor or to have a matured claim in order to proceed under subsection (a). See § 1(3) and (4) supra; American Surety Co. v. Conner, 251 N.Y. 1, 166 N.E. 783,

65 A.L.R. 244 (1929); 1 G. Glenn, Fraudulent Conveyances and Preferences 129 (Rev.ed. 1940).

(5) The provision in subsection (b) for a creditor to levy execution on a fraudulently transferred asset continues the availability of a remedy provided in § 9(b) of the Uniform Fraudulent Conveyance Act. See, e.g., Doland v. Burns Lbr. Co., 156 Minn. 238, 194 N.W. 636 (1923); Montana Ass'n of Credit Management v. Hergert, 181 Mont. 442, 449, 453, 593 P.2d 1059, 1063, 1065 (1979); Corbett v. Hunter, 292 Pa.Super. 123, 128, 436 A.2d 1036, 1038 (1981); see also American Surety Co. v. Conner, 251 N.Y. 1, 6, 166 N.E. 783, 784, 65 A.L.R. 244, 247 (1929) ("In such circumstances he [the creditor] might find it necessary to indemnify the sheriff and, when the seizure was erroneous, assumed the risk of error"); McLaughlin, Application of the Uniform Fraudulent Conveyance Act, 46 Harv.L.Rev. 404, 441-42 (1933).

(6) The remedies specified in § 7, like those enumerated in §§ 9 and 10 of the Uniform Fraudulent Conveyance Act, are cumulative. Lind v. O. N. Johnson Co., 204 Minn. 30, 40, 282 N.W. 661, 667, 119 A.L.R. 940 (1939) (Uniform Fraudulent Conveyance Act held not to impair or limit availability of the "old practice" of obtaining judgment and execution returned unsatisfied before proceeding in equity to set aside a transfer); Conemaugh Iron Works Co. v. Delano Coal Co., Inc., 298 Pa. 182, 186, 148 A. 94, 95 (1929) (Uniform Fraudulent Conveyance Act held to give an "additional optional remedy" and not to "deprive a creditor of the right, as formerly, to work out his remedy at law"); 1 G. Glenn, Fraudulent Conveyances and Preferences 120, 130, 150 (Rev.ed. 1940).

Section 8. Defenses, Liability, and Protection of Transferee.

(a) A transfer or obligation is not voidable under Section 4(a)(1) against a person who took in good faith and for a reasonably equivalent value or against any subsequent transferee or obligee.

(b) Except as otherwise provided in this section, to the extent a transfer is voidable in an action by a creditor under Section 7(a)(1), the creditor may recover judgment for the value of the asset transferred, as adjusted under subsection (c), or the amount necessary to satisfy the creditor's claim, whichever is less. The judgment may be entered against:

(1) the first transferee of the asset or the person for whose benefit the transfer was made; or

(2) any subsequent transferee other than a good-faith transferee or obligee who took for value or from any subsequent transferee or obligee.

(c) If the judgment under subsection (b) is based upon the value of the asset transferred, the judgment must be for an amount equal to the value of the asset at the time of the transfer, subject to adjustment as the equities may require.

(d) Notwithstanding voidability of a transfer or an obligation under this [Act], a good-faith transferee or obligee is entitled, to the extent of the value given the debtor for the transfer or obligation, to

(1) a lien on or a right to retain any interest in the asset transferred;

(2) enforcement of any obligation incurred; or

(3) a reduction in the amount of the liability on the judgment.

(e) A transfer is not voidable under Section 4(a)(2) or Section 5 if the transfer results from:

(1) termination of a lease upon default by the debtor when the termination is pursuant to the lease and applicable law; or

(2) enforcement of a security interest in compliance with Article 9 of the Uniform Commercial Code.

(f) A transfer is not voidable under Section 5(b):

(1) to the extent the insider gave new value to or for the benefit of the debtor after the transfer was made unless the new value was secured by a valid lien;

(2) if made in the ordinary course of business or financial affairs of the debtor and the insider; or

(3) if made pursuant to a good-faith effort to rehabilitate the debtor and the transfer secured present value given for that purpose as well as an antecedent debt of the debtor.

COMMENTS:

(1) Subsection (a) states the rule that applies when the transferee establishes a complete defense to the action for avoidance based on Section 4(a)(1). The subsection is an adaptation of the exception stated in § 9 of the Uniform Fraudulent Conveyance Act. The person who invokes this defense carries the burden of establishing good faith and the reasonable equivalence of the consideration exchanged. Chorost v. Grand Rapids Factory Showrooms, Inc., 77 F. Supp. 276, 280 (D.N.J. 1948), aff'd, 172 F.2d 327, 329 (3d Cir. 1949).

(2) Subsection (b) is derived from § 550(a) of the Bankruptcy Code. The value of the asset transferred is limited to the value of the levyable in-

terest on the transferor, exclusive of any interest encumbered by a valid lien. See § 1(2) supra.

(3) Subsection (c) is new. The measure of the recovery of a defrauded creditor against a fraudulent transferee is usually limited to the value of the asset transferred at the time of the transfer. See, e.g., United States v. Fernon, 640 F.2d 609, 611 (5th Cir. 1981); Hamilton Nat'l Bank of Boston v. Halstead, 134 N.Y. 520, 31 N.E. 900 (1892); cf. Buffum v. Peter Barceloux Co., 289 U.S. 227 (1932) (transferee's objection to trial court's award of highest value of asset between the date of the transfer and the date of the decree of avoidance rejected because an award measured by value as of time of the transfer plus interest from that date would have been larger). The premise of § 8(c) is that changes in value of the asset transferred that occur after the transfer should ordinarily not affect the amount of the creditor's recovery. Circumstances may require a departure from that measure of the recovery, however, as the cases decided under the Uniform Fraudulent Conveyance Act and other laws derived from the Statute of 13 Elizabeth illustrate. Thus, if the value of the asset at the time of levy and sale to enforce the judgment of the creditor has been enhanced by improvements of the asset transferred or discharge of liens on the property, a good faith transferee should be reimbursed for the outlay for such a purpose to the extent the sale proceeds were increased thereby. See Bankruptcy Code § 550(d); Janson v. Schier, 375 A.2d 1159, 1160 (N.H. 1977); Anno., 8 A.L.R. 527 (1920). If the value of the asset has been diminished by severance and disposition of timber or minerals or fixtures, the transferee should be liable for the amount of the resulting reduction. See Damazo v. Wahby, 269 Md. 252, 257, 305 A.2d 138, 142 (1973). If the transferee has collected rents, harvested crops, or derived other income from the use or occupancy of the asset after the transfer, the liability of the transferee should be limited in any event to the net income after deduction of the expense incurred in earning the income. Anno., 60 A.L.R.2d 593 (1958). On the other hand, adjustment for the equities does not warrant an award to the creditor of consequential damages alleged to accrue from mismanagement of the asset after the transfer.

(4) Subsection (d) is an adaptation of § 548(c) of the Bankruptcy Code. An insider who receives property or an obligation from an insolvent debtor as security for or in satisfaction of an antecedent debt of the transferor or obligor is not a good faith transferee or obligee if the insider has reasonable cause to believe that the debtor was insolvent at the time the transfer was made or the obligation was incurred.

(5) Subsection (e)(1) rejects the rule adopted in Darby v. Atkinson (In re Farris), 415 F.Supp. 33, 39-41 (W.D.Okla. 1976), that termination of a lease on default in accordance with its terms and applicable law may

constitute a fraudulent transfer. Subsection (e)(2) protects a transferee who acquires a debtor's interest in an asset as a result of the enforcement of a secured creditor's rights pursuant to and in compliance with the provisions of Part 5 of Article 9 of the Uniform Commercial Code. Cf. Calaiaro v. Pittsburgh Nat'l Bank (In re Ewing), 33 B.R. 288, 9 C.B.C.2d 526, CCH B.L.R. ¶ 69,460 (Bk.W.D.Pa. 1983) (sale of pledged stock held subject to avoidance as fraudulent transfer in § 548 of the Bankruptcy Code), rev'd, 36 B.R. 476 (W.D.Pa. 1984) (transfer held not voidable because deemed to have occurred more than one year before bankruptcy petition filed). Although a secured creditor may enforce rights in collateral without a sale under § 9-502 or § 9-505 of the Code, the creditor must proceed in good faith (U.C.C. § 9-103) and in a "commercially reasonable" manner. The "commercially reasonable" constraint is explicit in U.C.C. § 9-502(2) and is implicit in § 9-505. See 2 G. Gilmore, Security Interests in Personal Property 1224-27 (1965).

(6) Subsection (f) provides additional defenses against the avoidance of a preferential transfer to an insider under § 5(b).

Paragraph (1) is adapted from § 547(c)(4) of the Bankruptcy Code, which permits a preferred creditor to set off the amount of new value subsequently advanced against the recovery of a voidable preference by a trustee in bankruptcy to the debtor without security. The new value may consist not only of money, goods, or services delivered on unsecured credit but also of the release of a valid lien. See, e.g., In re Ira Haupt & Co., 424 F.2d 722, 724 (2d Cir. 1970); Baranow v. Gibraltor Factors Corp. (In re Hygrade Envelope Co.), 393 F.2d 60, 65-67 (2d Cir.), cert. denied, 393 U.S. 837 (1968); In re John Morrow & Co., 134 F.686, 688 (S.D.Ohio 1901). It does not include an obligation substituted for a prior obligation. If the insider receiving the preference thereafter extends new credit to the debtor but also takes security from the debtor, the injury to the other creditors resulting from the preference remains undiminished by the new credit. On the other hand, if a lien taken to secure the new credit is itself voidable by a judicial lien creditor of the debtor, the new value received by the debtor may appropriately be treated as unsecured and applied to reduce the liability of the insider for the preferential transfer.

Paragraph (2) is derived from § 546(c)(2) of the Bankruptcy Code, which excepts certain payments made in the ordinary course of business or financial affairs from avoidance by the trustee in bankruptcy as preferential transfers. Whether a transfer was in the "ordinary course" requires a consideration of the pattern of payments or secured transactions engaged in by the debtor and the insider prior to the transfer challenged under § 5(b). See Tait & Williams, Bankruptcy Preference Laws: The Scope of Section 547(c)(2), 99 Banking L.J. 55, 63-66 (1982). The defense provided by paragraph (2) is available, irrespective of whether the debtor or the insider or both are engaged in business, but the prior conduct or practice of both the debtor and the insider-transferee is relevant.

Paragraph (3) is new and reflects a policy judgment that an insider who has previously extended credit to a debtor should not be deterred from extending further credit to the debtor in a good faith effort to save the debtor from a forced liquidation in bankruptcy or otherwise. A similar rationale has sustained the taking of security from an insolvent debtor for an advance to enable the debtor to stave off bankruptcy and extricate itself from financial stringency. Blackman v. Bechtel, 80 F.2d 505, 508-09 (8th Cir. 1935); Olive v. Tyler (In re Chelan Land Co.), 257 F.497, 5 A.L.R. 561 (9th Cir. 1919); In re Robin Bros. Bakeries, Inc., 22 F.S. 662, 663-64 (N.D.Ill. 1937); see Dean v. Davis, 242 U.S. 438, 444 (1917). The amount of the present value given, the size of the antecedent debt secured, and the likelihood of success for the rehabilitative effort are relevant considerations in determining whether the transfer was in good faith.

Section 9. Extinguishment of [Claim for Relief] [Cause of Action].

A [claim for relief] [cause of action] with respect to a fraudulent transfer or obligation under this [Act] is extinguished unless action is brought:

(a) under Section 4(a)(1), within 4 years after the transfer was made or the obligation was incurred or, if later, within one year after the transfer or obligation was or could reasonably have been discovered by the claimant;

(b) under Section 4(a)(2) or 5(a), within 4 years after the transfer was made or the obligation was incurred; or

(c) under Section 5(b), within one year after the transfer was made or the obligation was incurred.

COMMENTS:

(1) This section is new. Its purpose is to make clear that lapse of the statutory periods prescribed by the section bars the right and not merely the remedy. See Restatement of Conflict of Laws 2d § 143 Comments (b) and (c) (1971). The section rejects the rule applied in United States v. Gleneagles Inv. Co., 565 F.S. 556, 583 (M.D.Pa. 1983) (state statute of limitations held not to apply to action by United States based on Uniform Fraudulent Conveyance Act).

(2) Statutes of limitations applicable to the avoidance of fraudulent transfers and obligations vary widely from state to state and are frequently subject to uncertainties in their application. See Hesson, The Statute of Limitations in Actions to Set Aside Fraudulent Conveyances and in Actions Against Directors by Creditors of Corporations, 32 Cornell L.Q. 222 (1946); Annos., 76 A.L.R. 864 (1932), 128 A.L.R. 1289 (1940), 133 A.L.R. 1311 (1941), 14 A.L.R.2d 598 (1950), and 100 A.L.R.2d 1094 (1965). Together with § 6, this section should mitigate the uncertainty and diversity that have characterized the decisions applying statutes of limitations to actions to fraudulent transfers and obligations. The periods prescribed apply, whether the action under this Act is brought by the creditor defrauded or by a purchaser at a sale on execution levied pursuant to § 7(b) and whether the action is brought against the original transferee or subsequent transferee. The prescription of statutory periods of limitation does not preclude the barring of an avoidance action for laches. See § 10 and the accompanying Comment infra.

Section 10. Supplementary Provisions.

Unless displaced by the provisions of this [Act], the principles of law and equity, including the law merchant and the law relating to principal and agent, estoppel, laches, fraud, misrepresentation, duress, coercion, mistake, insolvency, or other validating or invalidating cause, supplement its provisions.

COMMENTS:

This section is derived from § 11 of the Uniform Fraudulent Conveyance Act and § 1-103 of the Uniform Commercial Code. The section adds a reference to "laches" in recognition of the particular appropriateness of the application of this equitable doctrine to an untimely action to avoid a fraudulent transfer. See Louis Dreyfus Corp. v. Butler, 496 F.2d 806, 808 (6th Cir. 1974) (action to avoid transfers to debtor's wife when debtor was engaged in speculative business held to be barred by laches or applicable statutes of limitations); Cooch v. Grier, 30 Del.Ch. 255, 265-66, 59 A.2d 282, 287-88 (1948) (action under the Uniform Fraudulent Conveyance Act held barred by laches when the creditor was chargeable with inexcusable delay and the defendant was prejudiced by the delay).

Section 11. Uniformity of Application and Construction.

This [Act] shall be applied and construed to effectuate its general purpose to make uniform the law with respect to the subject of this [Act] among states enacting it.

Section 12. Short Title.

This [Act] may be cited as the Uniform Fraudulent Transfer Act.

Section 13. Repeal.

The following acts and all other acts and parts of acts inconsistent herewith are hereby repealed:

COMMENTS:

> If enacted by this State, the Uniform Fraudulent Conveyance Act should be listed among the statutes repealed.

APPENDIX 19:
IRS COLLECTION APPEAL REQUEST

Collection Appeal Request

1. Taxpayer's Name		2. Representative: (Form 2848, Power of Attorney Attached)	
3. SSN/EIN	4. Taxpayer's Business Phone	5. Taxpayer's Home Phone	6. Representative's Phone
7. Taxpayer's Street Address			
8. City		9. State	10. Zip Code
11. Type of Tax (Tax Form)	12. Tax Periods Being Appealed		13. Tax Due

Collection Action(s) Appealed

14. Please Check the Collection Action(s) You're Appealing:

☐ Federal Tax Lien   ☐ Denial of Installment Agreement

☐ Levy or Notice of Levy   ☐ Termination of Installment Agreement

☐ Seizure

Explanation

15. Please explain why you disagree with the collection action(s) you checked above and explain how you would resolve your tax problem. Attach additional pages if needed. Attach copies of any documents that you think will support your position.

Under penalties of perjury, I declare that I have examined this request and the attached documents, and to the best of my knowledge and belief, they are true, correct and complete. A submission by a representative, other than the taxpayer, is based on all information of which preparer has any knowledge.

16. Taxpayer's or Authorized Representative's Signature	17. Date
18. Collection Manager's Signature	19. Date Received

Form **9423** (Rev. 01-1999)   Catalog Number 14169I   Department of the Treasury – Internal Revenue Service
(Over)

Collection Appeal Rights

FOR LIENS, LEVIES, SEIZURES, AND DENIAL OR TERMINATION OF INSTALLMENT AGREEMENT

You may appeal a Notice of Federal Tax Lien, levy, seizure, or denial or termination of an installment agreement under these procedures. However, if you request an appeal after IRS makes a seizure, you must appeal to the Collection manager within 10 business days after the Notice of Seizure is provided to you or left at your home or business.

How to Appeal If You Disagree With One of These Actions

1. If you disagree with the decision of the Revenue Officer, and wish to appeal, you must first request a conference with a Collection manager.

2. If you do not resolve your disagreement with the Collection manager, you may request Appeals consideration by completing Form 9423, Collection Appeal Request.

3. On the Form 9423, check the Collection action(s) you disagree with and explain why you disagree. You must also explain your solution to resolve your tax problem. **THE COLLECTION OFFICE MUST RECEIVE YOUR REQUEST FOR AN APPEAL WITHIN 2 DAYS OF YOUR CONFERENCE WITH THE COLLECTION MANAGER OR WE WILL RESUME COLLECTION ACTION.**

What will happen when you appeal your case

Normally, we will stop the collection action(s) you disagree with until your appeal is settled, unless we have reason to believe that collection of the amount owed is at risk.

You may have a representative

You may represent yourself at your Appeals conference or you may be represented by an attorney, certified public accountant, or a person enrolled to practice before the IRS. If you want your representative to appear without you, you must provide a properly completed Form 2848, Power of Attorney and Declaration of Representative. You can obtain Form 2848 from your local IRS office or by calling 1-800-829-3676.

Decision on the appeal

Once the Appeals Officer makes a decision on your case, that decision is binding on both you and the IRS. This means that both you and the IRS are required to accept the decision and live up to its terms.

Note: Providing false information, failing to provide all pertinent information, or fraud will void Appeal's decision.

APPENDIX 20:
IRS REQUEST FOR A COLLECTION DUE PROCESS HEARING

Request for a Collection Due Process Hearing

Use this form to request a hearing with the IRS Office of Appeals only when you receive a **Notice of Federal Tax Lien Filing & Your Right To A Hearing Under IRC 6320**, a **Final Notice - Notice Of Intent to Levy & Your Notice Of a Right To A Hearing**, or a **Notice of Jeopardy Levy and Right of Appeal**. Complete this form and send it to the address shown on your lien or levy notice for expeditious handling. Include a copy of your lien or levy notice(s) to ensure proper handling of your request.

(Print) Taxpayer Name(s):_____

(Print) Address: _____

Daytime Telephone Number: _____ Type of Tax/Tax Form Number(s): _____

Taxable Period(s):_____

Social Security Number/Employer Identification Number(s): _____

Check the IRS action(s) that you do not agree with. Provide specific reasons why you don't agree. If you believe that your spouse or former spouse should be responsible for all or a portion of the tax liability from your tax return, check here [__] and attach Form 8857, Request for Innocent Spouse Relief, to this request.

____ **Filed Notice of Federal Tax Lien (Explain why you don't agree. Use extra sheets if necessary.)**

____ **Notice of Levy/Seizure (Explain why you don't agree. Use extra sheets if necessary.)**

I/we understand that the statutory period of limitations for collection is suspended during the Collection Due Process Hearing and any subsequent judicial review.

Taxpayer's or Authorized Representative's Signature and Date _____

Taxpayer's or Authorized Representative's Signature and Date _____

IRS Use Only:

IRS Employee *(Print)*: _____ IRS Received Date: _____

Employee Telephone Number: _____

Form 12153 (01-1999)   Catalog Number 26685D   Department of the Treasury - Internal Revenue Service

APPENDIX 21:
FEDERAL TAX LIEN ACT
(26 U.S.C. §6321, ET SEQ.)

Sec. 6321. Lien for taxes

If any person liable to pay any tax neglects or refuses to pay the same after demand, the amount (including any interest, additional amount, addition to tax, or assessable penalty, together with any costs that may accrue in addition thereto) shall be a lien in favor of the United States upon all property and rights to property, whether real or personal, belonging to such person.

Sec. 6322. Period of lien

Unless another date is specifically fixed by law, the lien imposed by section 6321 shall arise at the time the assessment is made and shall continue until the liability for the amount so assessed (or a judgment against the taxpayer arising out of such liability) is satisfied or becomes unenforceable by reason of lapse of time.

Sec. 6323. Validity and priority against certain persons

(a) Purchasers, holders of security interests, mechanic's lienors, and judgment lien creditors

The lien imposed by section 6321 shall not be valid as against any purchaser, holder of a security interest, mechanic's lienor, or judgment lien creditor until notice thereof which meets the requirements of subsection (f) has been filed by the Secretary.

(b) Protection for certain interests even though notice filed

Even though notice of a lien imposed by section 6321 has been filed, such lien shall not be valid:

(1) Securities

With respect to a security (as defined in subsection (h)(4)):

(A) as against a purchaser of such security who at the time of purchase did not have actual notice or knowledge of the existence of such lien; and

(B) as against a holder of a security interest in such security who, at the time such interest came into existence, did not have actual notice or knowledge of the existence of such lien.

(2) Motor vehicles

With respect to a motor vehicle (as defined in subsection (h)(3)), as against a purchaser of such motor vehicle, if:

(A) at the time of the purchase such purchaser did not have actual notice or knowledge of the existence of such lien, and

(B) before the purchaser obtains such notice or knowledge, he has acquired possession of such motor vehicle and has not thereafter relinquished possession of such motor vehicle to the seller or his agent.

(3) Personal property purchased at retail

With respect to tangible personal property purchased at retail, as against a purchaser in the ordinary course of the seller's trade or business, unless at the time of such purchase such purchaser intends such purchase to (or knows such purchase will) hinder, evade, or defeat the collection of any tax under this title.

(4) Personal property purchased in casual sale

With respect to household goods, personal effects, or other tangible personal property described in section 6334(a) purchased (not for resale) in a casual sale for less than $1,000, as against the purchaser, but only if such purchaser does not have actual notice or knowledge:

(A) of the existence of such lien, or

(B) that this sale is one of a series of sales.

(5) Personal property subject to possessory lien

With respect to tangible personal property subject to a lien under local law securing the reasonable price of the repair or improvement of such property, as against a holder of such a lien, if such holder is, and has been, continuously in possession of such property from the time such lien arose.

(6) Real property tax and special assessment liens

With respect to real property, as against a holder of a lien upon such property, if such lien is entitled under local law to priority over security interests in such property which are prior in time, and such lien secures payment of:

(A) a tax of general application levied by any taxing authority based upon the value of such property;

(B) a special assessment imposed directly upon such property by any taxing authority, if such assessment is imposed for the purpose of defraying the cost of any public improvement; or

(C) charges for utilities or public services furnished to such property by the United States, a State or political subdivision thereof, or an instrumentality of any one or more of the foregoing.

(7) Residential property subject to a mechanic's lien for certain repairs and improvements

With respect to real property subject to a lien for repair or improvement of a personal residence (containing not more than four dwelling units) occupied by the owner of such residence, as against a mechanic's lienor, but only if the contract price on the contract with the owner is not more than $5,000.

(8) Attorneys' liens

With respect to a judgment or other amount in settlement of a claim or of a cause of action, as against an attorney who, under local law, holds a lien upon or a contract enforceable against such judgment or amount, to the extent of his reasonable compensation for obtaining such judgment or procuring such settlement, except that this paragraph shall not apply to any judgment or amount in settlement of a claim or of a cause of action against the United States to the extent that the United States offsets such judgment or amount against any liability of the taxpayer to the United States.

(9) Certain insurance contracts

With respect to a life insurance, endowment, or annuity contract, as against the organization which is the insurer under such contract, at any time:

(A) before such organization had actual notice or knowledge of the existence of such lien;

(B) after such organization had such notice or knowledge, with respect to advances required to be made automatically to maintain such contract in force under an agreement entered into before such organization had such notice or knowledge; or

(C) after satisfaction of a levy pursuant to section 6332(b), unless and until the Secretary delivers to such organization a notice, executed after the date of such satisfaction, of the existence of such lien.

(10) Deposit-secured loans

With respect to a savings deposit, share, or other account with an institution described in section 581 or 591, to the extent of any loan made by such institution without actual notice or knowledge of the existence of such lien, as against such institution, if such loan is secured by such account.

(c) Protection for certain commercial transactions financing agreements, etc.

(1) In general

To the extent provided in this subsection, even though notice of a lien imposed by section 6321 has been filed, such lien shall not be valid with respect to a security interest which came into existence after tax lien filing but which:

(A) is in qualified property covered by the terms of a written agreement entered into before tax lien filing and constituting:

(i) a commercial transactions financing agreement,

(ii) a real property construction or improvement financing agreement, or

(iii) an obligatory disbursement agreement, and

(B) is protected under local law against a judgment lien arising, as of the time of tax lien filing, out of an unsecured obligation.

(2) Commercial transactions financing agreement

For purposes of this subsection:

(A) Definitions

The term "commercial transactions financing agreement" means an agreement (entered into by a person in the course of his trade or business):

(i) to make loans to the taxpayer to be secured by commercial financing security acquired by the taxpayer in the ordinary course of his trade or business, or

(ii) to purchase commercial financing security (other than inventory) acquired by the taxpayer in the ordinary course of his trade or business; but such an agreement shall be treated as coming within the term only to the extent that such loan or purchase is made before the 46th day after the date of tax lien filing or (if earlier) before the lender or purchaser had actual notice or knowledge of such tax lien filing.

(B) Limitation on qualified property

The term "qualified property", when used with respect to a commercial transactions financing agreement, includes only commercial financing security acquired by the taxpayer before the 46th day after the date of tax lien filing.

(C) Commercial financing security defined

The term "commercial financing security" means (i) paper of a kind ordinarily arising in commercial transactions, (ii) accounts receivable, (iii) mortgages on real property, and (iv) inventory.

(D) Purchaser treated as acquiring security interest

A person who satisfies subparagraph (A) by reason of clause (ii) thereof shall be treated as having acquired a security interest in commercial financing security

(3) Real property construction or improvement financing agreement

For purposes of this subsection:

(A) Definition

The term "real property construction or improvement financing agreement" means an agreement to make cash disbursements to finance—

(i) the construction or improvement of real property,

(ii) a contract to construct or improve real property, or

(iii) the raising or harvesting of a farm crop or the raising of livestock or other animals.

For purposes of clause (iii), the furnishing of goods and services shall be treated as the disbursement of cash.

(B) Limitation on qualified property

The term "qualified property", when used with respect to a real property construction or improvement financing agreement, includes only:

(i) in the case of subparagraph (A)(i), the real property with respect to which the construction or improvement has been or is to be made,

(ii) in the case of subparagraph (A)(ii), the proceeds of the contract described therein, and

(iii) in the case of subparagraph (A)(iii), property subject to the lien imposed by section 6321 at the time of tax lien filing and the crop or the livestock or other animals referred to in subparagraph (A)(iii).

(4) Obligatory disbursement agreement

For purposes of this subsection:

(A) Definition

The term "obligatory disbursement agreement" means an agreement (entered into by a person in the course of his trade or business) to make disbursements, but such an agreement shall be treated as coming within the term only to the extent of disbursements which are required to be made by reason of the intervention of the rights of a person other than the taxpayer.

(B) Limitation on qualified property

The term "qualified property", when used with respect to an obligatory disbursement agreement, means property subject to the lien imposed by section 6321 at the time of tax lien filing and (to the extent that the acquisition is directly traceable to the disbursements referred to in subparagraph (A)) property acquired by the taxpayer after tax lien filing.

(C) Special rules for surety agreements

Where the obligatory disbursement agreement is an agreement ensuring the performance of a contract between the taxpayer and another person:

(i) the term "qualified property" shall be treated as also including the proceeds of the contract the performance of which was ensured, and

(ii) if the contract the performance of which was ensured was a contract to construct or improve real property, to produce goods, or to furnish services, the term "qualified property" shall be treated as also including any tangible personal property used by the taxpayer in the performance of such ensured contract.

(d) 45-day period for making disbursements

Even though notice of a lien imposed by section 6321 has been filed, such lien shall not be valid with respect to a security interest which came into existence after tax lien filing by reason of disbursements made before the 46th day after the date of tax lien filing, or (if earlier) before the person making such disbursements had actual notice or knowledge of tax lien filing, but only if such security interest:

(1) is in property (A) subject, at the time of tax lien filing, to the lien imposed by section 6321, and (B) covered by the terms of a written agreement entered into before tax lien filing, and

(2) is protected under local law against a judgment lien arising, as of the time of tax lien filing, out of an unsecured obligation.

(e) Priority of interest and expenses

If the lien imposed by section 6321 is not valid as against a lien or security interest, the priority of such lien or security interest shall extend to:

(1) any interest or carrying charges upon the obligation secured,

(2) the reasonable charges and expenses of an indenture trustee or agent holding the security interest for the benefit of the holder of the security interest,

(3) the reasonable expenses, including reasonable compensation for attorneys, actually incurred in collecting or enforcing the obligation secured,

(4) the reasonable costs of insuring, preserving, or repairing the property to which the lien or security interest relates,

(5) the reasonable costs of insuring payment of the obligation secured, and

(6) amounts paid to satisfy any lien on the property to which the lien or security interest relates, but only if the lien so satisfied is entitled to priority over the lien imposed by section 6321, to the extent that, under local law, any such item has the same priority as the lien or security interest to which it relates.

(f) Place for filing notice; form

(1) Place for filing

The notice referred to in subsection (a) shall be filed—

(A) Under State laws

(i) Real property

In the case of real property, in one office within the State (or the county, or other governmental subdivision), as designated by the laws of such State, in which the property subject to the lien is situated; and

(ii) Personal property

In the case of personal property, whether tangible or intangible, in one office within the State (or the county, or other governmental subdivision), as designated by the laws of such State, in which the property subject to the lien is situated, except that State law merely conforming to or reenacting Federal law establishing a national filing system does not constitute a second office for filing as designated by the laws of such State; or

(B) With clerk of district court

In the office of the clerk of the United States district court for the judicial district in which the property subject to the lien is situated, whenever the State has not by law designated one office which meets the requirements of subparagraph (A); or

(C) With Recorder of Deeds of the District of Columbia

In the office of the Recorder of Deeds of the District of Columbia, if the property subject to the lien is situated in the District of Columbia.

(2) Situs of property subject to lien

For purposes of paragraphs (1) and (4), property shall be deemed to be situated:

(A) Real property

In the case of real property, at its physical location; or

(B) Personal property

In the case of personal property, whether tangible or intangible, at the residence of the taxpayer at the time the notice of lien is filed.

For purposes of paragraph (2)(B), the residence of a corporation or partnership shall be deemed to be the place at which the principal executive office of the business is located, and the residence of a taxpayer whose residence is without the United States shall be deemed to be in the District of Columbia.

(3) Form

The form and content of the notice referred to in subsection (a) shall be prescribed by the Secretary. Such notice shall be valid notwithstanding any other provision of law regarding the form or content of a notice of lien.

(4) Indexing required with respect to certain real property

In the case of real property, if:

(A) under the laws of the State in which the real property is located, a deed is not valid as against a purchaser of the property who (at the time of purchase) does not have actual notice or knowledge of the existence of such deed unless the fact of filing of such deed has been entered and recorded in a public index at the place of filing in such a manner that a reasonable inspection of the index will reveal the existence of the deed, and

(B) there is maintained (at the applicable office under paragraph (1)) an adequate system for the public indexing of Federal tax liens, then the notice of lien referred to in subsection (a) shall not be treated as meeting the filing requirements under paragraph (1) unless the fact of filing is entered and recorded in the index referred to in subparagraph (B) in such a manner that a reasonable inspection of the index will reveal the existence of the lien.

(5) National filing systems

The filing of a notice of lien shall be governed solely by this title and shall not be subject to any other Federal law establishing a place or places for the filing of liens or encumbrances under a national filing system.

(g) Refiling of notice

For purposes of this section—

(1) General rule

Unless notice of lien is refiled in the manner prescribed in paragraph (2) during the required refiling period, such notice of lien shall be treated as filed on the date on which it is filed (in accordance with subsection (f)) after the expiration of such refiling period.

(2) Place for filing

A notice of lien refiled during the required refiling period shall be effective only:

(A) if—

(i) such notice of lien is refiled in the office in which the prior notice of lien was filed, and

(ii) in the case of real property, the fact of refiling is entered and recorded in an index to the extent required by subsection (f)(4); and

(B) in any case in which, 90 days or more prior to the date of a refiling of notice of lien under subparagraph (A), the Secretary received written information (in the manner prescribed in regulations issued by the Secretary) concerning a change in the taxpayer's residence, if a notice of such lien is also filed in accordance with subsection (f) in the State in which such residence is located.

(3) Required refiling period

In the case of any notice of lien, the term "required refiling period" means:

(A) the one-year period ending 30 days after the expiration of 10 years after the date of the assessment of the tax, and

(B) the one-year period ending with the expiration of 10 years after the close of the preceding required refiling period for such notice of lien.

(4) Transitional rule

Notwithstanding paragraph (3), if the assessment of the tax was made before January 1, 1962, the first required refiling period shall be the calendar year 1967.

(h) Definitions

For purposes of this section and section 6324—

(1) Security interest

The term "security interest" means any interest in property acquired by contract for the purpose of securing payment or performance of an obligation or indemnifying against loss or liability. A security interest exists at any time (A) if, at such time, the property is in existence and the interest has become protected under local law against a subsequent judgment lien arising out of an unsecured obligation, and (B) to the extent that, at such time, the holder has parted with money or money's worth.

(2) Mechanic's lienor

The term "mechanic's lienor" means any person who under local law has a lien on real property (or on the proceeds of a contract relating to real property) for services, labor, or materials furnished in connection with the construction or improvement of such property. For purposes of the preceding sentence, a person has a lien on the earliest date such lien becomes valid under local law against subsequent purchasers without actual notice, but not before he begins to furnish the services, labor, or materials.

(3) Motor vehicle

The term "motor vehicle" means a self-propelled vehicle which is registered for highway use under the laws of any State or foreign country.

(4) Security

The term "security" means any bond, debenture, note, or certificate or other evidence of indebtedness, issued by a corporation or a government or political subdivision thereof, with interest coupons or in registered form, share of stock, voting trust certificate, or any certificate of interest or participation in, certificate of deposit or receipt for, temporary or interim certificate for, or warrant or right to subscribe to or purchase, any of the foregoing; negotiable instrument; or money.

(5) Tax lien filing

The term "tax lien filing" means the filing of notice (referred to in subsection (a)) of the lien imposed by section 6321.

(6) Purchaser

The term "purchaser" means a person who, for adequate and full consideration in money or money's worth, acquires an interest (other than a lien or security interest) in property which is valid under local law against subsequent purchasers without actual notice. In applying the preceding sentence for purposes of subsection (a) of this section, and for purposes of section 6324:

(A) a lease of property,

(B) a written executory contract to purchase or lease property,

(C) an option to purchase or lease property or any interest therein, or

(D) an option to renew or extend a lease of property, which is not a lien or security interest shall be treated as an interest in property.

(i) Special rules

(1) Actual notice or knowledge

For purposes of this subchapter, an organization shall be deemed for purposes of a particular transaction to have actual notice or knowledge of any fact from the time such fact is brought to the attention of the individual conducting such transaction, and in any event from the time such fact would have been brought to such individual's attention if the organization had exercised due diligence. An organization exercises due diligence if it maintains reasonable routines for communicating significant information to the person conducting the transaction and there is reasonable compliance with the routine. Due diligence does not require an individual acting for the organization to communicate information unless such communication is part of his regular duties or unless he has reason to know of the transaction and that the transaction would be materially affected by the information.

(2) Subrogation

Where, under local law, one person is subrogated to the rights of another with respect to a lien or interest, such person shall be subrogated to such rights for purposes of any lien imposed by section 6321 or 6324.

(3) Forfeitures

For purposes of this subchapter, a forfeiture under local law of property seized by a law enforcement agency of a State, county, or other local governmental subdivision shall relate back to the time of seizure, except that this paragraph shall not apply to the extent that under local law the holder of an intervening claim or interest would have priority over the interest of the State, county, or other local governmental subdivision in the property.

(4) Cost-of-living adjustment

In the case of notices of liens imposed by section 6321 which are filed in any calendar year after 1998, each of the dollar amounts under paragraph (4) or (7) of subsection (b) shall be increased by an amount equal to:

(A) such dollar amount, multiplied by

(B) the cost-of-living adjustment determined under section 1(f)(3) for the calendar year, determined by substituting "calendar year 1996" for "calendar year 1992" in subparagraph (B) thereof. If any amount as adjusted under the preceding sentence is not a multiple of $10, such amount shall be rounded to the nearest multiple of $10.

(j) Withdrawal of notice in certain circumstances

(1) In general

The Secretary may withdraw a notice of a lien filed under this section and this chapter shall be applied as if the withdrawn notice had not been filed, if the Secretary determines that:

(A) the filing of such notice was premature or otherwise not in accordance with administrative procedures of the Secretary,

(B) the taxpayer has entered into an agreement under section 6159 to satisfy the tax liability for which the lien was imposed by means of installment payments, unless such agreement provides otherwise,

(C) the withdrawal of such notice will facilitate the collection of the tax liability, or

(D) with the consent of the taxpayer or the National Taxpayer Advocate, the withdrawal of such notice would be in the best interests of the taxpayer (as determined by the National Taxpayer Advocate) and the United States. Any such withdrawal shall be made by filing notice at the same office as the withdrawn notice. A copy of such notice of withdrawal shall be provided to the taxpayer.

(2) Notice to credit agencies, etc.

Upon written request by the taxpayer with respect to whom a notice of a lien was withdrawn under paragraph (1), the Secretary shall promptly make reasonable efforts to notify credit reporting agencies, and any financial institution or creditor whose name and address is specified in such request, of the withdrawal of such notice. Any such request shall be in such form as the Secretary may prescribe.

Sec. 6324. Special liens for estate and gift taxes

(a) Liens for estate tax

Except as otherwise provided in subsection (c)—

(1) Upon gross estate

Unless the estate tax imposed by chapter 11 is sooner paid in full, or becomes unenforceable by reason of lapse of time, it shall be a lien upon the gross estate of the decedent for 10 years from the date of death, except that such part of the gross estate as is used for the payment of charges against the estate and expenses of its administration, allowed by any court having jurisdiction thereof, shall be divested of such lien.

(2) Liability of transferees and others

If the estate tax imposed by chapter 11 is not paid when due, then the spouse, transferee, trustee (except the trustee of an employees' trust which meets the requirements of section 401(a)), surviving tenant, person in possession of the property by reason of the exercise, nonexercise, or release of a power of appointment, or beneficiary, who receives, or has on the date of the decedent's death, property included in the gross estate under sections 2034 to 2042, inclusive, to the extent of the value, at the time of the decedent's death, of such property, shall be personally liable for such tax. Any part of such property transferred by (or transferred by a transferee of) such spouse, transferee, trustee, surviving tenant, person in possession, or beneficiary, to a purchaser or holder of a security interest shall be divested of the lien provided in paragraph (1) and a like lien shall then attach to all the property of such spouse, transferee, trustee, surviving tenant, person in possession, or beneficiary, or transferee of any such person, except any part transferred to a purchaser or a holder of a security interest.

(3) Continuance after discharge of fiduciary

The provisions of section 2204 (relating to discharge of fiduciary from personal liability) shall not operate as a release of any part of the gross estate from the lien for any deficiency that may thereafter be determined to be due, unless such part of the gross estate (or any interest therein) has been transferred to a purchaser or a holder of a security interest, in which case such part (or such interest) shall not be subject to a lien or to any claim or demand for any such deficiency, but the lien shall attach to the consideration received from such purchaser or holder of a security interest, by the heirs, legatees, devisees, or distributees.

(b) Lien for gift tax

Except as otherwise provided in subsection (c), unless the gift tax imposed by chapter 12 is sooner paid in full or becomes unenforceable by reason of lapse of time, such tax shall be a lien upon all gifts made during the period for which the return was filed, for 10 years from the date the gifts are made. If the tax is not paid when due, the donee of any gift shall be personally liable for such tax to the extent of the value of such gift. Any part of the property comprised in the gift transferred by the donee (or by a transferee of the donee) to a purchaser or holder of a security interest shall be divested of the lien imposed by this subsection and such lien, to the extent of the value of such gift, shall attach to all the property (including after-acquired property) of the donee (or the transferee) except any part transferred to a purchaser or holder of a security interest.

(c) Exceptions

(1) The lien imposed by subsection (a) or (b) shall not be valid as against a mechanic's lienor and, subject to the conditions provided by section 6323(b) (relating to protection for certain interests even though notice filed), shall not be valid with respect to any lien or interest described in section 6323(b).

(2) If a lien imposed by subsection (a) or (b) is not valid as against a lien or security interest, the priority of such lien or security interest shall extend to any item described in section 6323(e) (relating to priority of interest and expenses) to the extent that, under local law, such item has the same priority as the lien or security interest to which it relates.

Sec. 6324A. Special lien for estate tax deferred under section 6166

(a) General rule

In the case of any estate with respect to which an election has been made under section 6166, if the executor makes an election under this section (at such time and in such manner as the Secretary shall by regulations prescribe) and files the agreement referred to in subsection (c), the deferred amount (plus any interest, additional amount, addition to tax, assessable penalty, and costs attributable to the deferred amount) shall be a lien in favor of the United States on the section 6166 lien property.

(b) Section 6166 lien property

(1) In general

For purposes of this section, the term "section 6166 lien property" means interests in real and other property to the extent such interests:

(A) can be expected to survive the deferral period, and

(B) are designated in the agreement referred to in subsection (c).

(2) Maximum value of required property

The maximum value of the property which the Secretary may require as section 6166 lien property with respect to any estate shall be a value which is not greater than the sum of:

(A) the deferred amount, and

(B) the required interest amount.

For purposes of the preceding sentence, the value of any property shall be determined as of the date prescribed by section 6151(a) for payment of the tax imposed by chapter 11 and shall be determined by taking into account any encumbrance such as a lien under section 6324B.

(3) Partial substitution of bond for lien

If the value required as section 6166 lien property pursuant to paragraph (2) exceeds the value of the interests in property covered by the agreement referred to in subsection (c), the Secretary may accept bond in an amount equal to such excess conditioned on the payment of the amount extended in accordance with the terms of such extension.

(c) Agreement

The agreement referred to in this subsection is a written agreement signed by each person in being who has an interest (whether or not in possession) in any property designated in such agreement:

(1) consenting to the creation of the lien under this section with respect to such property, and

(2) designating a responsible person who shall be the agent for the beneficiaries of the estate and for the persons who have consented to the creation of the lien in dealings with the Secretary on matters arising under section 6166 or this section.

(d) Special rules

(1) Requirement that lien be filed

The lien imposed by this section shall not be valid as against any purchaser, holder of a security interest, mechanic's lien, or judgment lien creditor until notice thereof which meets the requirements of section 6323(f) has been filed by the Secretary. Such notice shall not be required to be refiled.

(2) Period of lien

The lien imposed by this section shall arise at the time the executor is discharged from liability under section 2204 (or, if earlier, at the time notice is filed pursuant to paragraph (1)) and shall continue until the liability for the deferred amount is satisfied or becomes unenforceable by reason of lapse of time.

(3) Priorities

Even though notice of a lien imposed by this section has been filed as provided in paragraph (1), such lien shall not be valid:

(A) Real property tax and special assessment liens

To the extent provided in section 6323(b)(6).

(B) Real property subject to a mechanic's lien for repairs and improvement

In the case of any real property subject to a lien for repair or improvement, as against a mechanic's lienor.

(C) Real property construction or improvement financing agreement

As against any security interest set forth in paragraph (3) of section 6323(c) (whether such security interest came into existence before or after tax lien filing).

Subparagraphs (B) and (C) shall not apply to any security interest which came into existence after the date on which the Secretary filed notice (in a manner similar to notice filed under section 6323(f)) that payment of the deferred amount has been accelerated under section 6166(g).

(4) Lien to be in lieu of section 6324 lien

If there is a lien under this section on any property with respect to any estate, there shall not be any lien under section 6324 on such property

(5) Additional lien property required in certain cases

If at any time the value of the property covered by the agreement is less than the unpaid portion of the deferred amount and the required interest amount, the Secretary may require the addition of property to the agreement (but he may not require under this paragraph that the value of the property covered by the agreement exceed such unpaid portion). If property having the required value is not added to the property covered by the agreement (or if other security equal to the required value is not furnished) within 90 days after notice and demand therefor by the Secretary, the failure to comply with the preceding sentence shall be treated as an act accelerating payment of the installments under section 6166(g).

(6) Lien to be in lieu of bond

The Secretary may not require under section 6165 the furnishing of any bond for the payment of any tax to which an agreement which meets the requirements of subsection (c) applies.

(e) Definitions

For purposes of this section—

(1) Deferred amount

The term "deferred amount" means the aggregate amount deferred under section 6166 (determined as of the date prescribed by section 6151(a) for payment of the tax imposed by chapter 11).

(2) Required interest amount

The term "required interest amount" means the aggregate amount of interest which will be payable over the first 4 years of the deferral period with respect to the deferred amount (determined as of the date prescribed by section 6151(a) for the payment of the tax imposed by chapter 11).

(3) Deferral period

The term "deferral period" means the period for which the payment of tax is deferred pursuant to the election under section 6166.

(4) Application of definitions in case of deficiencies

In the case of a deficiency, a separate deferred amount, required interest amount, and deferral period shall be determined as of the due date of the first installment after the deficiency is prorated to installments under section 6166.

Sec. 6324B. Special lien for additional estate tax attributable to farm, etc., valuation

(a) General rule

In the case of any interest in qualified real property (within the meaning of section 2032A(b)), an amount equal to the adjusted tax difference attributable to such interest (within the meaning of section 2032A(c)(2)(B)) shall be a lien in favor of the United States on the property in which such interest exists.

(b) Period of lien

The lien imposed by this section shall arise at the time an election is filed under section 2032A and shall continue with respect to any interest in the qualified real property:

(1) until the liability for tax under subsection (c) of section 2032A with respect to such interest has been satisfied or has become unenforceable by reason of lapse of time, or

(2) until it is established to the satisfaction of the Secretary that no further tax liability may arise under section 2032A(c) with respect to such interest.

(c) Certain rules and definitions made applicable

(1) In general

The rule set forth in paragraphs (1), (3), and (4) of section 6324A(d) shall apply with respect to the lien imposed by this section as if it were a lien imposed by section 6324A.

(2) Qualified real property

For purposes of this section, the term "qualified real property" includes qualified replacement property (within the meaning of section 2032A(h)(3)(B)) and qualified exchange property (within the meaning of section 2032A(i)(3)).

(d) Substitution of security for lien

To the extent provided in regulations prescribed by the Secretary, the furnishing of security may be substituted for the lien imposed by this section.

Sec. 6325. Release of lien or discharge of property

(a) Release of lien

Subject to such regulations as the Secretary may prescribe, the Secretary shall issue a certificate of release of any lien imposed with respect to any internal revenue tax not later than 30 days after the day on which:

(1) Liability satisfied or unenforceable

The Secretary finds that the liability for the amount assessed, together with all interest in respect thereof, has been fully satisfied or has become legally unenforceable; or

(2) Bond accepted

There is furnished to the Secretary and accepted by him a bond that is conditioned upon the payment of the amount assessed, together with all interest in respect thereof, within the time prescribed by law (including any extension of such time), and that is in accordance with such requirements relating to terms, conditions, and form of the bond and sureties thereon, as may be specified by such regulations.

(b) Discharge of property

(1) Property double the amount of the liability

Subject to such regulations as the Secretary may prescribe, the Secretary may issue a certificate of discharge of any part of the property subject to any lien imposed under this chapter if the Secretary finds that the fair market value of that part of such property remaining subject to the lien is at least double the amount of the unsatisfied liability secured by such lien and the amount of all other liens upon such property which have priority over such lien.

(2) Part payment; interest of United States valueless

Subject to such regulations as the Secretary may prescribe, the Secretary may issue a certificate of discharge of any part of the property subject to the lien if:

(A) there is paid over to the Secretary in partial satisfaction of the liability secured by the lien an amount determined by the Secretary, which shall not be less than the value, as determined by the Secretary, of the interest of the United States in the part to be so discharged, or

(B) the Secretary determines at any time that the interest of the United States in the part to be so discharged has no value. In determining the value of the interest of the United States in the part to be so discharged, the Secretary shall give consideration to the value of such part and to such liens thereon as have priority over the lien of the United States.

(3) Substitution of proceeds of sale

Subject to such regulations as the Secretary may prescribe, the Secretary may issue a certificate of discharge of any part of the property subject to the lien if such part of the property is sold and, pursuant to an agreement with the Secretary, the proceeds of such sale are to be held, as a fund subject to the liens and claims of the United States, in the same manner and with the same priority as such liens and claims had with respect to the discharged property.

(4) Right of substitution of value

(A) In general

At the request of the owner of any property subject to any lien imposed by this chapter, the Secretary shall issue a certificate of discharge of such property if such owner:

(i) deposits with the Secretary an amount of money equal to the value of the interest of the United States (as determined by the Secretary) in the property; or

(ii) furnishes a bond acceptable to the Secretary in a like amount.

(B) Refund of deposit with interest and release of bond

The Secretary shall refund the amount so deposited (and shall pay interest at the overpayment rate under section 6621), and shall release such bond, to the extent that the Secretary determines that:

(i) the unsatisfied liability giving rise to the lien can be satisfied from a source other than such property; or

(ii) the value of the interest of the United States in the property is less than the Secretary's prior determination of such value.

(C) Use of deposit, etc., if action to contest lien not filed

If no action is filed under section 7426(a)(4) within the period prescribed therefor, the Secretary shall, within 60 days after the expiration of such period:

(i) apply the amount deposited, or collect on such bond, to the extent necessary to satisfy the unsatisfied liability secured by the lien; and

(ii) refund (with interest as described in subparagraph (B)) any portion of the amount deposited which is not used to satisfy such liability.

(D) Exception

Subparagraph (A) shall not apply if the owner of the property is the person whose unsatisfied liability gave rise to the lien.

(c) Estate or gift tax

Subject to such regulations as the Secretary may prescribe, the Secretary may issue a certificate of discharge of any or all of the property subject to any lien imposed by section 6324 if the Secretary finds that the liability secured by such lien has been fully satisfied or provided for.

(d) Subordination of lien

Subject to such regulations as the Secretary may prescribe, the Secretary may issue a certificate of subordination of any lien imposed by this chapter upon any part of the property subject to such lien if:

(1) there is paid over to the Secretary an amount equal to the amount of the lien or interest to which the certificate subordinates the lien of the United States,

(2) the Secretary believes that the amount realizable by the United States from the property to which the certificate relates, or from any other property subject to the lien, will ultimately be increased by reason of the issuance of such certificate and that the ultimate collection of the tax liability will be facilitated by such subordination, or

(3) in the case of any lien imposed by section 6324B, if the Secretary determines that the United States will be adequately secured after such subordination.

(e) Nonattachment of lien

If the Secretary determines that, because of confusion of names or otherwise, any person (other than the person against whom the tax was assessed) is or may be injured by the appearance that a notice of lien filed under section 6323 refers to such person, the Secretary may issue a certificate that the lien does not attach to the property of such person.

(f) Effect of certificate

(1) Conclusiveness

Except as provided in paragraphs (2) and (3), if a certificate is issued pursuant to this section by the Secretary and is filed in the same office as the notice of lien to which it relates (if such notice of lien has been filed) such certificate shall have the following effect:

(A) in the case of a certificate of release, such certificate shall be conclusive that the lien referred to in such certificate is extinguished;

(B) in the case of a certificate of discharge, such certificate shall be conclusive that the property covered by such certificate is discharged from the lien;

(C) in the case of a certificate of subordination, such certificate shall be conclusive that the lien or interest to which the lien of the United States is subordinated is superior to the lien of the United States; and

(D) in the case of a certificate of nonattachment, such certificate shall be conclusive that the lien of the United States does not attach to the property of the person referred to in such certificate.

(2) Revocation of certificate of release or nonattachment

If the Secretary determines that a certificate of release or nonattachment of a lien imposed by section 6321 was issued erroneously or improvidently, or if a certificate of release of such lien was issued pursuant to a collateral agreement entered into in connection with a compromise under section 7122 which has been breached, and if the period of limitation on collection after assessment has not expired, the Secretary may revoke such certificate and reinstate the lien:

(A) by mailing notice of such revocation to the person against whom the tax was assessed at his last known address, and

(B) by filing notice of such revocation in the same office in which the notice of lien to which it relates was filed (if such notice of lien had been filed).

Such reinstated lien (i) shall be effective on the date notice of revocation is mailed to the taxpayer in accordance with the provisions of subparagraph (A), but not earlier than the date on which any required filing of notice of revocation is filed in accordance with the provisions of subparagraph (B), and (ii) shall have the same force and effect (as of such date), until the expiration of the period of limitation on collection after assessment, as a lien imposed by section 6321 (relating to lien for taxes).

(3) Certificates void under certain conditions

Notwithstanding any other provision of this subtitle, any lien imposed by this chapter shall attach to any property with respect to which a certificate of discharge has been issued if the person liable for the tax reacquires such property after such certificate has been issued.

(g) Filing of certificates and notices

If a certificate or notice issued pursuant to this section may not be filed in the office designated by State law in which the notice of lien imposed by section 6321 is filed, such certificate or notice shall be effective if filed in the office of the clerk of the United States district court for the judicial district in which such office is situated.

(h) Cross reference

For provisions relating to bonds, see chapter 73 (sec. 7101 and following).

Sec. 6326. Administrative appeal of liens

(a) In general

In such form and at such time as the Secretary shall prescribe by regulations, any person shall be allowed to appeal to the Secretary after the filing of a notice of a lien under this subchapter on the property or the rights to property of such person for a release of such lien alleging an error in the filing of the notice of such lien.

(b) Certificate of release

If the Secretary determines that the filing of the notice of any lien was erroneous, the Secretary shall expeditiously (and, to the extent practicable, within 14 days after such determination) issue a certificate of release of such lien and shall include in such certificate a statement that such filing was erroneous.

GLOSSARY

Abuse of Process The improper and malicious use of the criminal or civil process.

Acceptance Acceptance refers to one's consent to the terms of an offer, which consent creates a contract.

Accord and Satisfaction Accord and satisfaction refers to the payment of money, or other thing of value, which is usually less than the amount owed or demanded, in exchange for extinguishment of the debt.

Accrue To occur or come into existence.

Action at Law A judicial proceeding whereby one party prosecutes another for a wrong done.

Actionable Giving rise to a cause of action.

Actual Damages Actual damages are those damages directly referable to the breach or tortious act, and which can be readily proven to have been sustained, and for which the injured party should be compensated as a matter of right.

Adhesion Contract An adhesion contract is a standardized contract form offered to consumers of goods and services on a "take it or leave it" basis without affording the consumer a realistic opportunity to bargain, and under such conditions that infer coercion.

Affirmative Defense In a pleading, a matter constituting a defense.

American Arbitration Association (AAA) National organization of arbitrators from whose panel arbitrators are selected for labor and civil disputes.

Annual Percentage Rate (APR) The annual percentage rate is the actual cost of borrowing money, expressed in the form of an annual rate to make it easy for one to compare the cost of borrowing money among several lenders.

Answer In a civil proceeding, the principal pleading on the part of the defendant in response to the plaintiff's complaint.

Anticipatory Breach of Contract A breach committed before the arrival of the actual time of required performance.

Appearance To come into court, personally or through an attorney, after being summoned.

Arbitration The reference of a dispute to an impartial person chosen by the parties to the dispute who agree in advance to abide by the arbitrator's award issued after a hearing at which both parties have an opportunity to be heard.

Arbitration Clause A clause inserted in a contract providing for compulsory arbitration in case of a dispute as to the rights or liabilities under such contract.

Arbitrator A private, disinterested person, chosen by the parties to a disputed question, for the purpose of hearing their contention, and awarding judgment to the prevailing party.

Arrears Payments which are due but not yet paid.

Asset The entirety of a person's property, either real or personal.

Assignee An assignee is a person to whom an assignment is made, also known as a grantee.

Assignment	An assignment is the transfer of an interest in a right or property from one party to another.
Attachment	The act or process of taking, apprehending, or seizing persons or property, by virtue of a writ, summons, or other judicial order, and bringing the same into the custody of the court for the purpose of securing satisfaction of the judgment ultimately to be entered in the action.
Attachment Execution	A name given in some states to a process of garnishment for the satisfaction of a judgment.
Bad Faith	A willful failure to comply with one's statutory or contractual obligations.
Bankrupt	The state or condition of one who is unable to pay his debts as they are, or become, due.
Bankruptcy	The legal process governed by federal law designed to assist the debtor in a new financial start while insuring fairness among creditors.
Bankruptcy Code	Refers to the Bankruptcy Act of 1978, the federal law which governs bankruptcy actions.
Bankruptcy Court	The forum in which most bankruptcy proceedings are conducted.
Bankruptcy Trustee	The person, appointed by the bankruptcy judge or selected by the creditors, who takes legal title to the property of the debtor and holds it "in trust" for equitable distribution among the creditors.
Boilerplate	Refers to standard language found almost universally in certain documents.
Breach of Contract	The failure, without any legal excuse, to perform any promise which forms the whole or the part of a contract.
Burden of Proof	The duty of a party to substantiate an allegation or issue to convince the trier of fact as to the truth of their claim.

Capacity	Capacity is the legal qualification concerning the ability of one to understand the nature and effects of one's acts.
Cause of Action	The factual basis for bringing a lawsuit.
Caveat Emptor	Latin for "let the buyer beware."
Civil Action	An action maintained to protect a private, civil right as opposed to a criminal action.
Civil Court	The court designed to resolve disputes arising under the common law and civil statutes.
Civil Law	Law which applies to non-criminal actions.
Clean Hands Doctrine	The concept that claimants who seek equitable relief must not themselves have indulged in any impropriety in relation to the transaction upon which relief is sought.
Collateral	Property which is pledged as additional security for a debt, such as a loan.
Confession of Judgment	An admission of a debt by the debtor which may be entered as a judgment without the necessity of a formal legal proceeding.
Consequential Damages	Consequential damages are those damages which are caused by an injury, but which are not a necessary result of the injury, and must be specially pleaded and proven in order to be awarded.
Consideration	Something of value exchanged between parties to a contract, which is a requirement of a valid contract.
Contract	A contract is an agreement between two or more persons which creates an obligation to do or not to do a particular thing.
Court	The branch of government responsible for the resolution of disputes arising under the laws of the government.

Credit	Credit is that which is extended to the buyer or borrower on the seller or lender's belief that that which is given will be repaid.
Creditor	A person to whom a debt is owing by a debtor.
Credit Report	A credit report refers to the document from a credit reporting agency setting forth a credit rating and pertinent financial data concerning a person or a company, which is used in evaluating the applicant's financial stability.
Damages	In general, damages refers to monetary compensation which the law awards to one who has been injured by the actions of another, such as in the case of tortious conduct or breach of contractual obligations.
Debt	A sum of money due by a certain or express agreement.
Debtor	One who owes a debt, payment or other performance of the obligation secured, whether or not he owns or has rights in the collateral.
Defamation	The publication of an injurious statement about the reputation of another
Default	Default is a failure to discharge a duty or do that which ought to be done.
Defendant	In a civil proceeding, the party responding to the complaint.
Defense	Opposition to the truth or validity of the plaintiff's claims.
Demand for Arbitration	A unilateral filing of a claim in arbitration based on the filer's contractual or statutory right to do so.

Disclaimer	Words or conduct which tend to negate or limit warranty in the sale of goods, which in certain instances must be conspicuous and refer to the specific warranty to be excluded.
Down Payment	A partial payment of the purchase price.
Duress	Refers to the action of one person which compels another to do something he or she would not otherwise do.
Execution	Carrying out some act or course of conduct to its completion. Execution upon a money judgment is the legal process of enforcing the judgment, usually by seizing and selling property of the debtor.
Exemption	A privilege allowed by law to a judgment debtor, by which he may hold property to a certain amount or certain classes of property, free from all liability to levy and sale on execution or attachment.
Finance Charge	Any charge for an extension of credit, such as interest.
Fixed Income	Income which is unchangeable.
Foreclosure	The procedure by which mortgaged property is sold on default of the mortgagor in satisfaction of mortgage debt.
Fraud	A false representation of a matter of fact, whether by words or by conduct, by false or misleading allegations, or by concealment of that which should have been disclosed, which deceives and is intended to deceive another, and thereby causes injury to that person.
Fraudulent Conveyance	The transfer of property for the purpose of delaying or defrauding creditors.
Garnish	To attach the wages or property of an individual.

Garnishee	A person who receives notice to hold the assets of another, which are in his or her possession, until such time as a court orders the disposition of the property.
Garnishment	A statutory proceeding whereby a person's property, money, or credits in possession or under control of, or owing by, another are applied to payment of former's debt to third person by proper statutory process against debtor and garnishee.
General Damages	General damages are those damages directly referable to the breach or tortious act and which can be readily proven to have been sustained, and for which the injured party should be compensated as a matter of right.
Grace Period	In contract law, a period specified in a contract which is beyond the due date but during which time payment will be accepted without penalty.
Guarantor	One who makes a guaranty.
Guaranty	An agreement to perform in the place of another if that person reneges on a promise contained in an underlying agreement.
Homestead	The house, outbuilding, and land owned and used as a dwelling by the head of the family.
Homestead Exemption	Laws passed in most of the states allowing a householder or head of a family to designate a house and land as his homestead and exempt the same homestead from execution for his general debts.
Impound	To place property in the custody of an official.
In Rem	Refers to actions that are against property, and concerned with the disposition of that property, rather than against the person.

Indemnification Clause	An indemnification clause in a contract refers to the agreement by one party to secure the other party against loss or damage which may occur in the future in connection with performance of the contract.
Indemnify	To hold another harmless for loss or damage which has already occurred, or which may occur in the future.
Injunction	A judicial remedy either requiring a party to perform an act, or restricting a party from continuing a particular act.
Injury	Any damage done to another's person, rights, reputation or property.
Installment Contract	An installment contract is one in which the obligation, such as the payment of money, is divided into a series of successive performances over a period of time.
Interest	An amount of money paid by a borrower to a lender for the use of the lender's money.
Interest Rate	The percentage of a sum of money charged for its use.
Judge	The individual who presides over a court, and whose function it is to determine controversies.
Judgment	A judgment is a final determination by a court of law concerning the rights of the parties to a lawsuit.
Judgment Creditor	A creditor who has obtained a judgment against a debtor, which judgment may be enforced to obtain payment of the amount due.
Judgment Debtor	An individual who owes a sum of money, and against whom a judgment has been awarded for that debt.

Judgment Execution The formal or written evidence of the judgment which commands the officer to seize the goods and property of the judgment debtor to satisfy the judgment.

Judgment Proof Refers to the status of an individual who does not have the financial resources or assets necessary to satisfy a judgment.

Legal Capacity Referring to the legal capacity to sue, it is the requirement that a person bringing the lawsuit have a sound mind, be of lawful age, and be under no restraint or legal disability.

Levy To seize property in order to satisfy a judgment.

Liability Liability refers to one's obligation to do or refrain from doing something, such as the payment of a debt.

Libel The false and malicious publication, in printed form, for the purpose of defaming another.

Lien A claim against the property of another as security for a debt. witness to the crime may attempt an identification.

Liquidated Damages An amount stipulated in a contract as a reasonable estimate of damages to be paid in the event the contract is breached.

Loan Principal The loan principal is the amount of the debt not including interest or any other additions.

Maker As used in commercial law, the individual who executes a note.

Malicious Abuse of Legal Process Wilfully misapplying court process to obtain object not intended by law.

Malicious Prosecution One begun in malice without probable cause to believe the charges can be sustained.

Material Breach	A material breach refers to a substantial breach of contract which excuses further performance by the innocent party and gives rise to an action for breach of contract by the injured party.
Maturity Date	The date upon which a creditor is designated to receive payment of a debt, such as payment of the principal value of a bond to a bondholder by the issuing company or governmental entity.
Mechanic's Lien	A claim created by law for the purpose of securing a priority of payment of the price of work performed and materials furnished.
Mediation	The act of a third person in intermediating between two contending parties with a view to persuading them to adjust or settle their dispute but without the authority to make a binding decision.
Minor	A person who has not yet reached the age of legal competence, which is designated as 18 in most states.
Mortgage	A written instrument, duly executed and delivered, that creates a lien upon real estate as security for the payment of a specific debt.
Mutual Agreement	Mutual agreement refers to the meeting of the minds of the parties to a contract concerning the subject matter of the contract.
Negotiable Instrument	A signed writing which contains an unconditional promise to pay a sum of money, either on demand or at a specified time, payable to the order of the bearer.
Net Income	Gross income less deductions and exemptions proscribed by law.
Net Worth	The difference between one's assets and liabilities.
Nominal Damages	A trivial sum of money which is awarded as recognition that a legal injury was sustained, although slight.

Note	A writing which promises payment of a debt.
Novation	A novation refers to the substitution of a new party and the discharge of an original party to a contract, with the assent of all parties.
Obligee	An obligee is one who is entitled to receive a sum of money or performance from the obligor.
Obligor	An obligor is one who promises to perform or pay a sum of money under a contract.
Offeree	An offeree is the person to whom an offer is made.
Offeror	An offeror is the person who makes an offer.
Oral Agreement	An oral agreement is one which is not in writing or not signed by the parties.
Parties	The disputants.
Pecuniary	A term relating to monetary matters.
Performance	Performance refers to the completion of one's contractual obligation.
Referee's Deed	A deed given by a referee or other public officer pursuant to a court order for the sale of property.
Reformation	An equitable remedy which calls for the rewriting of a contract involving a mutual mistake or fraud.
Release	A document signed by one party, releasing claims he or she may have against another party, usually as part of a settlement agreement.
Repudiation	In contract law, refers to the declaration of one of the parties to the contract that he or she will not perform under the contract.

Rescission	The cancellation of a contract which returns the parties to the positions they were in before the contract was made.
Restitution	The act of making an aggrieved party whole by compensating him or her for any loss or damage sustained.
Sale	An agreement to transfer property from the seller to the buyer for a stated sum of money.
Sale and Leaseback	An agreement whereby the seller transfers property to the buyer who immediately leases the property back to the seller.
Satisfaction	The discharge and release of an obligation.
Service of Process	The delivery of legal court documents, such as a complaint, to the defendant.
Settlement	An agreement by the parties to a dispute on a resolution of the claims, usually requiring some mutual action, such as payment of money in consideration of a release of claims.
Special Damages	Special damages are those damages which are the natural, but not the necessary and inevitable result of the wrongful act.
Statute of Limitations	Any law which fixes the time within which parties must take judicial action to enforce rights or thereafter be barred from enforcing them.
Stay	A judicial order suspending some action until further court order lifting the stay.
Stipulation	An admission or agreement made by parties to a lawsuit concerning the pending matter.
Subpoena	A court issued document compelling the appearance of a witness before the court.

Subpoena Duces Tecum	A court issued document requiring a witness to produce certain document in his or her possession or control.
Summons	A mandate requiring the appearance of the defendant in an action under penalty of having judgment.
Tangible Property	Property which is capable of being possessed, whether real or personal.
Tax	A sum of money assessed upon one's income, property and purchases, for the purpose of supporting the government.
Tax Court	A federal administrative agency which acts as a court for the purposes of determining disputes between individuals and the Internal Revenue Service.
Trial	The judicial procedure whereby disputes are determined based on the presentation of issues of law and fact. Issues of fact are decided by the trier of fact, either the judge or jury, and issues of law are decided by the judge.
Trial Court	The court of original jurisdiction over a particular matter.
Truth-In-Lending Act	A federal law which requires commercial lenders to provide applicants with detailed, accurate and understandable information relating to the cost of credit, so as to permit the borrower to make an informed decision.
Unconscionable	Refers to a bargain so one-sided as to amount to an absence of meaningful choice on the part of one of the parties, together with terms which are unreasonably favorable to the other party.
Undue Influence	The exertion of improper influence upon another for the purpose of destroying that person's free will in carrying out a particular act, such as entering into a contract.

Usurious Contract	A contract that imposes interest at a rate which exceeds the legally permissible rate.
Usury	An excessive rate of interest above the maximum permissible rate established by the state legislature.
Vitiate	To make void.
Void	Having no legal force or binding effect.
Voidable	Capable of being rendered void and unenforceable.

BIBLIOGRAPHY AND
SUGGESTED READING

Black's Law Dictionary, Fifth Edition. St. Paul, MN: West Publishing Company, 1979.

Cane, Michael Allen *The Five-Minute Lawyers' Guide to Bad Debts, Credit Problems and Bankruptcy*. New York, NY: Dell Publishing Company, 1995.

Hobbs, Robert *Fair Debt Collection, Third Edition*. Boston, MA:

Internal Revenue Service (Date Visited: June 2000) <http://www.irs.ustreas.gov>.

Lovett, William A. *Banking and Financial Institutions Law*. St. Paul, MN: West Publishing, 1988.

Munna, Raymond J. *Legal Power for Small Business Owners and Managers*. Kenner, LA: Granite Publishers, 1991.

Nickel, Gudrun M. *Debtors' Rights: A Legal Self Help Guide*. Clearwater, FL: Sphinx International, 1992.

Nolo On-Line Encyclopedia (Date Visited: June 2000) <http://www.nolo.com>.

Reitman, Jeffrey B., and Harold Weisblatt. *Banking Law*. New York, NY: Matthew Bender & Co., Inc. , 1981.

Smith, Craig W. *Negotiable Instruments and the Payments Mechanism*. Washington, DC: American Bankers Association, 1983.

United States Department of Labor (Date Visited: June 2000) <http://www.dol.gov>.

Warner, Ralph, Elias, Stephen *Billpayer's Rights*. Berkeley, CA: Nolo Press, 1986.

White, James J. *Traveler's Checks and Money Orders: Paper and Electronic Payments Litigation*. Chicago, IL: ALI-ABA Continuing Professional Education Series, 1984.